T0142899

Human–Computer Interaction Series

Editors-in-Chief

Desney Tan
Microsoft Research, Redmond, WA, USA

Jean Vanderdonckt
Louvain School of Management, Université catholique de Louvain,
Louvain-La-Neuve, Belgium

The Human–Computer Interaction Series, launched in 2004, publishes books that advance the science and technology of developing systems which are effective and satisfying for people in a wide variety of contexts. Titles focus on theoretical perspectives (such as formal approaches drawn from a variety of behavioural sciences), practical approaches (such as techniques for effectively integrating user needs in system development), and social issues (such as the determinants of utility, usability and acceptability).

HCI is a multidisciplinary field and focuses on the human aspects in the development of computer technology. As technology becomes increasingly more pervasive the need to take a human-centred approach in the design and development of computer-based systems becomes ever more important.

Titles published within the Human–Computer Interaction Series are included in Thomson Reuters' Book Citation Index, The DBLP Computer Science Bibliography and The HCI Bibliography.

More information about this series at http://www.springer.com/series/6033

Vivian Genaro Motti

Wearable Interaction

Vivian Genaro Motti
George Mason University
Fairfax, VA, USA

ISSN 1571-5035   ISSN 2524-4477   (electronic)
Human–Computer Interaction Series
ISBN 978-3-030-27113-8   ISBN 978-3-030-27111-4   (eBook)
https://doi.org/10.1007/978-3-030-27111-4

This Springer imprint is published by the registered company Springer Nature Switzerland AG
The registered company address is: Gewerbestrasse 11, 6330 Cham, Switzerland

This book is dedicated to my grandparents, Antônio Genaro (in memorian) and Encarnação Flores Genaro, my guiding stars and fortress.

Foreword by Massimo Zancanaro

Wearable devices are at the same time a huge market potential and a lively research topic. Sales of wristbands, smartwatches, and ear-worn devices are growing steadily in the last few years and an even stronger growth has been foreseen for the near future [3]. Research is rampant in different areas including core technical challenges such as standardization [8] or processing [5] as well as in specific application fields such as precision medicine [2], sport [4], or operation in difficult environments [6], just to name a few literature surveys recently published.

Nevertheless, there is a huge gap in understanding and designing the user experience. First because, despite their apparent minimalism, wearable devices may be complex to use, if not properly designed and understood by the users [1]. Second because, even in the fields where they have longer been applied such as sport, for example, innovation seems largely focused on technical aspects rather than on how people appropriate and use wearable devices in the long term as well as how these devices can eventually change the experience of physical activity [4].

Therefore, wearable interaction, with its emphasis on interface and interaction aspects, is timely. Vivian Genaro Motti brings in this book her personal research experience together with a detailed analysis of the extant literature to provide a unifying picture on the knowledge on interface solutions for wearable technologies.

Wearable computing is not a new research field, as the first chapter dutifully illustrates, but it is sparse and, in many respects, incomplete. An overview about wearable computers was long needed starting by a reflection on basic definitions and fundamental concepts up to discussing more advanced aspects like the tension between universal use and adaptation.

Since the market is becoming more mature, the competition is going to move from the novelty effect to usefulness and usability. In this respect, the extensive list of design principles and patterns, together with guidelines and recommendations to design and evaluate wearable solutions, offers an important contribution as didactic material to train a new generation of professionals in this area.

Wearable Interaction is a fascinating book offering a comprehensive view on a lively research field and at the same time an interesting reference for designers and professionals.

July 2019   Massimo Zancanaro
Professor of Human–Computer Interaction
Department of Psychology and Cognitive Science
University of Trento, Trento, Italy

References

1. Benbunan-Fich R (2019) An affordance lens for wearable information systems. Eur J Inf Syst 28(3):256–271
2. Cheol Jeong I, Bychkov D, Searson PC (2018) Wearable devices for precision medicine and health state monitoring. IEEE Trans Biomed Eng 66(5):1242–1258
3. IDC Press Release "IDC Reports Strong Growth in the Worldwide Wearables Market, Led by Holiday Shipments of Smartwatches, Wrist Bands, and Ear-Worn Devices". March, 5th 2019 https://www.idc.com/getdoc.jsp?containerId=prUS44901819
4. Mencarini E, Rapp A, Tirabeni L, Zancanaro M (2019) Designing wearable systems for sports: a review of trends and opportunities in human–computer interaction. IEEE Tran Human–Mach Syst 1–12. https://doi.org/10.1109/THMS.2019.2919702
5. Nweke HF, Teh YW, Mujtaba G, Al-Garadi MA (2019) Data fusion and multiple classifier systems for human activity detection and health monitoring: review and open research directions. Inf Fusion 46:147–170
6. Stirling L, Siu HC, Jones E, Duda K (2018) Human factors considerations for enabling functional use of exosystems in operational environments. IEEE Syst J 13(1):1072–1083
7. Welk GJ, Bai Y, Lee JM, Godino J, Saint-Maurice PF, Carr L (2019) Standardizing analytic methods and reporting in activity monitor validation studies. Med Sci Sports Exerc 51(8):1767–1780
8. Xie H, Chu HC, Hwang GJ, Wang CC (2019) Trends and development in technology-enhanced adaptive/personalized learning: a systematic review of journal publications from 2007 to 2017. Comput Educ 103599

Foreword by Gerrit Meixner

When I got the invitation from Vivian Genaro Motti, I was happy to support her, encouraging her book project about wearable interaction. Concerning myself, I am professor for Human–Computer Interaction and working in the area for 15 years now. I know Vivian since she was a Ph.D. student at UCL in Belgium.

Writing a book about such an ongoing topic like wearable computing and having a focus on the interaction part of wearable computer is quite ambitious, because quick innovations change this area rapidly.

The book consists of five chapters beginning with an introduction to wearable computers. The introduction is typically the most interesting part for me—here I decide if I go on reading the rest of the book. In the case of this book, I very much like the historical background of the technology. I have several lectures at my university talking only about the historical background, how technology has evolved over the last decades and how it changed human's life. This is very important, because you get to know why things failed in early times and why they became successful later. The last part of the introduction concerning application domains of wearable computers gives a nice overview of use scenarios in our real world.

The second chapter is about design considerations. A wearable computer is a (mostly tiny) complex electronic product you wear on your body. Developing it is like developing a new Personal Computer—with a dozen problems more (I can tell you… we once had a project developing a wearable computer—a ring—for a big German company). Therefore, please, put the user in the center of your development and be as close as possible toward ISO 9241-210. Your customer and user will be very thankful.

The third chapter is about wearable interaction. There are so many ways of interacting with a wearable computer and this chapter helps you thinking about the right interaction modality.

The fourth chapter is about design guidelines and evaluation. By using (good) guidelines, you ensure that you do not do the same mistakes as many people did before you. Evaluating your designs, sketches, (physical) prototypes is indispensable for developing your new great gadget in a user-centered way. The fifth and last chapter is about future trends in wearable computing. It discusses several directions research will go or may go.

For me, the future of wearable interaction is very promising. In some years, humans will be highly extended with wearable computers on their bodies—ranging from smart eyewear to smart shoes.

July 2019   Prof. Dr.-Ing. Gerrit Meixner
                                                         UniTyLab, Heilbronn University
                                                         Heilbronn, Germany

Preface

Wearable Interaction provides readers with a comprehensive view about wearable computing, focusing on the design of the user interface, input entries, and output responses across form factors and application domains.

This book originates from the author's idea to unify the knowledge on interface solutions for wearable technologies. The intended audience includes designers and developers, from academia or industry, interested in learning about multimodal interfaces for wearables that are effective for end users to interact with. This book presents and discusses diverse interaction modalities, including approaches for input entry and output responses, with feedback that leverages on audio, graphic, haptic, and tactile solutions. The examples presented in the book were extracted from scientific literature but include commercial devices as well. The devices presented cut across multiple form factors, ranging from head-mounted displays to wrist-worn devices.

Wearable interaction provides an overview about wearable computers, focusing on human factors, user experience, and interaction design. The book is structured in five chapters.

In brief, Chap. 1 provides basic definitions and fundamental concepts in the domain, including a historic view and multiple examples of wearable technologies, illustrated through different form factors, including wrist-worn wearables, head-mounted displays, and smart garments. Eight application domains are discussed, including healthcare, education, and user interaction. Chapter 2 discusses the design considerations necessary to create interactive solutions for wearables, describing human factors, technological constraints, and universal design concerning customization choices for input entry and output responses. Chapter 3 focuses on the design of multimodal user interfaces and interactive solutions for diverse wearables. The examples of designs presented consider multiple modalities for input entry and output responses and multiple form factors as well. References from scientific literature and commercial examples are combined for illustration. This chapter emphasizes the different contexts of use where the wearable interaction takes place, discussing how different contextual factors impact the user experience with wearable computers. Chapter 4 provides a theoretical foundation to facilitate the design process, including guidelines, principles, and interaction paradigms that support the development life cycle and the evaluation of interactive applications for wearable technologies. To identify and discuss the main benefits and drawbacks involved in wearable interaction, several quality factors are described. Chapter 5 discusses future trends and concerns in the domain, illustrating examples of seamless solutions that are embedded or projected on the users' bodies. It also provides a critical reflection on the design of interactive solutions according to the design considerations, privacy concerns, and quality criteria described.

Each chapter of wearable interaction is summarized as follows:

Chapter 1	In the Introduction to wearable computers, the readers have an overview about the history of wearable computers, including different form factors, sensors, and actuators. The versatility of wearable computers to support everyday activities is emphasized, explaining multiple application domains that benefit from wearable solutions.
Chapter 2	In design considerations, a conceptual view of wearable computers is defined, including different placements on the user body, and multiple factors involved in the interaction design. This chapter emphasizes the constraints of the devices and the heterogeneous contexts of use where wearables are used. It also explains why microinteractions are important in such dynamic contexts, highlighting the diversity of users and considerations concerning ergonomic aspects. Lastly, the main design challenges are discussed, including trade-offs when universal design and customization must be considered to ensure acceptability among users.
Chapter 3	In wearable interaction, a number of interactive solutions for input and output are presented, as well as interaction paradigms and multimodal interfaces across form factors. The user interaction is illustrated for wrist-worn devices and head-mounted devices. Alternative form factors, such as back-mounted devices and chest-mounted devices, are also discussed.
Chapter 4	In design guidelines and evaluation, the readers have access to an extensive list of design principles and patterns, guidelines, and recommendations that must be taken into account when stakeholders are creating or evaluating wearable solutions. The contents guide a design process by providing a comprehensive list of principles that must be employed by stakeholders when developing wearables and also inform the evaluation phases by providing multiple methods for assessing and improving wearable technologies.

Chapter 5   Future trends in wearable computing conclude the book by presenting
             a critical view of novel interfaces, focusing on the miniaturization of
             devices as well as on-body interfaces. This chapter discusses electronic
             tattoos and implanted devices that are seamlessly connected to the
             users' body. It concludes with opportunities to further develop
             wearables.

Fairfax, USA   Vivian Genaro Motti
January 2019

Acknowledgements

The completion of this book would not have been possible without the support of many individuals. First and foremost, I thank my spouse, family members, and friends. I also acknowledge all my previous advisors, colleagues and ex-colleagues who strongly advised and inspired me throughout this journey, enduring the challenges that compiling a large number of scattered references involves. I am grateful not only to the support of the National Center for Faculty Development and Diversity for organizing the Writing Challenge but also to the librarians at George Mason University, who besides providing resources, materials, and space, organized a writing retreat facilitating the realization of this book. I am thankful to the funding agencies that provided financial support for me to complete my work, including CNPq, EU FP7, and NSF. Last, but not least, I thank the students from the Human–Centric Design Lab whose continuous growth inspires me in my academic endeavors.

Contents

About the Author

Vivian Genaro Motti is an Assistant Professor on Human–Computer Interaction in the Department of Information Sciences and Technology at George Mason University (GMU) where she leads the Human–Centric Design Lab (HCD Lab). Her research focuses on Human–Computer Interaction, Ubiquitous Computing, Wearable Health, and Usable Privacy. Before joining GMU, she was a Postdoctoral Research Fellow and a Research Assistant Professor in the Human-Centered Computing division at the School of Computing in Clemson University. During her postdoc, she contributed to the NSF-funded Amulet project, investigating human factors, usability, and privacy of wearable devices for health care.

Dr. Motti received her Ph.D. from the Université Catholique de Louvain (Louvain la Neuve, Belgium) in 2013. During her Ph.D., she investigated the multidimensional adaptation of user interfaces to the context of use. She earned a B.Sc. and a Masters degree from University of São Paulo. In her Master's thesis, she investigated usability issues in a ubiquitous computing environment for distributed meetings (DiGaE) in learning environments. The ultimate goal of her research is to bridge the gap between what users need and what technology actually provides them.

Acronyms

2D	Two dimensional
3D	Three dimensional
ACM	Association for Computing Machinery
ANT+	Adaptive Network Topology
AR	Augmented Reality
BAN	Body-Area Network
BCI	Brain–Computer Interface
BLE	Bluetooth Low Energy
BP	Blood Pressure
BVP	Blood Volume Pulse
COTS	Commercial off-the-shelf
CRS	Comfort Rate Scale
DIY	Do-it-yourself
DOF	Degree of Freedom
ECG	Electrocardiogram
EDA	Electrodermal Activity
EEG	Electroencephalogram
EMG	Electromyogram
EOG	Electrooculogram
FRAM	Ferroelectric Random Access Memory
GB	Gigabyte
GDPR	General Data Protection Regulation
GMU	George Mason University
GSR	Galvanic Skin Response
GUI	Graphic User Interface
HMD	Head-Mounted Devices
Hz	Hertz
I/O	Input and Output
ICU	Intensive Care Unit
IEEE	Institute of Electrical and Electronic Engineers

IR	Infrared
LED	Light-Emitting Diode
MHz	Mega-hertz
mm	Millimeters
NDD	Neurodevelopmental Disorders
NFC	Near-Field Communication
OS	Operating System
PAN	Personal Area Network
PC	Personal Computer
pH	Potential of Hydrogen
PPG	Photoplethysmograph
REBA	Rapid Entire Body Assessment
RFID	Radio-Frequency Identification
RTC	Real-time clock
SD	Secure Digital
SMS	Short Message Service
UI	User Interface
USB	Universal Serial Bus
VR	Virtual Reality
WC	Wearable Computing
WIMP	Window icon menu pointer
WIVR	Wearable Immersive Virtual Reality
WWW	Wrist-Worn Wearables

Chapter 1
Introduction to Wearable Computers

Abstract This chapter introduces wearable computing, beginning with fundamental concepts and definitions about wearable technologies. Then, it provides a historic view of the field, describing how wearable technologies evolved since 1970 throughout the past decades. To illustrate several different examples of wearable devices, a variety of form factors are presented, ranging from wrist-worn wearables and head-mounted displays to smart garments. This chapter also describes wearable sensors used to collect inward data from users, such as physiological signals, as well as environmental clues from the users' surroundings, such as temperature, light levels, and humidity. The main features of wearable technologies are characterized, concerning data collection, processing, and delivery of information, services, and resources for end users. The last part of the chapter concludes with an extensive list of examples of application domains in which wearables have been successfully employed thus far. Specifically, the examples describe wearable applications implemented to support human activities in education, health care, industry, fitness and sports, assistive technologies, music, leisure, arts and entertainment, safety critical systems and the military, and user interaction.

1.1 Introduction

Wearable technologies are characterized by body-worn devices, including smart clothes, such as e-textiles and interactive accessories as well. The term "wearable computer" encompasses a broad range of devices and concepts of use [1]. However, in general, wearables are technologies that use the human body as a support for computational solutions that embed electronics [2]. Wearables include garments and accessories that are capable of sensing users' data, processing and interpreting it seeking to provide users relevant information, services, and resources [3].

For Dunne and Smyth [4], wearables are electronic devices worn on the user body [4]. These devices are capable to function autonomously for a long period of time [5]. Unlike traditional mobile devices, for wearable computers to be successful, the devices should not interfere with the users' motions that are required for daily routine activities. Wearables should also be invisible to those around the user [6]. By

© Springer Nature Switzerland AG 2020   1
V. G. Motti, *Wearable Interaction*, Human–Computer Interaction Series,
https://doi.org/10.1007/978-3-030-27111-4_1

being virtually invisible, wearables should not hinder the main activities performed by the user; still the device should always be active, available, and operational when users need it, but without requiring their continuous attention [7].

Wearables are commercially available in different form factors, ranging in dimension from small rings to large exoeskeletons and space suits [8]. By sensing and processing data from the environment and their users, and by providing interventions, alerts, and reminders, wearables are portable technologies for which the human body serves as a platform.

To provide relevant features, services, and resources for users, the functionalities of wearable devices vary, including the analysis of air quality, monitoring of the users' activities, regulation of the body temperature, and emergency response [9]. The end users of wearable technologies are also commonly known as *wearers*.

By being continuously worn and accessible, wearables often enable hands-free interaction and timely notifications. Their interaction strives to require minimum efforts from wearers, and also to avoid disturbing, distracting, and overwhelming wearers with constant notifications. Wearables are capable of sensing the users' contexts and promptly getting the wearer's attention when necessary, be it through brief vibration, beeps, sounds, blinking lights, or graphic displays [10].

While some wearable technologies are meant to be used continuously (like fitness trackers), other devices have very specific purposes, like virtual reality headsets used for gaming, often used for a few hours consecutively. Wearable technologies can include actual computers with standard capabilities for input entry and output responses [1]. For output responses, the information is often provided to the wearer with one or multiple stimuli. Those are perceivable through human senses, including the visual, auditory, or haptic system [1]. Wearables cover some extent of the wearer body, but they can also be tiny, small embedded devices with very limited capabilities [1].

An important characteristic of the design of a wearable computer, and especially smart clothes, is that the device is considered to be part of the wearer; thus, the technology becomes also an integral part of the user's clothing [2]. The benefits of wearable appliances include (1) their ability to be an integral part of the wearer personal space [11], (2) their appeal to multiple sensory channels of the user, and (3) their engagement with all aspects of human embodiment, including senses, intellect, and emotions [12]. Also, because wearable computers are always switched on, they are easily accessible to their wearers. For Billinghurst and Starner [11], both the operational and interactional constancy sets wearable technologies apart from conventional forms of portable computers [11].

Since the production of the first sensors that were small enough to be carried on the body, wearable devices have rapidly evolved. Wearable computing is also considered as one of the areas of computer sciences with a major growth in recent years [13]. The miniaturization of microelectronics enabled novel applications to be implemented using new sensors. Miniaturized signal processing and advances in communication capabilities also emerged, allowing digital wearables to flourish [14]. The evolution of wearables applies not only to hardware, through the miniaturization of technologies, but it includes also improvements in batteries, the creation of novel sensors, and flexible electronics.

The future projections for wearable computing estimate a continued growth, as manufacturers develop new chips and sensors that have potential to make wearable devices even more powerful [15]. Due to their versatility, wearable devices have been applied in diverse domains, from entertainment (see Sect. 1.6.6) to safety-critical systems for the military sector (see Sect. 1.6.7). Sensors support multiple human activities by collecting and processing data from end users and their environments. The main activities currently supported involve monitoring vital signs (such as heart rate, respiration rate, skin temperature, oxygenation), augmenting human abilities and skills (such as strength, memory, communication skills) [16, 17], replacing sensory organs, or alerting users in case of emergencies that require urgent responses.

Improvements in electronics and algorithms for data collection, processing and storage, wireless standards for data exchange, energy-efficient batteries, and advances in material science all contributed to further the research and development in wearable computing [18]. Additionally, e-textiles and smart fabrics with computational capabilities facilitate the communication with machines for advanced data manipulation, management, and visualization. Innovative fabrics allow users to augment their perception of reality, thanks to the exchange of information with the external environment [19]. E-textiles have seen some rapid development recently as well, with advancements in fabrics, technology, and textile-friendly microcontrollers [20].

Advances in hardware and software, including miniaturized electronic components, resulted in more compact devices [5]. These advances, summed with more efficient energy sources, improved network connections, data storage, and transmission solutions [5, 8], led to an increased number of wearable computers available and a wider user adoption. In 2016, the worldwide sales of wearables reached 23 million devices, and by 2020 the sales are expected to increase to 213 million devices [21].

Development toolkits (such as Lilypad Arduino[1] [22] and Teknikio[2] [23]) became available. Consequently, the number of wearable applications also raised. Development toolkits include components such as microcontrollers, temperature sensor, vibrator motor, and LEDs. The devices are built using printed circuit boards and fabric, which are stitched together with conductive thread [6]. These kits contain instructions that help to introduce e-textiles to novice users.

Dedicated operating systems (such as Android Wear OS [24] and Samsung Tizen [25]) also emerged, helping to further promote the development of wearables by enabling developers and designers to build on off-the-shelf technologies and create customized solutions of hardware prototypes and software applications as well [8]. The Fusion Band prototype, for instance (presented in Sect. 1.6.5), was designed from off-the-shelf parts including the Arduino Pro mini [26], and the bracelet for cyclists (presented in Sect. 1.6.4) was built using Lilypad Arduino [19]. Although commercial off-the-shelf boards may be limited in processing power and code efficiency, they make up for their small footprint, besides being easy to use [26]. Off-the-shelf

---

[1]https://www.sparkfun.com/categories/135.
[2]https://www.teknikio.com/.

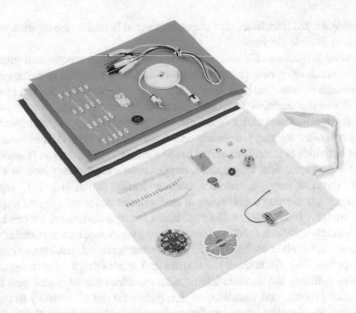

Fig. 1.1 Sparkfun electronics creates sewable electronic kits, such as the ChickTech Soft Circuits Kit illustrated. To facilitate the implementation of customized wearables, Sparkfun LilyPad Arduino provides kits containing sensors, actuators, and microcontrollers. These electronic components allow designers and developers to implement their own wearable prototypes. Photo credit by Juan Peña

components allow for custom-made applications; however, the supplied modules have no further potential for miniaturization [14].

Although wearables are not new, with the first devices dating from the 70s [27], advances in miniaturized, flexible, and autonomous technology have facilitated the implementation of new wearables [28], besides also fostering their commercialization. The higher availability of commercial wearables boosted users' acceptance and adoption. Existing development frameworks and do-it-yourself (DIY) toolkits, such as Android Wear [27], Arduino Wearables [29], LilyPad Arduino (see Fig. 1.1), [22, 23], facilitated the creation of customized applications with off-the-shelf components. Lilypad Arduino consists of a small, washable microcontroller designed for wearable computing [20]. Among other applications, it facilitates the design of a knee brace with Arduino Lilypad to monitor physical activity and exercise routine from end users [30].

To build wearable technologies, stakeholders benefit from multiple domains, including knowledge from research fields such as graphical design, psychology of perception and cognition, human–computer interaction, and Artificial Intelligence. These disciplines provide fundamental concepts and methods that facilitate the creation and deployment of wearable applications [1].

1.2 History

One of the first examples of a wearable is the abacus ring. Attributed to the Qing Chinese Dynasty, the ring allowed wearers to rapidly perform calculations by flipping pebbles directly on the artifact [31]. Other inventions from the sixteenth century associated to the foundations of wearable computers are pockets and wristwatches [32]. The modern wristwatch was popularized in 1907 by the Brazilian aviator Alberto Santos-Dumont, so that he could check the time while keeping both hands free [11]. Eyeglasses date from ca. 1286 [33], as assistive technologies that augment the wearer's vision compensating for visual deficits.

Regarding digital solutions, the roots of research on wearable computers can be traced back to the twentieth century [34]. The first scientific publication reporting an interactive wearable dates from 1955, when Edward Thorp and Steve Channon implemented a wearable system to predict the trajectory of the ball in casino roulette wheels, followed by a "gambling shoe" [35]. Despite the hardware limitations of the time, they succeeded to build a proof-of-concept prototype to predict the roulette behavior and effectively wear it as an earpiece with radio transmission in the casino while playing the roulette game.

Concerning head-mounted devices, Ivan Sutherland proposed a display that used mirrors to project a three-dimensional image to the wearer in 1968. This work focused on the specification of the equipment, and the device proposed is a precursor of current virtual reality headsets [36].

Thanks to the development and usage of several prototypes of recording devices in the form of headsets, glasses, and badges, Steve Mann is considered to be the father of wearable computing. In 1980, he developed the first of a headset series with embedded cameras and microphones to record daily activities [37].

The first wireless heart rate (HR) monitor was introduced in the 1980s by Polar, a Finnish company. The monitor consisted of a chest strap transmitter with a wrist-worn receiver [34]. In the early 1990s, in collaboration with Thad Starner and colleagues, Steve Mann started to pioneer modern-day wearable computing [32].

Further, in 1989–1990, Schoening and colleagues envisioned and designed a small wearable computer that was integrated with a wireless link and a head-mounted device to help soldiers in the battlefield [34].

In the 90s, wearable technologies were limited to academic research projects, mostly because the hardware was not popularized but could be explored by students from interdisciplinary fields, including Design, Computer Engineering, Computer Science, Human–Computer Interaction, and Management. Also, wearables were too risky for the industry to invest on, due to its unproven business model [38]. In addition to that, at that time, these devices were extremely limited concerning their functionalities; they were not comfortable to wear, being mostly used for very specific use case scenarios [34].

In 1993, an Australian investigator created the first underwater wearable computer. The WetPC featured a mask-mounted, high-contrast virtual display and an one-handed, five-key controller named Kordpad. Wires connected the devices to the computer which was attached to the air tank in a waterproof casing [39].

The first finger-mounted ring scanner dates from 1994. Thanks to refinements in early 1995, this prototype became an arm-mounted computer and finger scanner that would let post workers to scan parcels as they loaded them into trucks at warehouses [11].

In 1995, Starner characterized wearable interfaces as persistent and constant, meaning that they should be made continuously available to be used in parallel with the execution of user's tasks [1]. Constancy also allows the same wearable interface to be used in diverse situations.

By the mid-90s, wearables started to be commercialized. In 1997, BodyMedia was one of the first companies to commercially offer wearable sensors (it was later acquired by Jawbone) [38]. BodyMedia was a startup company whose vision integrated wearable computing (such as Sensewear) and Internet-based services (Body-Media.com) to provide products for users to track vital signs and monitor their personal health routines, and as such be proactive when managing their wellness [40].

In 1997, Steve Mann defined WearComp, a wearable system based on three attributes. By being "eudaemonics", the computational apparatus was situated as part of the wearer and disconnected from any stationary power supply. By being "existential", the system would enable wearers to control its computational capabilities without requiring conscious thought or effort. By being "ephemeral", the wearable avoids delays caused by interaction or operation, making it constant concerning its operation and potential for interaction [1]. The operational constancy implies in a wearable that is always active while being worn even when a power-saving mode exists [1].

Initial challenges faced in the development of wearables were associated with the miniaturization of computer hardware, head-mounted display technologies, connectivity, and battery life. However, as computing technology in general progressed, these technical issues, with the possible exception of battery lifetime, became less constraining [41]. Advances in technology are driven by solving technology bugs, reducing costs, and adapting applications to the new user interfaces that emerge [42]. Today, in addition to energy-efficient solutions, sustaining users' engagement with wearable technologies also remains as an open challenge [34].

Between the 90s and the year 2000, Smailagic and Siewiorek [42] estimated that two dozen wearable computers have been designed and built. To list the wearable computers produced between 1970 and 2001, a Family Tree of wearable computers was created and eight application categories emerged: plant operation, manufacturing, language translation, maintenance, medical applications, smart rooms, mobile workers, and navigation systems [42].

The evolution in wearable technologies faced a rapid development after the year 2000, with a parallel growth of scientific research and commercial devices, despite their specific, and somehow complementary, interests. As Fig. 1.2 indicates, the scientific publications including the term "wearable" increased exponentially between 1990 and 2010 according to search results from the digital library of the Associ-

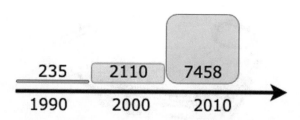

Fig. 1.2 The digital library of the Association of Computing Machinery (ACM) indicates an exponential growth in the number of scientific publications mentioning the term "wearables", beginning in the early 90s, the library results count today with almost 10,000 records (9,803 publications), being 235 in 1990, 2110 in 2000, and 7458 in 2010

ation for Computing Machinery (ACM). The number of publications raised from 235 in the 90s to 7,458 records in 2010. The continuous growth in the number of publications illustrates the increased interest in the domain. Among the scientific publications on wearables, two topics related to usability stand out as most discussed: (1) the device characteristics (such as screen size, battery life, screen display, elements (text/buttons), interaction techniques, etc.) and (2) the deployment categories (motion artifacts and wearing positions) [34].

After 2010, wearable technology became increasingly common on the commercial market [43]. In addition to that, the penetration rate of consumer wearable technology is also expected to accelerate [34], growing to around 89 million units by 2022 [44]. While industry representatives are usually concerned with cost and usefulness of the products, representatives from academia are often concerned with solving more theoretical problems and rapidly building and evaluating prototypes [1].

Wearable technologies are volatile, and some devices have been quickly discontinued after a few years in the market, for example, the Google Glass (a head-mounted device aimed at augmented reality applications), the Pebble watch (an interactive smartwatch), and the Thalmic Myo (an armband to support end user interaction through arm gestures).

Google Glass was a wearable computer running on Android. As Fig. 1.3 illustrates, the device served as an augmented reality computer with a camera, touchpad, battery, and microphone built into spectacle frames. Glass was designed to overlay information in the user's view without obstructing it [45]. Glass included also a monocular optical head-worn display, but end users could alternatively interact with the Glass using voice commands and a touchpad placed along the arm of the device. MyGlass was released as an application that enabled users to touch, swipe, or tap their mobile phones in order to provide input to Google Glass, as an alternative to using voice or gesture to control the device [46]. Glass-supported end users' activities such as taking pictures, recording videos, searching the web, browsing websites, and translating content on the go [45].

The rapid evolution in the field, followed by the popularization and widespread adoption of wearable devices, made them less expensive for consumers. Thanks to the production growth and novel technologies, head-mounted displays that initially

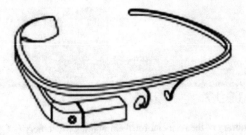

Fig. 1.3 Google Glass was a wearable computer running on Android that served as an augmented reality computer including a camera, touchpad, battery, and microphone built into spectacle frames. Glass was designed to overlay information in the user's view without obstructing it [45]

costed several thousand dollars at their inception [38] had their price substantially decreased since then.

On the implementation side, the availability of development frameworks also progressed dynamically. Wear OS, initially named Android Wear, for instance, has been constantly updated to meet the developers' needs and to match the requirements of newer technologies.

Leading high-technology companies, such as Google, Microsoft, and Sony, have already launched wearable products, and are constantly in the process of creating new technologies to fuel the next wave of exponential growth in the consumer market [47]. Despite the volatility of the market and obsolescence of technology, wearable devices—from bracelets to monitor physical activity and sleeping patterns, to clothes with built-in sensors—are considered to be one of the next big technology waves [47].

1.3 Form Factors

Wearable computing is characterized by body-worn devices, including smart clothing, interactive accessories, and garments. By integrating computational capabilities in a garment, wearables provide useful features to end users. A wearable computer serves thus dual functions; it provides computational features, besides incorporating the purposes of clothing and accessories, be those protective (like a jacket to keep the user body warm or sunglasses to protect the user's eyes against ultraviolet radiation) or purely aesthetics (like an earring or necklace) [7].

Depending on their specific application goals, wearable devices are available in many form factors, ranging in terms of body placement—from head-mounted to shoe-mounted devices, and dimensions—from small-scale rings to large-scale space suits. As illustrated in Fig. 1.4, jewelry has a large potential to carry computational solution on the users' body, thanks to their widespread usage, large-scale adoption, conventional formats, and versatility concerning placement, dimensions, materials, and fit.

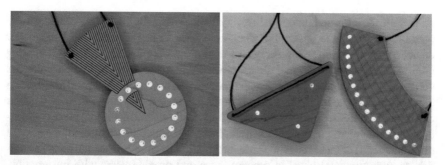

Fig. 1.4 Jewelry pieces, such as necklaces, have a large potential for application in wearable computing, due to its widespread adoption, conventional look, and versatility. Credit: Sophy Wong. Available at https://sophywong.com

Wearables also vary concerning their materials, with stiff hardware pieces and soft electronic textiles. Whereas some wearable technologies are self-contained and stand-alone, others are portable and can be integrated in different form factors. For Siewiorek (2017), control devices should also be enough flexible to mount on different parts of the body, facilitating user acceptance [38]. Clothes, inserts facilitate the creation of wearable technologies, including: layers of paddings, interfacing or other materials intended to give shape, strength or protective function to the garment, facilitate the creation wearable technologies. A shoulder pad, for example, can be augmented with an embedded vibrotactile display [48].

Despite wrist-worn wearables (such as smartwatches and fitness trackers) and head-mounted devices (such as virtual reality and augmented reality headsets) being the most popular form factors in use nowadays, wearable computers largely vary in their format. Examples of form factors include but are not limited to armband [49], anklet [50], badge [43], bracelet [51], belt [52], chest-mounted devices [53], contact lenses [54], earpieces [55], necklace [56], glasses [57], gloves [58], goggles [59], jacket [60], ring [61], shoes [62], vest [63], and watches [64].

Thanks to its versatility, wearable computing offers support and has already been applied to various applications: from safety-critical domains, for aircraft control, health care, monitoring vital signs [49], for accessible communication [65], to leisure [60], gaming [66], sports [62], and user interaction [59]. By employing different sensors and actuators, wearable devices support many human activities, providing a large potential for applications, especially when the integration of diverse electronics—including multimodal sensors and actuators—is considered.

The form factors of wearables vary in dimension, placement, proximity to the human body, stiffness, and functionality. In a small-scale, tooth-implanted devices, mouth-worn devices, jewelry pieces, earpieces, and accessories stand out, including rings, pendants, bottom pins, and clipped devices that serve very specific functions. SunSprite[3] is an example of such a device, aimed at measuring the level of ultraviolet radiation in the air to communicate it to the user.

---

[3]https://www.sunsprite.com/.

Despite their limited functionality, tiny devices offer the advantage of being more portable and easier to customize when compared to larger devices. Also, smaller devices tend to require less energy to operate. Medium-scale devices, including t-shirts, vests, backpacks, and shoes, cover more surface of the human body. As accessories, wearable technologies include scarves, umbrellas, and hats. Large-scale devices are best exemplified by exoskeletons that restore and augment human power and motor functions, uniforms for the military, with several electronic pieces embedded and integrated, ensembles for firefighters and spacesuits that combine several different pieces of technology to sense information from an astronaut's body in addition to environmental clues to process those and provide users with information, alerts, notifications, and services.

Depending on their placement on the wearer body, the access to the technology can be facilitated or hindered. Also, certain placements make it obvious for bystanders to notice the device, while other placements conceal the technology enabling more discrete usage. Certain garment features, such as pockets, decorations, fasteners, and its edges, afford wearers an easier access and a more obvious interaction approach [43].

To supplement their input and output capabilities, extend their features, and augment their autonomy, sensing, and processing power, wearables are often combined forming "body-area networks" that are characterized by multiple devices connected through communication channels. For Billinghurst and Starner [11], most wearable applications combine several devices, for instance, a belt or backpack PC, a head-mounted display with wireless communications, hardware, and some input devices, such as a touchpad [11].

In an experiment with electrooculogram EOG goggles, Bulling et al. [59] used a head-up display with an eye-tracker and a wearable hand-mounted keyboard (named Twiddler 2). To run the experiment software, a laptop was placed in a backpack, allowing users to move while interacting with the goggle. The keyboard allowed users to control the software [59]. For health monitoring, four physiological signals were collected: Electromyography (EMG), Blood Volume Pulse (BVP), respiration, and skin conductance. The EMG was placed on the left trapezius muscle, the Galvanic Skin Response (GSR) electrodes were placed on the index and middle finger of the right hand of the user, the BVP sensor was placed on the ring finger of his/her right hand, and the respiration sensor was placed around his/her diaphragm [67].

1.4 Sensors

To enable data collection for wearable computers, sensors acquire data about the users, their behaviors, activities, location, or environment [1]. A sensor measures a property of the physical world and produces a signal to be processed by an algorithm [1]. There are several different sensors available to measure different physical properties [1, 68]. Acceleration sensors collect data about the user activity and movements, GPS (Global Positioning System) sensors provide the user's location, and temperature sensors measure temperature levels [1]. Motion sensors, such as gyroscopes and accelerometers, measure the rate of rotation and acceleration of the user, and EMG (Electromyography) sensors measure a very small electric potential (in mV) produced during muscle activation [26].

Sensors can be classified based on their physical properties. Physical sensors are hardware sensors, such as a microphone or accelerometer [69]. While hard sensors are built of hard electronic components, soft sensors are embedded in clothing (for instance, through knitting) [70].

Soft sensors can also be considered as those sensors that record data regarding the usage of a software executed in a given device. Soft sensors can, for instance, register when and for how long the user communicates with a contact, when the device is being charged, or the frequency of use of various applications [69].

Sensors embedded in textiles can be integrated in garments to sense users' movements and to recognize their activities, for instance, a knitwear and garment designed as a sport top to detect eleven degrees of limb and upper body movement [70] and also to help monitoring physiological signals from human wearers [71]. Wearable physiological sensors that are noninvasive are used in a variety of applications, such as home health care and elderly monitoring of older adults, sensing signals such as heart rate, movement from accelerometers, and skin surface temperature [49].

For sport and health care, wearable systems can measure skin temperature, using a color and a sweat pH sensor from a functional e-textile [47]. SensVest is an example of a shirt containing accelerometers that measure body and arm movement, and the shirt also includes thermometers to measure body temperature, and monitor heart rate [2]. To sense heart rate with commercial sensors, the Garmin HRM-Run sensor and the Garmin 920xt watch are available devices [72].

Soft sensors that are inexpensive and wearable are an alternative to expensive and obtrusive sensors and trackers for long-term monitoring. If the sensors are integrated in clothing, gesture and activity recognition is no longer bound to a location and can be performed at any place at any time [70].

Accelerometers have had an extensive uptake, thanks to their availability, small size, relatively low cost, in addition to as their easy integration with existing platforms for sensor networks [64]. By collecting inertial measurement units, accelerometers are versatile, enabling a large variety of applications.

To conduct human performance assessment, advances in computing power and microelectronics were fundamental [73]. In this process, the choice of sensors for a wearable technology is driven by the need of data collection, its frequency, accuracy, the sensors' availability, and costs [70, 74]. Still, to ensure that users are comfortable when wearing a device, its sensors must be lightweight, small, and easy to attach to clothes [75].

Sensors employed in wearable technologies collect either inward data from users, including physiological and vital signals about the wearer, or outward data, including clues about the wearer environment, temperature, humidity levels, and noise, among others. When the sensor is in direct physical contact to the wearer, the material employed has to be safe and biocompatible [14]. The fixation of the sensors in place aims at ensuring that they do not fall, shift, or slip away [72], hindering the quality of

Table 1.1 Examples of sensors explored to collect data from the users' environment, activities, or physiological signs

Data type	Sensors
Environmental	Microphone, Camera, Brightness, Humidity, Proximity, RFID, GPS, Gas, Smoke
Activity	Accelerometer, Gyroscope, Magnetometer, Compass, Inertial Measurement Units
Physiological	BVP, Rate, Temperature, GSR, ECG, EEG, EMG, EOG, GSR, EDA, ECG, PPG

the readings, still they must be comfortable to wear for the user, not bothering daily life activities and human movement [76].

Inward sensors can be concealed under users' garments, whereas exposed sensors face the users' surroundings to environmental clues. Respiration sensors can be worn around the chest on top of a t-shirt, EMG sensors can be worn around the wearer bicep, a blood volume pulse (BVP) can be attached to the user wrist and a GSR sensor can be worn on two fingers. Examples of hidden sensors include the respiration sensor worn under the shirt, the EMG sensor on the trapezius (back shoulder) muscle, the galvanic skin response (GSR) sensor on the wearer foot, and the BVP sensor on the side of the neck. To integrate and conceal different sensors, a wearable computer can be hidden, for instance, in a backpack, purse, pocket, or in a tote [67].

Depending on accuracy and precision requirements of a wearable system, multiple sensors can be employed to improve the quality, validity, and reliability of the measurements. Although it is well known that the position of the sensors is important for activity classification, the sensor placement depends on the activity being monitored, and thus far few comparative studies have investigated optimal sensor placement for activities of daily living [64]. Skin conductivity, for instance, can be effectively measured from the palm of the user hand or from the sole of the user' foot. While the users foot is a discreet place to collect data, the user hands are usually busy with numerous daily activities, which create motion artifacts. Also, hand washing affects the skin conductivity. However, the skin conductance measured from the user foot can also be subject to pressure artifacts when the wearer is walking [67].

Table 1.1 lists examples of sensors used in wearables to collect data from the user's environment, activities, and physiological signals. Although few devices provide the flexibility to be placed at different locations on the body, there are sensors with specific body placements that are unique. For sensors that can be placed in multiple locations on the wearer's body and still serve the same functionality, additional requirements can be considered, for example, the interference of the placement with the user movement, the user interaction, and individual preferences.

Alternative orientations may also be possible for sensor placement, because the orientation of acceleration sensors influences the data collection, it is an important design consideration. Therefore, sensors should be oriented according to the coordinate system associated with the user body to facilitate the analysis of data

collected [76]. The sensor placement determines the level of accuracy in the readings. Jalaliniya and Pederson placed a pulse sensor in an armband and noticed that
the heart rate data from the armband was too noisy when compared to data sensed
from the ear lobe of the user [49]. For electrodermal activity (EDA) measurements,
the wrist and the ankle are not standard locations for measuring it, because the sweat
glands there are less densely distributed than those on the palm or fingers where EDA
is often measured [74]. Still EDA sensors are promising to measure stress or anxiety,
especially when such affective states cannot be communicated verbally or socially
[18].

For SpO_2, the blood oxygen saturation proxy sensor, the wrist is a non-standard
placement because a reflective sensor is required, and standard sensors transmit light
through the fingertip [14]. For kinematic features in running activities, sensors placed
on the wearer's foot and on the shin suffice to cover all the inertial measurement units
(IMU) needed to monitor fatigue and provide assistance [77]. For long-term monitoring of heart rate, a wearable belt was proposed. This device can be comfortably
worn either on the user chest or waist [78].

Although the best positioning for the sensors still poses interesting research challenges [64], if alternative placements for the same sensors are possible, it is recommended to take the users' preferences into account. For running activities and
physiological monitoring, for instance, the responses of study participants to a questionnaire indicated that they prefer to use the watch during their running activities,
instead of a glass or arm-mounted smartphone [72]. For cyclists, the choice of the
user's wrist as a placement was motivated by the fact that it supports easy and effective
actions of the wearer (to record memories) while riding a bike [19].

For electrocardiogram (ECG) monitoring, when two placements are available, the
device worn on the user's chest senses ECG with best signal quality; however, when
worn on the user waist, the device is perceived to be more comfortable, especially
for female users [78].

The choice of IMUs—their placement and number—also depends on the degrees
of freedom (DOF) of the user movement to be analyzed (as Fig. 1.5 illustrates).

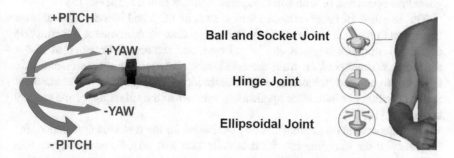

Fig. 1.5 The degrees of freedom associated to the user movement to be monitored help to inform
the placement and number of IMU sensors [26]. U.S. Government work not protected by U.S.
copyright

Placing accelerometers on too many positions is not only cumbersome for end users but it also makes the data collection prone to errors [64]. A rigid body has six degrees of freedom, three for the linear position of the center of gravity and three for the orientation [76]. For a knee brace to monitor exercise in patients with knee injury, indirect accelerometer sensors were used to gather data. By measuring the force of gravity with three degrees of freedom, measured by one sensor above and another below the knee, it was feasible to detect the angle the user joint moved [30]. Using optical fiber curvature sensors, two or more degrees of freedom of motion can be measured [75].

Applied to measure movement, the Euler angles are defined as follows [76]:

1. Rotation around the Z-axis, the yaw angle.
2. Rotation around the Y-axis, the pitch angle.
3. Rotation around the X-axis, the roll angle.

The pitch angle measures the body balance. The roll angle measures the body rotation around the longitudinal axis. The yaw angle measures the direction, which cannot be determined with the accelerometer, because the rotation axis is parallel to the gravity [76].

For EOG, the eye movements are tracked by analyzing the changes in the signal collected. While electrode pairs are able to capture the horizontal and the vertical components of eye motion, a good electrode placement is required on the eyes' horizontal and vertical axes of motion. Otherwise, there is an increased crosstalk between both components. Signal crosstalk hinders a robust detection of eye movement events and eye gaze tracking. In addition to a good fit of the device, electrodes should be appropriately placed. Dry skin of users, for instance, can compromise the reading of signals even when the EOG goggles have a good fit [59].

For measuring the human body motion for motor-impaired users, optical fiber (OF) curvature sensors can be employed. Optical fibers are suitable for sensors that measure the body motions because of their flexibility, lightness, small size, and low cost. Calibration and mapping methods are needed, but the sensors allow for extracting 2-DOF from human shoulder motions, being constructed either with simple geometric equations, or with a multilayered artificial neural network [75].

The selection of health-related sensors, such as ECG and blood pressure, must be subject to medical validation [14]. For temperature measurements, a thermopile or a thermistor measurement can be selected, and the results investigated to opt for more accurate choices. Still, the relationship between the measurement, skin temperature, and body temperature is a research topic that requires further assessment and exploration per individual application, even when the validation of the sensors is required [14].

Also, depending on the functionality envisaged for the wearable application, the frequency of the sampling rate for data collection will vary. Some data types will require continuous data collection, like heart rate or body temperature, and other applications may require discrete data collection, like hours of sleep. The inherent trade-off of the frequency of data collection involves battery level and storage. For instance, seeking to avoid battery depletion, the developer may decide to record location information every five minutes, or due to privacy concerns, location can be collected only from Mondays to Fridays from 9am to 2pm [69].

In terms of interaction, some sensors require explicit interaction from wearers, like capacitive screens or touchpads, whereas passive sensors, such as microphones, require no user attention [11]. Self-reports, including ecological momentary sampling, also aid in data collection and annotations. Concerning their popularity, some sensors are commonly encountered in various mobile devices (like microphones, GPS, and accelerometers available in smartphones [79]), whereas others are very specific and may even require individual calibration [80]—like the EMG, EOG, ECG, and EEG.

In health care, wearable sensors for long-term measurement of electrodermal activity, temperature, motor activity, and photoplethysmography are encountered mostly in dedicated applications [74]. While plethysmography is a noninvasive technique to measure volume changes in the body (such as those caused by blood being forced into vessels) [81], photoplethysmography (PPG), for instance, helps detecting the blood volume pulse by measuring the relative absorption of near infrared light on the wearer skin. Since oxygenated and de-oxygenated blood exhibits different light absorptions, the measurement at two wavelengths can be used to calculate the relative oxygen saturation in the blood (SpO_2) [18]. For HealthGear, for illustration, to constantly monitor and analyze the user's blood oxygen level (SpO_2), heart rate, and plethysmographic signals, an oximeter was used [81].

In healthcare, a wearable device that senses ECG, PPG signals, and indirectly estimates arterial blood pressure levels has an immeasurable value for continuous monitoring of users' physiological signals [82].

Also concerning healthcare sensors, the EQ01 is a chest-mounted device for monitoring physiological signals. It senses electrocardiogram (from which is derived the heart rate), respiration at 25.6 Hz through an embedded strain gauge, motion (acceleration at 25.6 Hz), and body skin temperature [83].

The design decisions of device placement, number, and type of sensors involve several trade-offs, depending mostly on the system requirements, be those functional (in what regards the data to be collected) or nonfunctional ones, concerning quality factors such as the user comfort. Requirements under consideration include the user and the system needs for accuracy, comfort, utility, and safety, among others. The placement of devices at limbs can be perceived as obtrusive if the device dimensions and weight exceed low limits.

While wearing a watch at the wrist is often assumed to be comfortable concerning size and weight for upper limbs, certain types of shoes may be too cumbersome for users to execute everyday activities [7]. EMG can be used for an all-in-one recognition system. However, to perform simple and intuitive gestures, several electrodes are needed, which makes EMG sensors complex to position. Using several EMG sensors also requires significant signal processing, which is overly complex for most users, especially for novice and non-experts [26].

While small, lightweight sensor embodiment is preferable, oftentimes, the maximum information content in fine granularity levels is also needed [64]. Small form factors increase wearability and users' comfort levels; however, a more detailed data collection, combining various signals from multiple sensors, has the advantage of avoiding the time-consuming manual data labeling task, often necessary to annotate different user activities [64].

To facilitate the identification of ideal placements for data gathering, and experiment with inertial measurement unit (IMU) sensor, Munoz et al. [30] used Velcro-backed patches of neoprene and attached the sensors to these patches so that they could move the sensors to different positions on the knee brace as needed. Moving the sensors' placement allows stakehoders to check the quality levels of multiple different readings [30]. For the optical fiber curvature sensor, the position of the sensor was selected by searching for the position where the maximum amount of change of sensor data was found [75].

To ensure high quality and accuracy in the data collection, investigators should also ensure that sensors are attached well to the users' skin. Seuter et al. [72] used markers placed using double-sided tape to that end. Also, an elastic fixation tape between the skin and the double-sided tape was used to prevent markers from falling off when in contact with sweat in an experiment involving running activities [72]. Although no marker fell in the experiment because fixation addressed potential problems with sweat and movement, the markers attached to the skin may have bothered participants, even if they did not report to feel uncomfortable [72].

Multiple types and placements of sensors can be combined to ensure accuracy in the data collection [68]. Accelerometers alone, for instance, are not enough to provide context information; thus they need to be combined with other sensors, including microphones, gyroscopes, and ECG sensors, seeking to facilitate accurate activity classification [64]. For Cannan and Hu [26], by combining sensors, such as gyroscope and accelerometers, the wearer control for input via armbands can be improved [26]. To detect user activity with a jacket, for instance, 11 knitted sensor strips can be placed over the elbow and shoulder joints of the wearer. In the initial version of such a garment, investigators first distributed six sensors on the right side of the user, enabling the measurement of his/her right elbow movement using one sensor along the joint. In the same project, to measure the position and movements of the right upper arm, three sensors were used: two for measuring upper arm movements in a vertical axis. The investigators placed the sensors on the wearer shoulder and at his/her armpit. Another sensor strip was positioned on the upper back and shoulder of the wearer to measure position and movements of the upper arm in a horizontal axis. Lastly, to detect bending forward, a sensor was placed below the chest of the wearers and also diagonally across the center of his/her back [70].

Concerning the placement for EDA sensors, the main benefit of sensing it from the wrist or ankle is that "the sensor can be comfortably worn for long periods of time (days and weeks) by adults and by small children (ages 3–6) without interfering with activities of daily living, such as sleeping, washing hands, or typing" [74]. For acceleration, the choice of sensor can consider the measurement of constant and varying accelerations as well as its financial cost [70]. For measuring human posture, three accelerometers have been attached to the wearer trunk, thigh, and calf. Also, a gyro-sensor was attached to the thigh and the walking speed was calculated from the thigh angle changes, walking cycle and leg length [84]. A gyroscope provides the rate of rotation in degrees per second, which is linear, and thus does not require significant processing [26].

Concerning PPG, besides using a wristband form factor, other body placements and form factors (earpiece and earphones) have also been explored for heart rate measurement using PPG [18]. To exchange information through handshaking an infrared (IR) transceiver alignment can be combined with a sensed up-and-down motion. IR transmission is only activated when the wearers' hands or wrists are already in a pre-calibrated handshaking orientation [85].

For EDA and ECG, data collected via gel sensors (such as the Ambu Blue Sensor) was considered to provide high-fidelity measures. The other benefits of gel sensors include they being disposable, gentle on the user skin, and alcohol-free. Concerning data collection, ECG sensors can be placed on the upper part of each user arm, and EDA can be collected with sensors placed on the sole of the foot of the wearer [86].

For sports and exercise monitoring, sensor units capture data and signals about the user speed, distance completed, and heart rate, among others. Such data inform users about their performance and physical condition [76].

To build a wearable augmented reality audio terminal, microphones in a binaural headset can be used, requiring no additional hardware for tracking data. Those binaural signals can also help localizing unknown sources of sound and estimating the acoustic properties of the user environment, facilitating thus context recognition [87].

The merits of electronic and fabric sensors strongly depend on their individual applications. In this context, design decisions are mainly driven by the availability and costs of the components. Their reduced dimensions and portability are particularly beneficial for sensors well suited to be worn with any other clothing [70].

Through sensors and actuators embedded in garments and wearable devices, physiological data previously considered as private can become visually represented and aesthetically displayed. Such representations create an extended experience of the user by explicitly communicating information to others [88].

1.5 Features

The availability of a wide range of sensors on wearables, including physiological sensors, activity sensors, and audiovisual sensors, has facilitated the creation of several applications across domains [89]. Wearable computers are able to assist users in numerous activities of daily living, including shopping, sports, and leisure [7]. For the workplace, wearable devices can serve different purposes for activities such as monitoring, augmenting, assisting, delivering, and tracking, all of which, when well implemented, facilitate the adoption of devices by wearers [34, 90].

Wearable technologies provide solutions to users in scenarios varying from authentication to assistive support, be it when wearers have situation-induced impairments or are busy with main tasks, such as driving or running. For Nunez and Loke

[88], ubiquitous computing allows interaction designers to create wearable technologies that amplify human senses through the environment [88].

Overall, the features available on wearables include data collection and processing to provide useful information, resources, and services for end users. Wearable features augment users' abilities or help systems to better understand the contexts where the user is located, for example, using badges or jackets that collect and use the information in a favorable way [70]. Main abstract features include reading and storing sensor data, feature extraction, and classifying information based on pattern and statistical modeling [7]. For Scheffler and Hirt [14], key requirements for a successful wearable application, in addition to data collection and processing, include computational power (with low power consumption), mobile data storage, and wireless communication capabilities [14].

The specific features of a wearable technology depend on the application goal and domain. For Smailagic and Siewiorek [42], wearables support mainly information access through graphics and text, communication, collaboration and assistance, maintenance, and context sensing [42]. Some wearables are purely passive, sensing information from the users' environment, while others are active, requiring explicit interaction from the wearer to respond appropriately.

For activity recognition, body-area networks combining sensors on the wearers' calf and trunk [84] as well as wearable badges have been explored to detect when users are standing, lying (face up or down), sitting, walking, or running [70]. Advances in sensors allow wearable devices to be deployed for human activity recognition (HAR) and to enable continuous long-term activity monitoring [68].

In health care, wearables aim at making patients more independent of their physician, providing them the opportunity to conduct simple measurements on their own and as such more actively participate in their medical care. "Wearable" (and not only portable) ensures that the technologies are so small and unobtrusive that they accompany the user to any place and at any time [14].

Wearables allow for monitoring human activities, be it through wearable cameras [91] or with other sensors used to detect users' motion, when they stand up, walk, and sit, or with physiological sensors, such as a blood oximeter to monitor the user's blood oxygen level and pulse [81] and blood pressure measuring pulse transit times (PTT) [92]. In the recognition of human activity, wearables assess physical movements and exercising, e.g., climbing stairs or using an elevator, determining eating habits, social contacts, emotional status as well as stress levels [7]. Motion features are useful for rehabilitation as well as long-term care [84]. To monitor and classify the physical activity of a wearer, temperature sensors and accelerometers are often used [18]. To record everyday activities of children with autism, caregivers can wear recording devices. Despite some impact on their everyday instructional and caregiving activities, wearable devices facilitate note-taking in certain situations [91].

In fitness applications, potential involve monitoring fatigue, as well as training assistance [77]. To enable in situ data collection through wearables using embedded or attached sensors, local data storage is necessary to maintain the data collected [93].

To support text entry, forearm-mounted keyboards have been explored [94]. In health care, low-cost wearable devices have potential to manage chronic health problems, prevent diseases, help in earlier diagnosis, provide continuous monitoring, therapeutic, and rehabilitation functions. From a cost perspective, the primary goal of wearable health is to steer health care from hospital, clinics, and emergency rooms toward preemptive care and outpatient monitoring, focusing on technologies that enable continuous health monitoring [18].

The benefits of wearable health include reducing medical expenses and healthcare costs by shifting the care to a more patient-centric, personalized, and preventive approach [95–97]. Also, new wearable materials, coupled with small long-lasting batteries, enable data collection over time in nonclinical settings [74].

Besides enabling information access available from any place and at any time, the wearable computing system should be aware of the user's context to respond in an appropriate way according to the user's cognitive and social state, anticipating his/her intentions and needs [42].

1.6 Application Domains

By meeting basic needs for data collection, wearable applications are well suited to meet requirements from numerous cyber-physical applications. The domains explored thus far include but are not limited to environmental monitoring, health care, security, and industrial applications [47]. Concerning basic human activities, wearables are able to support human language skills, augmenting memory, cognition, and executive functions [98]. By replacing, restoring, and augmenting users' abilities, wearable computers can also aid communication and collaboration [11], besides helping users with activities that range from inspection, maintenance, manufacturing, and navigation to on-the-move collaboration, position sensing, and real-time speech recognition and language translation [42]. With the variety of form factors for wearable technologies, their benefits impact not only the individual wearer but organizational settings as well [34].

Initially, wearable computers began to be used in niche applications that required the wearer to be mobile and have hands-free access to information and computing power. Early-stage applications viewed the human–computer interaction as a secondary task [11]. However, with advances in technology, wearable applications spread out across sectors, finding multiple opportunities for useful task support. Applications started to appear in military and medical emergency response, warehouse inventory, vehicle maintenance [11], and farming [99].

Because wearables are more easily accessible than conventional mobile devices, they improve users' lives in several ways for health and fitness, personal abilities, self-confidence, and infotainment [45]. In health care, they support monitoring and reminder tasks, helping diabetic patients with glucometers and insulin pumps, and veterans with adherence for medication intake. As assistive technologies, they aid people with visual, hearing, motor, and cognitive impairments [98].

Table 1.2 provides a list of applications of wearable computers in eight domains, specifying their goals and form factors. In entertainment, wearables provide gaming tools, painting support, and decorative artifacts. In beauty and fashion, they augment nail polish, makeup, and garments [100]. In the military, they also serve to monitor physiological signals in the battlefield, and to communicate health conditions in real time. In the workplace, they help stakeholders to complete their activities with higher performance in annotation tasks [101] and car manufacturing [102], among others.

1.6.1 Education

Wearable technology has a promising potential to be an agent of transformation in schools [103]. In education, wearables can help students to interact with their instructors, and instructors to receive guidance in real time through augmented reality devices [103]. In education, wearable features range from data collection and monitoring of students' behaviors and affective states, for later retrieval of experiences [91], to timely delivery of personalized notifications, alerts, and reminders [8].

In educational settings, the wearability of the device as well as the end user attitudes influence the user intention to adopt a wearable. Moreover, the application performance and required interaction efforts regarding users' expectations impact the wearer's attitude. Additionally, privacy concerns and social influences are related to the intention to use. Lastly, the design and physical characteristics of a device have significant influences on the wearer intentions to use a device [34].

Concerning the monitoring of users' daily activities, wearable technologies are often integrated in a body-area network. The integration of head-mounted devices with belt buckles allows for the recognition of social interactions and other activities of students, including discussions, lecture, meetings, phone calls, physical exercises, eating, and drinking habits [7]. Prior work on wearable education involves the usage of handheld devices for note-taking [91], wrist-worn devices, and head-mounted displays. Wearable applications in educational settings improve teaching and learning experiences, for instance, by aiding to teach children about math, science, and physical education [104, 105], teenagers about physics and sciences [22, 104, 106], young adults about programming, computing, engineering, environmental and cognitive sciences [107–109], and instructors for improved communication [107].

Although the prevalence of wearable technologies for teaching and learning is currently unclear, the limited literature in this domain suggests that wearable technologies are not yet being fully harnessed for education [110].

Concerning the integration of wearable computing in the educational curriculum, wearable-based inquiry has been previously explored. In the context of elementary classrooms, live physiological sensing and visualization tools were used to provide age-appropriate scaffolds for students, adapting the class contents according to the teacher perspectives. In this experiment, a 2-year, iterative process was followed to develop scaffolds and implement them in four elementary classrooms. The participatory designed scaffolds were able to impact the inquiry experiences of the learners through a wearable-based, authentic approach [111]. Wearables also hold great potential to motivate students to learn more about technology and computing in a context that is considered to be futuristic, innovative, and creative as well [20].

1.6.2 Health Care

To collect health monitoring data, wearable devices not only provide local processing capabilities but can also grant access to cloud functionalities, be those for storage purposes or for advanced analytic features [83]. Wearable technology stands out in health care, mostly because electronic smart devices have a large potential to monitor the vital signs of patients. Additionally, wearables can empower practitioners to diagnose diseases in early stages [47]. Wearable sensors that are less obtrusive and stand-alone also allow for low-cost healthcare systems to be applied in a wide range of medical interventions and therapies [18]. Wearable health solutions are numerous and varied. While continuously monitoring patient health data, wearables allow doctors to predict diseases and also to provide optimal treatment. In this context, healthcare costs can be reduced, avoiding medical treatments in later disease stages with earlier diagnosis [14].

The increasing prevalence of wearable sensors that are low cost makes health monitoring an impactful and appealing target for wearable computing [86]. In health care, wearable applications focus primarily on monitoring [84] and alerting patients [112], for instance, through wearable sensors for long-term measurement of electro-dermal activity, temperature, motor activity, and photoplethysmography [74]. Wearable technology can support additional sensing modalities, including pulse oximetry, blood pressure, electrocardiography, and glucose [113]. In this context, companies compete to release wearable devices that provide health-related functions, including the monitoring, collection, and presentation of information concerning quality of sleep, distance traveled, calories burned [114], and eating habits [115]. Examples of such applications include HealthGear [81], MoodWing [86], and Auracle [115].

HealthGear uses noninvasive sensors wirelessly connected via Bluetooth to a cell phone to provide a real-time wearable system that monitors physiological signals from end users. The system stores, transmits, and analyzes the physiological data, presenting the analysis results to the user [81]. In MoodWing, eight biosignal channels are collected, including EDA and ECG, to monitor stress levels of the user [86].

In Auracle, an earpiece was designed to detect chewing and as such monitor eating habits of end users. Auracle uses an off-the-shelf contact microphone which is positioned behind the user's ear [115].

Three main features are enabled by wearables for health: long-term monitoring, recording, and prevention [41]. Thanks to such potential, wearables facilitate the treatment and management of many chronic illnesses, neurological disorders, and mental health issues [18]. Examples of medical conditions that can benefit from wearable technologies include but are not limited to diabetes, autism spectrum disorder (ASD), depression, drug addition, and anxiety disorders [18].

Additionally, wearable technologies can also aid caregivers and physicians to better understand medical conditions, longitudinally and in a large scale, allowing medical studies with more diverse populations to ensure generalizability and minimize the overfitting in predictive models [113].

Thus, not only the data collected from one patient can be considered for health assessment and care, but also aggregated records from a number of patients that share similar conditions. This massive collection and processing of health data has potential to greatly boost the medical understanding, leading to an optimal provision of care. In the long run, the data collected could be further processed to infer information about the users' physiological conditions, or even to determine certain behavioral patterns of specific user groups, including older adults and users with diverse needs [34, 83].

The key beneficiaries of wearable health include thus as primary stakeholders, patients, and medical practitioners as end users, as well as secondary stakeholders, caregivers and scientific investigators that can be informed by the data collected through wearable sensors. Interactive dashboards and visualization tools facilitate the aggregation, analysis, and interpretation of the data collected [30]. In PhysioDroid, for instance, remotely stored health data were accessible to doctors, or any other authorized third party, such as a clinician, so that they could monitor the patients' information [83].

In MoodWings, a visualization enabled the researcher to determine when users were stressed. The visualization showed 30 seconds of raw ECG data, bandpass-filtered ECG data (without background noise), lowpass-filtered ECG data (showing respiration rate), and raw EDA data [86]. Such a visualization tool can enable investigators to rescale data streams to incorporate new maxima or minima, and to compare local or global contexts [86].

For telemonitoring, a portable system was implemented to provide the clinician direct access to patient's information. This system included a head-mounted display (HMD) powered by a wearable computer connected to a wireless network. A wrist-mounted keyboard and a hip-mounted mouse enabled data entry. Regarding patient's information (such as heart rate and blood pressure), webcam images transmitted via a wireless network provided access to for other clinicians [117].

Prior work on wearable health explored also prevention, diagnose, treatment, rehabilitation, and behavior change, targeting at chronic diseases, such as diabetes, Parkinson, and cardiac diseases. For alert and monitoring, wearable health systems have been explored for cardiac patients [118], for monitoring the users' postures [84, 119], respiration rates [120], temperature via long-wave infrared sensors and heart rate through PPG [55].

For rehabilitation, a knee brace was created to facilitate counting the repetitions and exercise routines of patients with knee injury. Such a device placed the locus of control externally, allowing the physical therapist to minimally interfere with the patients' lives [30]. For Gioberto et al. [121], smart fabrics allow for convenient wearable sensing solutions to monitor body movements during everyday activities [121]. Such monitoring is fundamental in several chronic diseases and specific medical conditions, for instance, to prevent and detect fall in older adults [52]. Another advantage is that wearables can be less stigmatizing, since they not always look like a medical device [14].

A number of design challenges remain open to be addressed before wearable health can be fully exploited, especially concerning users' and data privacy, device safety, regulatory legislation, and standards. Such concerns must be weighed carefully before advocating for large-scale adoption of wearable devices in clinical care [15].

1.6.3 Industry

The widespread popularity of wearable computing follows a shift from stationary desktop PCs to laptops, tablets, and smartphones that enabled individuals to be connected and work on the go [45]. Like the smartphone, wearables hold potential to transition from an individual usage to enterprise usage [122]. In industrial settings, wearable technologies can be beneficial for employers and employees as well, serving, for instance, to increase efficiency and productivity and to reduce operational costs [34]. In organizational settings, the technological, social, policy, and economic challenges related to the use of wearable devices strongly affect the adoption of wearable devices [34].

In industry, applications for wearables include mechanical assembly of vehicles, routine inspection and audit of machine components, and preparation of medical equipment in health care [1]. For instance, to support training procedures of blue-collar assembly line workers, a wearable solution (named KATO) was created. To provide trainees with information to perform production tasks, the wearable offered a mobile semi-autonomous training using context information. The production tasks were tracked via mobile sensors mounted on the worker body and in the environment. The application aids the trainees by detecting performance errors, displaying context-sensitive help and suggestions. The trainee interacted with the wearable system through voice or a HMD [1]. Using the KATO maintenance assistant, through the HMD the technician could access information about maintenance procedures, a defect list, and material of system failures to be fixed. Defect reports could be examined in detail, by browsing maintenance and troubleshooting manuals in the HMD using a gesture interface [1].

Although it may take several years before wearable computers become mainstream in the workplace, companies began to apply the technology in specific scenarios. Noteworthy projects demonstrate the benefits of using a general-purpose wearable computer to support collaboration and performance in workplace activities [11]. In the industrial sector, wearables have been explored for manufacturing [102], assembly [79], and to help picking items in warehouse and to monitor posture of workers [119]. In avionics, Boeing equipped mechanics with a wearable computer to access all the plane's documentation, guiding them in decision-making so that they could identify faults more quickly [11].

Wearable support systems for electronic performance provide an advantage to workers in jobs that require real-time information access, enabling mobility, as well as hands-free interaction and information access. The rise of mobile systems, such as the wearable check-out devices used by staff at automobile rental facilities, indicates an increasing interest in wearable solutions for industrial applications. The cost-effectiveness of these systems still needs to be further assessed by the research community though [123].

1.6.4 *Fitness and Sports*

In the lay market of fitness monitoring, wearable technology that tracks health-related parameters has been gaining popularity [113]. Although the most popular wearable sport technologies today are heart rate monitors, widely used to sense the heart rate of the athletes [76], the application of wearables in fitness and exercise activities vary largely, ranging from assessment of body movement, vibration-based muscle therapy, virtual coaching, sports performance monitoring and evaluation support [89].

For Nguyen et al. [68], wearables enable human activity analysis in sports, and by better understanding athletic movements, coaches and managers can assess their players' performance, predict injuries, optimize training programs, and support strategic decision-making [68].

Athletes as potential users can embrace wearable technologies, envisioning devices that facilitate data collection during workouts, with precise and real values, rather than estimated calculations based on standard norms [40].

Ubiquitous fitness trackers come in a variety of form factors, and their continuous tracking features help users to navigate everyday choice making, besides also better controlling their bites, sips, steps, and minutes of sleep [124]. Most trackers include an accelerometer to measure user movement and to estimate the number of steps taken, as well as total calories burned. Examples of exercises and sports already investigated for wearable technologies include climbing [125], cycling [19, 126], swimming [76], basketball [68], and running [72, 77].

Despite issues with battery life, privacy and data accuracy, for Seuter et al. [72], the use of wearable devices among runners particularly has become a commonplace [72]. For runners' kinematic analysis, measurements involve foot contact duration, the foot strike type, and the heel lift [77]. The features and capabilities of fitness trackers range from information related to physical activity, eating habits, and mental states. Many devices also include other sensors, such as a heart rate sensor, a sleep tracker, a skin conductance sensor, and light sensors [15]. While some devices are dedicated to passively sense users' data, others provide interventions and recommendations as well.

Mopet, for instance, is a wearable system to supervise physical fitness activity based on alternating jogging and fitness exercises in outdoor environments. The system combines real-time data from sensors with human-domain knowledge from experts, and a user model that is created and periodically updated with guided auto-tests [41].

The Fitbit Charge wristband, for instance, tracks steps taken, calories burned, floors climbed, and sleep quality. While some fitness trackers collect all the information via embedded sensors, others allow data entry via a mobile app or web application [127].

For monitoring swimming, a wearable assistant was implemented. It integrates acceleration sensors with microcontrollers and feedback interface modules to assist swimmers while exercising. The system monitors time per lane, the swimming velocity, and the number of strokes per lane, enabling continuous swim performance evaluation. Body balance and body rotation can be analyzed by the system too [76].

For the analysis of games, a wearable board was created combining an accelerometer and magnetometer system with a gyroscope system. The board included also a pressure sensor to detect falls or movements based on altitude changes (mainly postural transitions) using a MEMS (microelectromechanical systems), a pressure sensor, and a barometric sensor [68].

For cyclists to capture their memories while riding their bikes, a bracelet instrumented with LilyPad Arduino was created. Called thimble, the input device integrated a LilyPad Button Board connected to a Lilypad and sewn in a bracelet using e-textiles. This input device is able to activate the camera of a mobile phone. Also, it records the position and the speed of the user and the weather conditions using the device sensors placed on a bike [19].

For Bachlin et al. [76], the typical wearable device for sport monitoring is worn on the user wrist, equipped with tiny buttons on the side, or on the top, for input entry. It should feature a small display to present information and control options for the wearer. Also, it should include a piezo-electric beeper for feedback and output responses [76].

1.6.5 Assistive Technologies

Assistive technologies have a long history of benefiting users with diverse needs and disabilities, enabling them to be more included in society [128]. With the proliferation of consumer wearable devices (such as smartwatches), it becomes more practical and affordable to use wearables as assistive technologies [129]. Wearable real-time assistive technologies, for instance, can aid people with social disabilities in their communication and social interaction [128].

Due to their data collection and prompt response capabilities, wearable technologies have a promising potential as assistive technologies [130–132]. Through unobtrusive monitoring and prompt interventions, wrist-worn devices are well suited to provide continuous and consistent support for people with diverse needs regardless of their location [133]. For innovations in assistive technology, wearables are an active and exciting area [134]. Commercial wearables are the best example of an emergent technology that serves as a suitable vehicle for assistive technologies for cognition, with promising potential for inclusion and acceptance [131].

As assistive technologies, wearable applications have been explored for sign language recognition [135], and to support users with visual impairments (such as color-blindness [136], and blindness [137]), hearing impairments (deaf, deafened, and hard of hearing) [138–140], cognitive impairments [129, 132], neurodevelopmental disorders [141], and motor impairments [26, 142].

For people with spinal injury who can move their neck and shoulders but cannot move their legs and arms, a wearable master device was created to measure the movements of their neck or shoulder and as such help them to drive a wheelchair [75].

For children with neurodevelopmental disorders (NDD), particularly autism spectrum disorders, Wearable Immersive Virtual Reality (WIVR) can be applied. Be Trendy is a WIVR application that benefits from immersive virtual reality to challenge the cognitive capabilities of children, to improve learning, attention span, memory, and social skills. The application is modular and remote, and it can be embedded in current NDD interventions [141].

For young adults with intellectual disabilities following an inclusive postsecondary education program, a smartwatch application, WELI, was created to help them with emotional regulation, reminders, and interventions. The watch is controlled by a mobile application, and interventions can be triggered remotely by an assistant [143, 144].

For caregivers of children with autism, a handheld device for monitoring activities and buffering experiences has been explored [91]. For motor impairments of individuals with some arm movement and arm voluntary muscle contraction control, an input device, called a GE-Fusion Band, was created. This armband fuses signals from Gyro and EMG sensors, serving for various potential applications [26].

For children with profound hearing loss, a tactile sensory aid in the form of a belt was created. The belt is worn around the user abdomen, and it displays sound frequencies as touch patterns [139].

For raising users' awareness about their affective states, MoodWing is a wearable device mounted on users' wrist and foot. MoodWing is recommended for people who are less capable of affective expression, such as babies, ill children, and elderly people in nursing homes [86].

To support adults with mild dementia, in work environments, wearables can address issues related to health, family, and productivity support as well [129].

1.6.6 Music, Leisure, Arts, and Entertainment

In music and arts contexts, wearable gloves have been explored to train piano players, and augmented costumes have been explored in the entertainment industry. As Fig. 1.6 illustrates, glasses and shirts can be augmented with lights. In the fashion industry, the goal of wearables is to make a positive impact on appearance and to

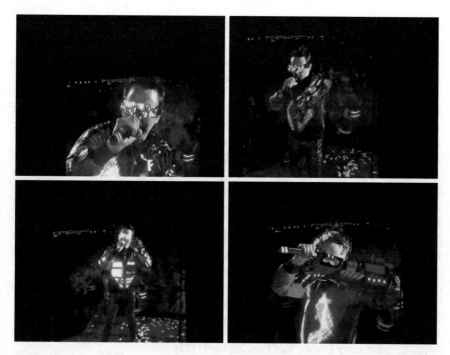

Fig. 1.6 Singer wearing augmented glasses with lights, instrumented shirt, and sleeves. Personal archive

create fascinating fashion pieces, including decorative displays, light adornments, and tracking displays of emotions on clothing items [89].

By insulating electronics in silver and polyester and directly weaving them into clothing, a German company developed an approach to integrate microprocessors and sensors into clothing that can be washed and dry-cleaned. In 2002, the company introduced a wearable MP3 player with a half-inch-square chip, small battery, and multimedia card-sewn into a jacket and activated by voice commands [39].

Using earpieces, Song et al. [145] proposed a wearable audio player system to playback the digital audio signal transmitted through the wearer's body. To reduce the power consumption for audio transmission, the system uses a wideband signaling human body communication scheme [145].

Concerning wearable art installations, the Eloquent Robes is a project for the visualization of heartbeat data on the body to explicitly communicate intimate physiological data [88]. Wearers dress with an undergarment containing a large pocket situated between their shoulder blades. This pocket contains electronic components, such as an Arduino UNO, wireless communication devices (XBee), a pulse sensor, and batteries. A white paper garment covers the undergarment. Biofeedback with colored circles was generated from a pulse sensor attached to the earlobe of the user, and projected on the garment. The colors of the heartbeat were divided in six ranges: the warmer the color, the faster the heartbeat [88].

1.6.7 Safety-Critical Systems and Military Applications

Wearable technologies have useful military applications if they are acceptable by soldiers, able to provide important actionable information [73], and to stand harsh users' environments [38]. Devices must be small and light enough to be carried in a pocket or embedded in fabric. Also, they must be durable to withstand harsh conditions, including rain and the turbulence they are subjected to in a washing machine. In hazardous environments, it is necessary to consider that users must wear the right personal protective equipment [34].

Military applications must have a low probability of detection and interception [39]. Additional requirements include ensuring the validation of algorithms to make real-time computed information useful, and opening the architectural design to allow integration with the ecosystem of devices and technologies from soldiers [73]. For Billinghurst and Starner [11], the combination of several different wearable devices can dramatically improve user performance in applications such as aircraft maintenance, navigational assistance, and vehicle inspection [11].

Friedl [73] highlights several applications of wearables for physiological monitoring related to soldier status (or "readiness score"). The signals involved comprise thermal work limits, alertness and fitness for duty status, musculoskeletal fatigue limits, neuropsychological status, and mission-specific physiological status (such as hypoxia, pulmonary threats, and freezing cold) [73].

For firefighters, gloves augmented with tactile feedback can aid in low vision settings [146]. For soldiers, physiological monitoring through wearables can predict an individual's health and performance [73]. For aeronautics, inspections can be facilitated through wearable systems. The Navigator 2, for instance, was a back-mounted device created to facilitate an aircraft sheet metal inspection. The device trial was conducted on KC-135 refueling tankers at the Air Logistics Command in Sacramento, CA [38]. Regardless of their goal, wearables for the military and safety-critical solutions should carefully consider the users' contexts, main activities, and their inherent requirements and constraints. As Siewiorek [38] highlights, aircraft workers need to squeeze into tight places and do not want anything to add dimension to their body; also, sailors on aircraft carriers use their shoulders to carry tie-down chains [38].

For firefighters, some of the physiological sensors that wearable devices include are heart rate (HR), respiratory rate (RR), skin temperature (Tsk), oxygen saturation (SaO_2), tidal volume (VT), and minute ventilation (VE). Plethysmographic sensors are usually integrated in vests, stored onto a small, portable data recorder carried in a pouch and telemetered in real time to a laptop computer [147].

1.6.8 Interaction Support

Physiological signals, including EMG and EOG, can also be used to control multimodal systems. While EMG arises from electrical activity caused by muscle contractions, EOG is generated by blinking and other eye movements as well [45].

Wearable input devices include commercial armbands—like the Thalmic Myo. The Myo was a gesture-controlled armband that used electromyography (EMG) sensors and a nine-axis inertial measurement unit (IMU) to sense motion, orientation, and rotation of the user forearm [46]. It detected arm gestures of the user with EMG sensors and translated it to input commands. Although Myo was discontinued in 2018, it served as a good demonstration of how wearables can assist the user interaction. Handheld devices and gloves, such as the interactive glove illustrated in Fig. 1.7, have also been explored as input entry interface. The Argot glove, for instance, allowed wearers to type letters, numbers, and symbols. The glove employed weak magnetic interactions for "key" presses to provide passive haptic feedback and reduce the need for precision in proprioceptive hand positioning [148].

Data gloves support hand gesture as input interaction. For that end, the glove hardware can feature 3D acceleration sensors, or a tilt sensor. The hardware should also include a multichannel reusable sensor board that can be accessed via Bluetooth, a Bluetooth keyboard, and an integrated RFID reader [1]. For text entry, three keyboard versions have been explored, including a forearm-mounted keyboard (FK), a virtual keyboard (VK), and a Kordic keypad (KK) [94]. For handshake detection, a bracelet was investigated, enabling the wearers to exchange information about themselves and their relationships [85].

The Fusion armband (described in the Sect. 1.6.5) was created to support input entry for users with motor impairments. Among the applications envisioned, the authors remarked control of mobile phones, interfaces with electronic wheelchairs, control of computer mouse, 3D object manipulation, virtual reality, robot controls, robotic arm control, virtual witting, virtual signature used for passwords, document signature, TV remote controls, rehabilitation, and games console [26].

To support the wearer interaction with a hands-free approach, eye gestures can be efficiently recognized from EOG signals from goggles. Using a camera to instrument a regular glass, Arai [149] developed a wearable device for input entry. The head-

Fig. 1.7 Interactive gloves instrumented with sensors and actuators can support the user interaction, serving also as assistive technologies for users with motor or situational impairments. Credit: Sophy Wong. At https://sophywong.com

Table 1.2 Examples of applications of wearable computing across domains

Domain	Goal	Form factor	References
Education	Experience buffer	Handheld device	[91]
	Student tracker	Belt buckle	[7]
Fitness and sports	Running monitoring	Anklet and shoe	[77]
	Basketball monitoring	Back-mounted	[68]
	Climbing	Body-area	[125]
	Swimming monitoring	Body-area	[76]
Interaction	Text entry	Forearm keyboard	[94]
	Eye-based input entry	Glass	[149]
	Eye tracking	Goggle	[59]
	Haptic display	Finger-mounted	[151]
Assistive device	Input control	Armband	[26]
	Emotion regulation	Smartwatch	[143]
	Tactile feedback for sounds	Belt	[139]
	Motion detection for motor-impaired	Chest-mounted	[75]
Health care	Health monitoring	Vest	[112]
	Mental health monitoring	Headband	[152]
	Physiological monitoring for apnea	Finger-mounted	[81]
	Monitoring of eating habits	Earpiece	[115]
	Rehabilitation	Knee Brace	[30]
	Fall detection	Belt	[52]
	Heart rate monitoring (PPG)	Earpiece	[55]
	Heart rate monitoring (ECG)	Chest-mounted	[53]
	Respiration rate (breathing)	Textile	[71]
Entertainment	Music player	Earpiece	[145]
	Piano practice	Glove	[153]
	Physiological awareness	Body-area	[88]
Safety-critical	Vital sign detection	Body-area	[154]
	Augmented reality for firefighters	Glove	[146]
	Aircraft inspection	Back-mounted	[38]
Social interaction	Handshake	Bracelet	[85]

[a]The list is not exhaustive

mounted display is coupled with a mobile phone and a tablet for processing the data [149]. A major advantage of using EOG to support wearer interaction is the minimal requirements of power and computation for signal processing [59]. For Bulling et al. [59], "EOG-based eye input allows for versatile human–computer interaction and may eventually provide new means of lightweight interaction in mobile settings by complementing current input modalities."

Specifically, to create a lightweight system, with dry electrodes integrated into the frame can be combined with a small pocket-worn computer with a powerful micro-controller for EOG signal processing. Such a system is able to capture sequences of eye movements (or eye gestures) that can be efficiently recognized for user interaction purposes (input entry commands). The device proposed, a goggle, is a self-contained solution that allows for seamless eye motion sensing in everyday environments [150].

Summary

This chapter provides an overview of wearable technologies, including funda-mental concepts about form factors, sensors, and features. This chapter begins with an introduction to wearable computers, and then describes a historic view of wearable computing explaining how the field evolved, since the first wear-ables were created in the 70s. The versatility of wearables, with a variety of form factors and sensors, allows their application in different domains, from military and safety- critical to arts and entertainment. This chapter illustrates devices and sensors that have been employed in wearable technologies to col-lect data, be it physiological measurements from users or data about their environment, surroundings, and contexts of use. The chapter ends with exam-ples of wearable applications in education, to support teaching and learning, in health care, to support monitoring and diagnosis, in industry, to support maintenance and information retrieval, in fitness and sports, to track users, as assistive technologies, to address users' impairments, in arts and entertainment for leisure, in safety critical fields to augment users' senses and monitor their physiological status and in user interaction, to support input entry and output responses in multiple modalities.

References

1. Witt H (2007) Human-computer interfaces for wearable computers. PhD thesis
2. Knight JF, Baber C (2005) A tool to assess the comfort of wearable computers. Human Fact 47(1):77–91
3. Motti VG, Caine K (2014) Human factors considerations in the design of wearable devices. In: Proceedings of the human factors and ergonomics society annual meeting 2014 Sep (Vol 58, No 1, pp 1820–1824). Sage CA: Los Angeles, CA: SAGE Publications

4. Dunne LE, Smyth B (2007) Psychophysical elements of wearability. In: Proceedings of the SIGCHI conference on Human factors in computing systems 2007 Apr 29 (pp 299–302). ACM
5. Berglund ME, Duvall J, Dunne LE (2016) A survey of the historical scope and current trends of wearable technology applications. In: Proceedings of the 2016 ACM international symposium on wearable computers 2016 Sep 12 (pp 40–43). ACM
6. Martin T, Healey J (2007) 2006's wearable computing advances and fashions. IEEE Pervasive Comput 6(1):14–6
7. Amft O, Lauffer M, Ossevoort S, Macaluso F, Lukowicz P, Troster G (2004) Design of the QBIC wearable computing platform. In: Proceedings 15th IEEE international conference on application-specific systems, architectures and processors, 2004. 2004 Sep 27 (pp 398–410). IEEE
8. Motti VG (2019) Wearable technologies in education: a design space. In: International conference on universal access in human-computer interaction. Springer, Cham
9. Buenaflor C, Kim H (2013) Six human factors to acceptability of wearable computers. Int J Multimed Ubiquitous Eng 8(3):103–114
10. Rhodes BJ (1997) The wearable remembrance agent: a system for augmented memory. Personal Technol 1(4):218–24
11. Billinghurst M, Starner T (1999) Wearable devices: new ways to manage information. Computer 32(1):57–64
12. Cranny-Francis A, Hawkins C (2008) Wearable technology. Vis Commun 7(3):267–270
13. Brewster S, Lumsden J, Bell M, Hall M, Tasker S (2003) Multimodal eyes-free interaction techniques for wearable devices. In: Proceedings of the SIGCHI conference on human factors in computing systems 2003 Apr 5 (pp 473–480). ACM
14. Scheffler M, Hirt E (2004) Wearable devices for emerging healthcare applications. In: The 26th annual international conference of the IEEE engineering in medicine and biology society 2004 Sep 1 (Vol 2, pp 3301–3304). IEEE
15. Torous BJ, Gualtieri L (2016) Knowns and Unknowns. Psychiatric Times, Wearable Devices for Mental Health, pp 4–7
16. Rekimoto J, Nagao K (1999) The world through the computer: computer augmented interaction with real world environments. Desig Commun Collab Support Syst. 1999 Mar 22
17. Augmented Starner T, Computing Reality Through Wearable (1997) Presence. Special Issue on Augmented Reality, 6–4
18. Fletcher RR, Ming-Zher Poh RR, Eydgahi H (2010) Wearable sensors: opportunities and challenges for low-cost health care. In: Proceedings of the 2010 annual international conference of the IEEE engineering in medicine and biology society. 1763–1766
19. Matassa A, Rapp A, Simeoni R (2013) Wearable accessories for cycling: tracking memories in urban spaces. In: Atelier of smart garments and accessories, held in conjunction with 2013 acm international joint conference on pervasive and ubiquitous computing (UbiComp 2013) 2013 (pp 415–424). ACM
20. Lau WW, Ngai G, Chan SC, Cheung JC (2009) Learning programming through fashion and design: a pilot summer course in wearable computing for middle school students. ACM SIGCSE Bull 41(1):504–508. ACM
21. Spil TA, Kijl B, Romijnders V (2019) The adoption and diffusion of wearables. In: International working conference on transfer and diffusion of IT (2019) 21. Springer, Cham, pp 31–47
22. Buechley L, Eisenberg M (2008) The LilyPad Arduino: toward wearable engineering for everyone. IEEE Pervasive Comput 7(2):12–5
23. Teknikio. https://www.teknikio.com/ Accessed February 12th, 2019
24. Android Wear OS (Operating System). https://wearos.google.com/ Retrieved on January 24th, 2019
25. Tizen OS, Samsung. https://www.tizen.org/ Accessed February 12th, 2019
26. Cannan J, Hu H. A wearable sensor fusion armband for simple motion control and selection for disabled and non-disabled users. In: 2012 4th computer science and electronic engineering conference (CEEC) 2012 Sep 12 (pp 216–219). IEEE

27. Calvo A (2015) Beginning android wearables: with android wear and google glass SDKs. Apress; 2015 Apr 6
28. Mann S (1997) Wearable computing: a first step toward personal imaging. Computer 30(2):25–32
29. Olsson T (2012) Arduino wearables. Apress
30. Munoz D, Pruett A, Williams G. Knee: an everyday wearable goniometer for monitoring physical therapy adherence. In: CHI'14 extended abstracts on human factors in computing systems 2014 Apr 26 (pp 209–214). ACM
31. Motti VG, Caine K (2015) Users' privacy concerns about wearables. In: International conference on financial cryptography and data security. Springer, Berlin, Heidelberg, pp 231–244
32. Amft O, Lukowicz P (2009) From backpacks to smartphones: past, present, and future of wearable computers. IEEE Pervasive Comput 8(3):8–13
33. Ilardi V (2007) Renaissance vision from spectacles to telescopes. American Philosophical Society
34. Khakurel J. Enhancing the adoption of quantified self-tracking devices. (Doctoral dissertation, University of Technology, Lappeenranta, Finland) ISBN 978-952-335-318-3
35. Thorp EO (1998) The invention of the first wearable computer. In: Digest of Papers. Second international symposium on wearable computers (Cat. No. 98EX215) 1998 Oct 19 (pp 4–8). IEEE
36. Sutherland IE (1968) A head-mounted three dimensional display. In: Proceedings of the December 9–11, 1968, fall joint computer conference, part I 1968 Dec 9 (pp 757–764). ACM
37. Mann S (1998) Humanistic computing: "wearcomp" as a new framework and application for intelligent signal processing. Proc IEEE 86(11):2123–51
38. Siewiorek D (2017) Wearable Computing: Retrospectives on the first decade. GetMobile: Mobile Comput Commun 21(1):5–10
39. Roy L (2003) Next-generation wearable networks. IEEE Comput Pract, 31–39
40. Forlizzi J, McCormack M. Case study: user research to inform the design and development of integrated wearable computers and web-based services. In: Proceedings of the 3rd conference on Designing interactive systems: processes, practices, methods, and techniques 2000 Aug 1 (pp 275–279). ACM
41. Lukowicz P (2008) Wearable computing and artificial intelligence for healthcare applications. Artif Intell Med 42(2):95–98. https://doi.org/10.1016/j.artmed.2007.12.002
42. Smailagic A, Siewiorek D (2002) Application design for wearable and context-aware computers. IEEE Pervasive Comput 1(4):20–9
43. Dunne LE, Profita H, Zeagler C, Clawson J, Gilliland S, Do EY, Budd J (2014) The social comfort of wearable technology and gestural interaction. In: 2014 36th annual international conference of the IEEE engineering in medicine and biology society 2014 Aug 26 (pp 4159–4162). IEEE
44. Shanghong L. Projected smart/basic wearables unit shipments worldwide 2017–2021, Statista GmbH, available at: https://www.statista.com/statistics/296565/wearables-worldwide-shipments/
45. Powell C, Munetomo M, Schlueter M, Mizukoshi M (2013) Towards thought control of next-generation wearable computing devices. In: International conference on brain and health informatics. Springer, Cham, pp 427–438
46. Zucco JE, Thomas BH (2016) Design guidelines for wearable pointing devices. Front ICT 27(3):13
47. Magno M, Brunelli D, Sigrist L, Andri R, Cavigelli L, Gomez A, Benini L (2016) InfiniTime: multi-sensor wearable bracelet with human body harvesting. Sustai Comput: Inf Syst 1(11):38–49
48. Toney A, Dunne L, Thomas BH, Ashdown SP (2003) A shoulder pad insert vibrotactile display. IEEE
49. Jalaliniya S, Pederson T (2012) A wearable kids' health monitoring system on smartphone. In: Proceedings of the 7th Nordic conference on human-computer interaction: making sense through design 2012 Oct 14 (pp 791–792). ACM

50. Troshynski E, Lee C, Dourish P (2011) Accountabilities of presence: reframing location-based systems. Droit et cultures. Revue internationale interdisciplinaire. 1(61):171–93
51. Cheng HT, Griss M, Davis P, Li J, You D (2013) Towards zero-shot learning for human activity recognition using semantic attribute sequence model. In: Proceedings of the 2013 ACM international joint conference on Pervasive and ubiquitous computing 2013 Sep 8 (pp 355–358). ACM
52. Reich J, Wall C, Dunne LE (2015) Design and implementation of a textile-based wearable balance belt. J Med Dev 9(2):020919
53. Griffin L, Compton C, Dunne LE (2016) An analysis of the variability of anatomical body references within ready-to-wear garment sizes. In: Proceedings of the 2016 ACM international symposium on wearable computers 2016 Sep 12 (pp 84–91). ACM
54. Pandey J, Liao YT, Lingley A, Parviz B, Otis B (2009) Toward an active contact lens: integration of a wireless power harvesting IC. In: 2009 IEEE biomedical circuits and systems conference 2009 Nov 26 (pp 125–128). IEEE
55. Erickson K, McMahon M, Dunne LE, Larsen C, Olmstead B, Hipp J (2016) Design and analysis of a sensor-enabled in-ear device for physiological monitoring. J Med Dev 10(2):020966
56. Gamboa H, Silva F, Silva H (2010) Patient tracking system. In: 2010 4th international conference on pervasive computing technologies for healthcare 2010 Mar 22 (pp 1–2). IEEE
57. Kim MY, Yang S, Kim D (2012) Head-mounted binocular gaze detection for selective visual recognition systems. Sens Actuat A: Phys 1(187):29–36
58. Perng JK, Fisher B, Hollar S, Pister KS (1999) Acceleration sensing glove (ASG). In: Digest of Papers. Third International Symposium on Wearable Computers 1999 Oct 18 (pp 178–180). IEEE
59. Bulling A, Roggen D, Troster G (2008) It's in your eyes: towards context-awareness and mobile HCI using wearable EOG goggles. In: Proceedings of the 10th international conference on Ubiquitous computing 2008 Sep 21 (pp 84–93). ACM
60. Teh JK, Cheok AD, Peiris RL, Choi Y, Thuong V, Lai S (2008) Huggy Pajama: a mobile parent and child hugging communication system. In: Proceedings of the 7th international conference on Interaction design and children 2008 Jun 11 (pp 250–257). ACM
61. Werner J, Wettach R, Hornecker E (2008) United-pulse: feeling your partner's pulse. In: Proceedings of the 10th international conference on Human computer interaction with mobile devices and services 2008 Sep 2 (pp 535–538). ACM
62. Spelmezan D (2012) An investigation into the use of tactile instructions in snowboarding. In: Proceedings of the 14th international conference on Human-computer interaction with mobile devices and services 2012 Sep 21 (pp 417–426). ACM
63. Duvall JC, Dunne LE, Schleif N, Holschuh B (2016) Active hugging vest for deep touch pressure therapy. In: Proceedings of the 2016 ACM international joint conference on pervasive and ubiquitous computing: adjunct 2016 Sep 12 (pp 458–463). ACM
64. Atallah L, Lo B, King R, Yang GZ (2010) Sensor placement for activity detection using wearable accelerometers. In: 2010 international conference on body sensor networks 2010 Jun 7 (pp 24–29). IEEE
65. Lin R, Kreifeldt JG (2001) Ergonomics in wearable computer design. Int J Ind Ergon 27(4):259–69
66. Motti VG, Caine K (2014) Understanding the wearability of head-mounted devices from a human-centered perspective. In: Proceedings of the 2014 ACM international symposium on wearable computers 2014 Sep 13 (pp 83–86). ACM
67. Healey JA. Wearable and automotive systems for affect recognition from physiology (Doctoral dissertation, Massachusetts Institute of Technology)
68. Nguyen LN, Rodriguez-Martin D, Catala A, Perez-Lopez C, Sama A, Cavallaro A (2015) Basketball activity recognition using wearable inertial measurement units. In: Proceedings of the XVI international conference on Human Computer Interaction 2015 Sep 7 (p 60). ACM
69. Favela J (2017, October) Inferring human behavior using mobile and wearable devices. In: Proceedings of the 23rd Brazillian symposium on multimedia and the web (pp 11–13). ACM

70. Farringdon J, Moore AJ, Tilbury N, Church J, Biemond PD (1999) Wearable sensor badge & sensor jacket for context awareness. In: The proceedings of The third international symposium on wearable computers. San Francisco, CA, Oct. 18–19, 1999

71. Ramos-Garcia RI, Da Silva F, Kondi Y, Sazonov E, Dunne LE (2016) Analysis of a cover-stitched stretch sensor for monitoring of breathing. In: 2016 10th international conference on sensing technology (ICST) 2016 Nov 11 (pp 1–6). IEEE

72. Seuter M, Pfeiffer M, Bauer G, Zentgraf K, Kray C (2017) Running with technology: evaluating the impact of interacting with wearable devices on running movement. Proc ACM Interact Mobile Wearable Ubiquitous Technol 1(3):101

73. Friedl KE (2018) Military applications of soldier physiological monitoring. J Sci Med Sport 21(11):1147–53

74. Fletcher R, Dobson K (2010) iCalm: Wearable sensor and network architecture for wirelessly communicating and logging autonomic activity. IEEE Trans Inf Technol Biomed 14(2):215–223

75. Lee K, Kwon DS (2000) Wearable master device for spinal injured persons as a control device for motorized wheelchairs. Artif Life Robot 4(4):182–7

76. Bachlin M, Forster K, Troster G. SwimMaster: a wearable assistant for swimmer. In: Proceedings of the 11th international conference on Ubiquitous computing 2009 Sep 30 (pp 215–224). ACM

77. Strohrmann C, Harms H, Troster G, Hensler S, Muller R. Out of the lab and into the woods: kinematic analysis in running using wearable sensors. In: Proceedings of the 13th international conference on Ubiquitous computing 2011 Sep 17 (pp 119–122). ACM

78. Peng M, Wang T, Hu G, Zhang H. A wearable heart rate belt for ambulant ECG monitoring. In: 2012 IEEE 14th international conference on e-health networking, applications and services (Healthcom) 2012 Oct 10 (pp 371–374). IEEE

79. Ward JA, Lukowicz P, Troster G, Starner TE (2006) Activity recognition of assembly tasks using body-worn microphones and accelerometers. IEEE Trans Pattern Anal Mach Intell 28(10):1553–67

80. Brady S, Dunne LE, Lynch A, Smyth B, Diamond D (2005) Wearable Sensors? What is there to sense? Stud Health Technol Inf 1(117):80–8

81. Oliver N, Flores-Mangas F (2006) HealthGear: a real-time wearable system for monitoring and analyzing physiological signals. In: International workshop on wearable and implantable body sensor networks (BSN'06) 2006 Apr 3 (p 4-p). IEEE

82. Marques FA, Ribeiro DM, Colunas MF, Cunha JP (2011) A real time, wearable ECG and blood pressure monitoring system. In: 6th Iberian conference on information systems and technologies (CISTI 2011) 2011 Jun 15 (pp 1–4). IEEE

83. Banos O, Villalonga C, Damas M, Gloesekoetter P, Pomares H, Rojas I (2014) Physiodroid: combining wearable health sensors and mobile devices for a ubiquitous, continuous, and personal monitoring. Sci World J

84. Motoi K, Higashi Y, Kuwae Y, Yuji T, Tanaka S, Yamakoshi K (2006) Development of a wearable device capable of monitoring human activity for use in rehabilitation and certification of eligibility for long-term care. In: 2005 IEEE engineering in medicine and biology 27th annual conference 2006 Jan 17 (pp 1004–1007). IEEE

85. Kanis M, Winters N, Agamanolis S, Gavin A, Cullinan C (2005) Toward wearable social networking with iBand. In: CHI'05 extended abstracts on Human factors in computing systems 2005 Apr 2 (pp 1521–1524). ACM

86. MacLean D, Roseway A, Czerwinski M (2013) MoodWings: a wearable biofeedback device for real-time stress intervention. In: Proceedings of the 6th international conference on PErvasive technologies related to assistive environments 2013 May 29 (p 66). ACM

87. Tikander M, Harma A, Karjalainen M (2003) Binaural positioning system for wearable augmented reality audio. In: 2003 IEEE workshop on applications of signal processing to audio and acoustics (IEEE Cat. No. 03TH8684) 2003 Oct 19 (pp 153–156). IEEE

88. Nunez-Pacheco C, Loke L (2014) Crafting the body-tool: a body-centred perspective on wearable technology. In: Proceedings of the 2014 conference on Designing interactive systems 2014 Jun 21 (pp 553–566). ACM

89. Shrestha P, Saxena N (2017) An offensive and defensive exposition of wearable computing. ACM Comput Surv 50(6):1–39. https://doi.org/10.1145/3133837
90. Khakurel J, Melkas H, Porras J (2018) Tapping into the wearable device revolution in the work environment: a systematic review. Inf Technol People 31(3):791–818
91. Hayes GR, Truong KN (2005) Autism, environmental buffers, and wearable servers. IEEE Pervasive Comput 4(2):14–7
92. Poon CC, Wong YM, Zhang YT. M-health: the development of cuff-less and wearable blood pressure meters for use in body sensor networks. In: 2006 IEEE/NLM life science systems and applications workshop 2006 Jul 13 (pp 1–2). IEEE
93. Burgy C, Garrett JH (2002) Wearable computers: an interface between humans and smart infrastructure systems. Vdi Berichte 1668:385–98
94. Thomas B, Tyerman S, Grimmer K (1997) Evaluation of three input mechanisms for wearable computers. In: Digest of Papers. First international symposium on wearable computers 1997 Oct 13 (pp 2–9). IEEE
95. Hoof C van, Penders J (2013) Addressing the healthcare cost dilemma by managing health instead of managing illness –an opportunity for wearable wireless sensors. In: 2013 design, automation and test in europe conference and exhibition (DATE) 2013 Mar 18 (pp 1537–1539). IEEE
96. Zheng J, Shen Y, Zhang Z, Wu T, Zhang G, Lu H (2013) Emerging wearable medical devices towards personalized healthcare. In: Proceedings of the 8th international conference on body area networks 2013 Sep 30 (pp 427–431). ICST (Institute for Computer Sciences, Social-Informatics and Telecommunications Engineering)
97. Motti VG, Caine K (2015) Micro interactions and multi dimensional graphical user interfaces in the design of wrist worn wearables. In: Proceedings of the human factors and ergonomics society annual meeting 2015 Sep (Vol 59, No 1, pp 1712–1716). Sage CA: Los Angeles, CA: SAGE Publications
98. Motti VG (2019) Assistive wearables: opportunities and challenges. In: Proceedings of the 2019 ACM international joint conference on pervasive and ubiquitous computing and proceedings of the 2019 ACM international symposium on wearable computers (pp 1040–1043). ACM
99. Fukatsu T, Nanseki T (2009) Monitoring system for farming operations with wearable devices utilized sensor networks. Sensors 9(8):6171–84
100. Vega K, Fuks H (2014) Beauty tech nails: interactive technology at your fingertips. In: Proceedings of the 8th international conference on tangible, embedded and embodied interaction 2014 Feb 16 (pp 61–64). ACM
101. Kern N, Schiele B, Junker H, Lukowicz P, Troster G (2003) Wearable sensing to annotate meeting recordings. Personal Ubiquitous Comput 7(5):263–74
102. Stiefmeier T, Roggen D, Ogris G, Lukowicz P, Troster G (2008) Wearable activity tracking in car manufacturing. IEEE Pervasive Comput 1(2):42–50
103. Sandall BK (2016) Wearable technology and schools: where are we and where do we go from here? J Curric Teach Learn Leadership Educ 1(1):9
104. Engen BK, Giæver TH, Mifsud L (2018) Wearable technologies in the K-12 classroom–cross-disciplinary possibilities and privacy pitfalls. J Interact Learn Res 29(3):323–41
105. Garcia B, Chu SL, Nam B, Banigan C (2018) Wearables for learning: examining the smart-watch as a tool for situated science reflection. In: Proceedings of the 2018 CHI conference on human factors in computing systems 2018 Apr 21 (p 256). ACM
106. Lukowicz P, Poxrucker A, Weppner J, Bischke B, Kuhn J, Hirth M (2015) Glass-physics: using google glass to support high school physics experiments. In: Proceedings of the 2015 ACM international symposium on wearable computers 2015 Sep 7 (pp 151–154). ACM
107. Zarraonandia T, Diaz P, Montero A, Aedo I, Onorati T (2019) Using a google glass-based classroom feedback system to improve students to teacher communication. IEEE Access 7:16837–46
108. Ngai G, Chan SC, Cheung JC, Lau WW (2009) Deploying a wearable computing platform for computing education. IEEE Trans Learn Technol 3(1):45–55

109. Alvarez V, Bower M, de Freitas S, Gregory S, de Wit B (2016) The use of wearable technologies in Australian universities: examples from environmental science, cognitive and brain sciences and teacher training. Mobile Learn Futures-Sustain Qual Res Pract Mobile Learn 24:25

110. Bower M, Sturman D (2015) What are the educational affordances of wearable technologies? Comput Educ 1(88):343–53

111. Byrne VL, Kang S, Norooz L, Velez R, Katzen M, Clegg T. Scaffolding authentic wearable-based scientific inquiry for early elementary learners

112. Dittmar A, Lymberis A. Smart clothes and associated wearable devices for biomedical ambulatory monitoring. In: Digest of technical papers—international conference on solid state sensors and actuators and microsystems, TRANSDUCERS'05 (Vol 1, pp 221–227). https://doi.org/10.1109/SENSOR.2005.1496398

113. Burnham JP, Lu C, Yaeger LH, Bailey TC, Kollef MH (2018) Using wearable technology to predict health outcomes: a literature review. J Am Med Inf Assoc 25(9):1221–7

114. Cho H, Yoon H, Kim KJ, Shin DH. Wearable health information: effects of comparative feedback and presentation mode. In: Proceedings of the 33rd annual ACM conference extended abstracts on human factors in computing systems 2015 Apr 18 (pp 2073–2078). ACM

115. Bi S, Wang T, Tobias N, Nordrum J, Wang S, Halvorsen G, Sen S, Peterson R, Odame K, Caine K, Halter R (2018) Auracle: detecting eating episodes with an ear-mounted sensor. Proc ACM Interact Mobile Wearable Ubiquitous Technol 2(3):92

116. Motti VG (2019) Wearable health: opportunities and challenges. In Proceedings of the 13th EAI international conference on pervasive computing technologies for healthcare 2019 May 20 (pp 356–359). ACM

117. Weller P, Rakhmetova L, Ma Q, Mandersloot G (2010) Evaluation of a wearable computer system for telemonitoring in a critical environment. Personal Ubiquitous Comput 14(1):73–81

118. Anliker U, Ward JA, Lukowicz P, Troster G, Dolveck F, Baer M, Keita F, Schenker EB, Catarsi F, Coluccini L, Belardinelli A (2004) AMON: a wearable multiparameter medical monitoring and alert system. IEEE Trans Inf Technol Biomed 8(4):415–27

119. Walsh P, Dunne LE, Caulfield B, Smyth B (2006) Marker-based monitoring of seated spinal posture using a calibrated single-variable threshold model. In: 2006 international conference of the IEEE engineering in medicine and biology society 2006 Aug 30 (pp 5370–5373). IEEE

120. Brady S, Dunne LE, Tynan R, Diamond D, Smyth B, O'Hare GM (2005) Garment-based monitoring of respiration rate using a foam pressure sensor. In: Ninth IEEE international symposium on wearable computers (ISWC'05) 2005 Oct 18 (pp 214–215). IEEE

121. Gioberto G, Min CH, Compton C, Dunne LE (2014) Lower-limb goniometry using stitched sensors: effects of manufacturing and wear variables. In: Proceedings of the 2014 ACM international symposium on wearable computers 2014 Sep 13 (pp 131–132). ACM

122. Dibia V (2015) An affective, normative and functional approach to designing user experiences for wearables. Normative and Functional Approach to Designing User Experiences for Wearables (July 14, 2015)

123. Gobert D (2002) Designing wearable performance support: Insights from the early literature. Techn Commun 49(4):444–8

124. Schull ND (2016) Data for life : Wearable technology and the design of self-care. BioSocieties 1–17. https://doi.org/10.1057/biosoc.2015.47

125. Mencarini E, Leonardi C, Cappelletti A, Giovanelli D, De Angeli A, Zancanaro M (2019) Co-designing wearable devices for sports: the case study of sport climbing. Int J Human-Comput Stud (IJHCS) 124:26–43

126. Koo H, Dunne L (2012) Enhancing visibility in bicycling apparel using integrated flashing LEDs. InSmart Design 2012 (pp 41–47). Springer, London

127. Goyal R, Dragoni N, Spognardi A (2016) Mind the tracker you wear: a security analysis of wearable health trackers. In: Proceedings of the 31st annual ACM symposium on applied computing—SAC'16, 131–136. https://doi.org/10.1145/2851613.2851685

128. Kirkham R, Greenhalgh C (2015) Social access vs. privacy in wearable computing: a case study of autism. IEEE Pervasive Comput. 14(1):26–33

129. Dibia V, Trewin S, Ashoori M, Erickson T (2015) Exploring the potential of wearables to support employment for people with mild cognitive impairment. In: Proceedings of the 17th international ACM SIGACCESS conference on computers & accessibility 2015 Oct 26 (pp 401–402). ACM

130. Gomez J, Torrado JC, Montoro G (2016) Using smartwatches for behavioral issues in ASD. In: Proceedings of the XVII international conference on human computer interaction 2016 Sep 13 (p 28). ACM

131. Torrado JC, Gomez J, Montoro G (2017) Emotional self-regulation of individuals with autism spectrum disorders: smartwatches for monitoring and interaction. Sensors 17(6):1359

132. Vukovic M, Car Z, Pavlisa JI, Mandic L (2018) Smartwatch as an assistive technology: tracking system for detecting irregular user movement. Int J E-Health Med Commun (IJEHMC) 9(1):23–34

133. Baker J, Wennerlind R, Devine S, Nasir-Tucktuck M (2019) The use of smart technology on improving time management of college students with intellectual/developmental disability. J Incl Postsecond Educ 1(1)

134. Kane SK (2019) Wearables. In: Web accessibility 2019 (pp 701–714). Springer, London

135. Brashear H, Starner T, Lukowicz P, Junker H. Using multiple sensors for mobile sign language recognition. Georgia Institute of Technology

136. Tanuwidjaja E, Huynh D, Koa K, Nguyen C, Shao C, Torbett P, Emmenegger C, Weibel N (2014) Chroma: a wearable augmented-reality solution for color blindness. In: Proceedings of the 2014 ACM international joint conference on pervasive and ubiquitous computing 2014 Sep 13 (pp 799–810). ACM

137. Fiannaca A, Apostolopoulous I, Folmer E (2014) Headlock: a wearable navigation aid that helps blind cane users traverse large open spaces. In: Proceedings of the 16th international ACM SIGACCESS conference on Computers and accessibility 2014 Oct 20 (pp 19–26). ACM

138. Jain D, Findlater L, Gilkeson J, Holland B, Duraiswami R, Zotkin D, Vogler C, Froehlich JE (2015) Head-mounted display visualizations to support sound awareness for the deaf and hard of hearing. In: Proceedings of the 33rd annual ACM conference on human factors in computing systems 2015 Apr 18 (pp 241–250). ACM

139. Saunders FA, Hill WA, Franklin B (1981) A wearable tactile sensory aid for profoundly deaf children. J Med Syst 5(4):265–70

140. Mielke M, Bruck R (2015) A pilot study about the smartwatch as assistive device for deaf people. In: Proceedings of the 17th international ACM SIGACCESS conference on computers and accessibility 2015 Oct 26 (pp 301–302). ACM

141. Etchart M, Caprarelli A (2018) A wearable immersive web-virtual reality approach to remote neurodevelopmental disorder therapy. In: Proceedings of the 2018 international conference on advanced visual interfaces 2018 may 29 (p 61). ACM

142. Carrington P, Hurst A, Kane SK (2014) Wearables and chairables: inclusive design of mobile input and output techniques for power wheelchair users. In: Proceedings of the SIGCHI Conference on human factors in computing systems 2014 Apr 26 (pp 3103–3112). ACM

143. Zheng H, Genaro Motti V (2018) Assisting students with intellectual and developmental disabilities in inclusive education with smartwatches. In: Proceedings of the 2018 CHI conference on human factors in computing systems 2018 Apr 21 (p 350). ACM

144. Zheng H, Motti VG, Giwa-Lawal K, Evmenova A, Evaluating Graff H (2019) WELI: a wrist-worn application to assist young adults with neurodevelopmental disorders in inclusive classes. In: IFIP conference on human-computer interaction, (2019) September). Springer, Cham, pp 114–134

145. Song SJ, Lee SJ, Cho N, Yoo HJ (2006) Low power wearable audio player using human body communications. In: 2006 10th IEEE international symposium on wearable computers 2006 Oct 11 (pp 125–126). IEEE

146. Carton A, Dunne LE. Tactile distance feedback for firefighters: design and preliminary evaluation of a sensory augmentation glove. In: Proceedings of the 4th augmented human international conference 2013 Mar 7 (pp 58–64). ACM

147. Coca A, Roberge RJ, Williams WJ, Landsittel DP, Powell JB, Palmiero A (2009) Physiological monitoring in firefighter ensembles: wearable plethysmographic sensor vest versus standard equipment. J Occup Environ Hygiene 7(2):109–114

148. Peshock A, Duvall J, Dunne LE (2014) Argot: a wearable one-handed keyboard glove. In: Proceedings of the 2014 ACM international symposium on wearable computers: adjunct program 2014 Sep 13 (pp 87–92). ACM

149. Arai K (2013) Wearable computing system with input-output devices based on eye-based human computer interaction allowing location based web services. Int J Adv Res Artif Intell 2(8)

150. Bulling A, Roggen D, Troster G. Wearable EOG goggles: eye-based interaction in everyday environments. ACM; 2009 Apr 4

151. Minamizawa K, Fukamachi S, Kajimoto H, Kawakami N, Tachi S (2007) Gravity grabber: wearable haptic display to present virtual mass sensation. In: ACM SIGGRAPH 2007 emerging technologies 2007 Aug 5 (p 8). ACM

152. Roh T, Bong K, Hong S, Cho H, Yoo HJ (2012) Wearable mental-health monitoring platform with independent component analysis and nonlinear chaotic analysis. In: 2012 annual international conference of the IEEE engineering in medicine and biology society 2012 Aug 28 (pp 4541–4544). IEEE

153. Huang K, Do EYL, Starner T (2008) PianoTouch: a wearable haptic piano instruction system for passive learning of piano skills. In: 2008 12th IEEE international symposium on wearable computers 2008 Sep (pp 41–44). IEEE

154. Tharion WJ, Buller MJ, Karis AJ, Mullen SP (2007) Acceptability of a wearable vital sign detection system. In: Proceedings of the human factors and ergonomics society annual meeting 2007 Oct (Vol 51, No 17, pp 1006–1010). Sage CA: Los Angeles, CA: SAGE Publications

Chapter 2
Design Considerations

Abstract This chapter begins with the goals and objectives of wearable technologies, describing the different disciplines that contribute to constitute and advance wearable computing. This chapter includes also multiple dimensions that must be considered in the design, development, and evaluation of wearable technologies. Concerning hardware aspects, six implementation layers are defined and illustrated with examples from the literature. Concerning software aspects, systems, and applications, this chapter provides the objectives, features, and functionalities implemented with wearable computers. Concerning network and connectivity, this chapter provides examples of protocols and approaches for physical and virtual connections that enable data sharing and device synchronization. Additional topics discussed in the chapter include energy requirements and considerations for wearables, contexts of use where wearers interact with their devices, and common tasks they execute, emphasizing the advantages of wearable computers to support activities of daily living. This chapter highlights the diversity of users who benefit from wearables and the inherent trade-offs that emerge when universal design and customization must be considered altogether to ensure acceptability among diverse users' profiles. The chapter ends with an in-depth discussion of the main challenges faced by users when interacting with a wearable technology and by stakeholders when creating those technologies during the implementation phases. The main challenges highlighted cut across six different concerns: usability and wearability, implementation, power, network and sensors, safety, and privacy aspects.

2.1 Design Goals

Chapter 1 introduces wearable computing as an emergent field whose scientific research and industrial development have faced substantial advances since its inception. It stands out as key characteristics of wearable technologies their diverse deployments, with a variety of sensors, form factors, and applications. To come to fruition, in the design of wearable technologies, multiple considerations must be taken into account. To elicit such considerations, this chapter presents and discusses key fac-

© Springer Nature Switzerland AG 2020
V. G. Motti, *Wearable Interaction*, Human–Computer Interaction Series,
https://doi.org/10.1007/978-3-030-27111-4_2

Fig. 2.1 Wearable
computing is an
interdisciplinary field that
lies at the intersection of
several domains, inheriting
contributions from
disciplines that include but
are not limited to
Human–Computer
Interaction, Computer
Sciences, Electric
Engineering, Fashion, and
Cognitive Sciences

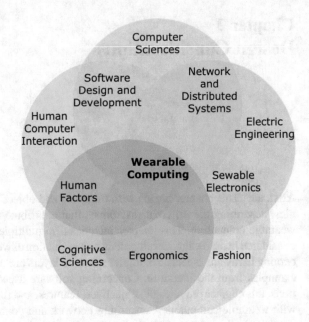

tors that structure, influence, and inform design decisions for wearable technologies, including diverse disciplines, domain knowledge, and cross-cutting design concerns.

Wearable computing is an active research area that involves a number of other fields as well [1]. For Cranny and[2] Hawkins , wearable computing brings together practitioners and theorists in fields that include fashion design, engineering, music, performance studies, architecture, cultural studies, and medicine [2]. Ten of the several different disciplines that contribute to the design, development, and evaluation of a wearable technology are illustrated in Fig. 2.1.

Contributions from Human–Computer Interaction, Human Factors, and Ergonomics facilitate the definitions of the interface design, attempting to bridge the gap between the users' expectations and needs to what technology effectively provides them. Contributions from Cognitive Sciences help to ensure wearers are neither overwhelmed nor annoyed with the constant notifications, perceiving output responses, easily learning how to use the device, accepting and adopting it in a comfortable and intuitive way. Electric Engineering contributes with the definitions of hardware pieces, power sources, communication protocols, assembly, and integration of components in an operational manner.

Computer Science helps to define the functionality of the devices, considering software design and development, processing units to read and interpret sensor data as well as algorithms to provide users with notifications that are both relevant and timely. The fashion industry also contributes to ensure the technology is socially acceptable, aesthetically pleasing, and comfortable for users to wear. In summary, any knowledge domain impacting human embodiment is potentially affected by the development of wearables including every field of human creativity, innovation, and thought [2].

Seeking to satisfy and meet the wearers' needs and to aid human users in task performance, making it easier, more productive, and efficient, wearables are primarily meant to be used by human users [3]. More specifically, wearable computers aim to satisfy three main goals [4]. First, the technology must be wearable, by definition, the technology must accompany the user wherever he or she goes in a comfortable manner. Second, wearable technologies must also augment the users' reality, by providing resources, services, features, or information in a relevant way, for instance, overlaying computer-generated images and audio on the real world according to users' needs [5]. Lastly, wearables must be context-sensitive, not only being aware of the wearer's surroundings and state, but reacting and responding to those accordingly. When designed in a truly intelligent manner, context-sensitive applications can harness and leverage the intimacy between wearer, computer, and environment [5].

For Rhodes [6], wearable computers are characterized by:

- being always portable while in operation;
- enabling hands-free or hand-limited use;
- being able to get the users' attention even if not in use, with high notice rates;
- being always available whenever users need it; and
- attempting to sense and interpret the wearer's context to provide a better service.

For Fletcher [7], besides providing privacy and security, wearable technologies should also be comfortable, simple to use, and unobtrusive [7].

For Amft [1], the three core concepts that characterize wearable computing are: [1]

- **Integration**: Blending the technology seamlessly with the outfits of the wearers, without hindering their physical activity or embarrassing them;
- **Interaction**: Allowing wearers to focus on their main tasks while interacting with the technology; and
- **Situational awareness**: Recognizing the contexts of use where the user interaction occurs and adapting the technology to actual wearers' needs in real time.

2.2 Design Dimensions

More than ubiquitous and mobile applications, wearable technologies bring computation to a very intimate proximity to the user body, which raises questions about the role of the human body in the interaction with technology [8]. In such an interaction, several dimensions and cross-cutting concerns must be considered: the contexts of use, the user group and profiles, the technology requirements, the wearers' need for safety, and ease of use. To be suitable for end users, the size, weight, placement, and attachment to the body of the technology must be altogether considered [3].

In practice, when considering multiple dimensions altogether conflicting requirements emerge, especially when taking into account low energy consumption, high computational performance, responsiveness and processing power, scalable connectivity to include multiple sensors and to access external devices and resources, extensibility to add new peripheric equipment if need be, and an ergonomic form factor [1]. To address conflicting requirements in this context, the domain knowledge, summed with the prioritization of needs and the user involvement, become essential [2].

For Toney et al. [9], the design of wearable computers requires consideration not only of function, but also of the wearer comfort, mobility, and social weight [9]. For Buenaflor and Kim [3], physical comfort and safety are essential considerations. Also, users value the opinions and beliefs of people close to them, which highly influences decision-making processes toward ensuring technology acceptance [3].

For Nunez and Loke [8], in the case of a wearable art installation project and technologies that provide self-awareness as a feature, the comfort with the device may be secondary when compared with other aspects, such as trust in data and reliability [8]. For Ha et al. [10], reliability stands out as the most fundamental issues that prevent widespread adoption of wearable sensors for health care [10].

For Jalaliniya and Pederson [11], putting the sensors on the most appropriate placement of the user body indeed increases quality of physiological measurements; however, it can also lead to lower acceptability of the device for children, mostly because children would not accept to put a temperature sensor in their ear for a long time [11].

For Zheng et al. [12], to provide wearable physiological monitoring without the discomfort of clips used for PPG measurement on the users' fingers and ears, eyeglasses become an alternative, as the device also serves to acquire photoplethysmogram (PPG) from readings on the user's nose bridge. Experimental results indicated that PPG measured from nose and ear is more resistant to motion artifacts when compared with PPG signals collected from the user's finger during exercise sessions [12].

For Khakurel [4], matching the functionality to the format is crucial but challenging too. More specifically, in organizational settings, primarily stakeholders need to identify the devices that are suitable for the purpose of use, including information about the context of the work and technological challenges. Wearable devices such as head-mounted displays (HMD) are not suitable for self-tracking purposes; therefore, they are better designed to deliver multimedia contents and games [4].

For Amft et al. [1], the wearable design should consider that the user's outfit is actually a complex, hierarchical system that encompasses several different "device" classes with a wide range of application domains and functionalities [1].

For Oliver and Flores-Manga [13], to be particularly suitable for wearable applications, sensors should be small, lightweight, flexible, and capable of long-term monitoring [13]. Their mechanical flexibility, however, along with size, weight, and cost remains among the main challenges to be addressed to enable next-generation wearable electronic devices [14].

For Dunne et al. [15], context awareness and intuitive device interfaces minimize disruption for wearers, but only when the technology is not physically intrusive, and the interface preserves the user's homeostatic comfort [15]. As Gioberto and Dunne

[16] highlight, wearable sensors are often subject to errors in the data collection due to the movement of the sensor over the body surface [16].

For Burgy and Garrett [17], to prevent errors in the data collection, understanding the users' tasks thoroughly is essential. Thus, extensive task analyses are necessary to understand the workflow that wearable computers support before actually designing and developing the system and deciding on sensors and data collection processes [17].

For Bulling et al. [38], to build a wearable device for eye tracking, the most important requirements cover functional aspects as well as quality factors, as follows.

- **On-board data storage and low power consumption**: To allow for stand-alone long-term recordings in daily life.
- **Real-time capability and responsiveness**: To perform online signal processing on the device.
- **Acceleration and light sensors**: To compensate for artifacts caused by physical activity and changes in ambient light.
- **Wearable and lightweight form factor**: To achieve a convenient and unobtrusive implementation design, minimizing eventual user distraction.

For Seuter et al. [18], the interference of the device with the main activity of the user and its context should inform the placement of the device on the wearer body and its form factor, for instance, reaching a phone strapped to the upper arm requires the opposing hand to travel further than to reach a wrist-worn watch [18]. Besides being light, small, and adjustable, wearable computer components should be mounted on the back and sides of the user's waist to avoid interfering with his or her main tasks and everyday activities [19]. Sensing data (such as PPG) through eyeglasses on the nose risks the equipment slipping down and introducing artifacts in the readings, especially during exercise [12]. To mitigate such risks and reduce potential interferences, adjustments in the device fit are as important as design choices of interaction approach, be it through touch, voice recognition, or user gestures [18].

Thus, regardless of the application purpose, the decisions concerning wearable design should carefully consider the relevance of fitting the device according to the wearer, and selecting the placement of the sensors striving to reduce noise and artifacts in the data collection and aiming at high accuracy of the data collected. Examples of requirements in a wearable design project include a smooth surface, ergonomics, adjustability, soft and breathable materials, and aesthetics [20].

2.2.1 Hardware

To define a wearable technology capable of monitoring the wearer as well as his/her environments, sensors, circuits, and wires are embedded in the user garment [3]. In this process, wearables usually contain three components: hardware sensors to sense the physical environments of the wearers, built-in processors to analyze the observations and data, and communication modules for data sharing [21]. To implement

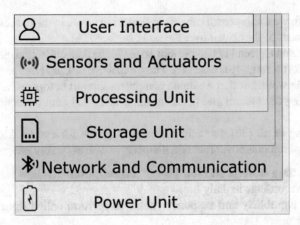

Fig. 2.2 Wearable technologies require the assembly and integration of an end user interface component, sensors and actuators for data collection and output responses (feedback), processing units for data management and control, storage for data management, access and retrieval, network and communication modules for data transmission and connectivity, and power sources

and integrate such components, wearables must accommodate various electronic pieces including sensors, cameras, microphones, wireless transceivers, along with a microprocessor, a battery, and memory. When assembling the device, a display is also needed, with a convenient placement and an intuitive user interface to convey meaningful information and feedback responses to wearers [22].

To assemble the standard electronic components in a circuit board, manufacturing technologies such as regular printed circuit boards (PCBs), with surface-mounted or soldered devices (SMDs), and even through-hole components are employed resulting in a reliable, but sometimes bulky, technology [23]. For Scheffler and Hirt [23], "high-density packaging uses a more sophisticated approach by mounting unhoused integrated circuits onto high-interconnection substrates," which saves size and weight as well (up to 75%). For them, miniaturizing the electronics improves the mechanical housing, yielding a significantly smaller system [23].

As Fig. 2.2 illustrates, in general, the hardware components of wearable include the end user interface, with a module for sensors and actuators, the processing unit, and the power source—be it a battery holder for stand-alone devices, or a charging port to connect wires for recharging the device. A storage unit (such as a memory card) and a connection unit (such as USB ports) are also common. To illustrate examples of how these components are instantiated, several wearable applications have been analyzed. As described next, they include fitness trackers and activity recognition applications, as well as health monitoring and emotional regulation applications.

For fitness trackers, the basic anatomy of the device includes a battery source, a Bluetooth chip, a power button, sensors according to data collection and required features, a connecting jack, and wrist strap [24]. For monitoring running activities, ETHOS is an example of an anklet that comprises a 3D accelerometer, a 3D gyro-scope, and a 3D magnetic field as sensor suite. For the central processing unit, a

16-bit dsPIC is used. Sampled data can be stored using a 2 GB microSD card or transmitted through a USB port. Wireless connectivity is provided by an integrated ultralow power ANT+ module that allows to interface with other ETHOS units, for instance, to sample data provided by external ANT+ compatible devices, such as heart rate belts or GPS receivers. Each ETHOS unit is equipped with a real-time clock (RTC) for synchronization of multiple devices [25].

For activity recognition, in a basketball monitoring context, a BSK board was created, including an inertial measurement unit (IMU) to capture inertial data requiring a long range of acceleration, as well as for experiments requiring barometric information. In addition to the IMU, the BSK board includes a storage unit and a small interface to send and receive commands. The board included also a power system, the microcontroller and its interface, the analog system, and the communications module [26].

For a low-power bracelet, the following specification was used: (i) a microcontroller subsystem built using a Texas Instruments MSP430FR5969, and including 64 kB of nonvolatile FRAM; (ii) a multi-sensor subsystem where a nano-power accelerometer, a temperature sensor, and an analog microphone are hosted on-board; (iii) a communication module consisting of an NFC/RFID tag IC transceiver; (iv) a display system based on ultralow power e-paper technology with a zero idle power graphical user interface; and (v) an energy harvester (solar and thermal) subsystem available directly on board. The energy component can recharge both Li-ion battery and supercapacitors depending on the application specification, and the conditioning circuitry counted with analog and digital signals, including an analog camera which can be connected to the main board using a dedicated connector [27].

To assemble a calming armband, the main casing included a steep metal base and a plastic cover. Such casing housed three main electronic components: a coin vibration motor to deliver tactile stimulus to the wearer, a low energy Bluetooth chip to communicate with an app or computer and allow users to upload new rhythms to the device, and a lithium–ion battery to power the armband [28].

For ECG monitoring, a wearable heart rate belt was proposed including several components. Active textile electrodes were designed to sense ECG signals. A battery-powered circuit board was developed including ECG signal conditioning circuits, a three-axis accelerator for body motion detection, a 12-bit AD converter, a DSP for signal processing, and a SD card for data storage. A wireless communication module was also included in the system to send heart rate data to a sport watch for visualization purposes [29].

For monitoring t-shirts, such as SensVest, the design and development process was based mainly on housing the sensors, wires, and electrical equipment in a large zipper-fastened pouch sewn over the chest, shoulder, and upper back of a 70% cotton and 30% polyester long-sleeved sweatshirt [30].

For monitoring health in children, a wearable device was built including a TMP102 digital temperature sensor breakout from Sparkfun; a pulse sensor to measure heart rate; a Mini Pro Arduino microcontroller (3 v) to collect data, remove outliers, and transmit data every 5 min; and a Bluetooth Mate Gold communication module from Sparkfun to send the data to a mobile application [11].

For chest-mounted devices to detect motion for motor-impaired users, an optical fiber curvature sensor was designed. It includes five parts: a light source, a light detector, an optical fiber, an electric circuit, and a power source. The light source and the detector are built with an IR LED and phototransistor. Also, the electric circuit includes one operational amplifier and several resistors and capacitors [31].

For communication bracelets, the electronics can be housed in a pocket in the device strap, hidden from the wearer view. The electronics include, for instance, a microcontroller and two-axis accelerometer. The adoption of a low-power design ensures that the circuit board and battery lay flat under the wrist. Placing the IR transceiver near the back of the thumb ensures it is visible by the IR transceiver embedded in another device when wearers are shaking hands [32].

In building a bracelet to record memories for cyclists, the device proposed employed a Lilypad board for communication with various sensors (accelerometer and temperature) and actuators (tricolor led), enabling users to capture additional information, such as the speed of travel and the temperature, to record a moment. The device was designed to allow continuous recording of the user behavior during his or her journey with the bicycle, and to minimize the user effort when registering places and moments [33].

For chest bands, the Equivital LifeMonitor device consisted of the sensor electronics module (SEM) and the monitoring belt. The SEM contained a battery, electronics, and software that processed the measurements from the monitoring belt. The monitoring belt held the SEM on the wearer body and contained fabric electrodes, which required contact with the user's skin to sense his or her vital signs [34].

For armbands, like the GE-Fusion Band, an assistive technology for input entry of users with motor impairments was implemented, including a microcontroller (8 MHz Arduino Pro Mini) and multiple sensors (a dual-channel EMG, and three-axis Gyroscope sensors, plus three electrodes). The entire device weighed less than 20 grams and was housed in a 60 mm × 35 mm × 20 mm project box, with external connections for three EMG electrodes. The strap of the armband was produced with elastic, allowing the device to be securely fastened to the wearer [35].

For knee braces to monitor user movement, the electronic components include an Arduino Pro Mini (3.3 V, 8 MHz), and two InterSense MPU-6050 accelerometers mounted on Sparkfun breakout boards. Also, microSD cards integrated with a Sparkfun OpenLog enable data storage. The choice of small components allowed the circuitry to be concealed avoiding thus to intimidate patients [36].

To monitor the wearer oxygenation with finger-mounted devices, the sensor can be connected to Nonin's XPod board, a processing unit that gathers and processes the raw analog sensor data. Such data are output from a digital serial stream containing SpO_2 and heart rate at 3 Hz. The board can also provide a plethysmographic signal sampled at 75 Hz. The XPod board is placed under the batteries, from which each LED drains 3 mW. With such configuration, HealthGear can run intermittently for 12 h using two AAA rechargeable batteries [13].

For a belt buckle, three important design decisions involve the properties system performance, connectivity, and extensibility, including the selection of an adequate processing unit, dimensioning of memory, and interface speeds [1].

For earpieces in augmented reality, to ensure the system becomes more viable for wearable devices, the user wears a binaural microphone array and the source anchor is placed in the environment since the power consumption of a loudspeaker is much higher than that of a receiver with a microphone array. Additionally, tracking information is facilitated when the system is worn by the user [37].

For eye-tracking goggles, the hardware can include two main components: Goggles with integrated electrodes above and below the lenses frame and a signal processing unit, with a credit card size of 82×56 mm. The pocket (external case) can be worn on the user body, for instance, in a bag fixed to the wearer upper arms. The system implemented by Bulling et al. [38] weighed 208 g and was powered by a 3.7 V / 1500 mAh Li-polymer battery attached to the pocket. In terms of duration, with this specific configuration the battery enabled more than 7 h of mobile eye movement recording [38].

For eye tracking with a cap, and commercial off-the-shelf devices, electrodes connected to Mobi from Twente Medical Systems International (TMSI) can be employed to record Electrooculography (EOG). Also, an infrared eye tracker (Dikablis from Ergoneers) can be used to record gaze, and a cap with an inertial measurement units (from XSens) can be used in connection with an XBus master to record head movements. To fuse the data, the signals from these three devices should be transferred to a computer, with an application to handle both synchronization and storage [39].

With foot-mounted sensors to monitor stress levels, GRASP was created. It is a real-time system, including sensor boards, a firmware, software libraries, and an API. Each sensor board has an MSP430 microprocessor, powered by a lithium-ion polymer (3.7V) battery. The boards sample up to eight biosignal channels (TI80S1298), including electrodermal activity (EDA) and electrocardiogram (ECG) data, both streamed directly to a PC via Bluetooth [40].

In a body-area network for swimming monitoring, a prototype consisting of three-axis accelerometer sensors and feedback modules was implemented. Three sensors were mounted on the swimmers back and wrist. A visual feedback swim goggles, with a tactile and an audio feedback device, provided output responses to wearers. The data gathered with the acceleration sensor were stored for offline processing. Concerning the hardware specification, three-axis accelerometers, a microcontroller, 1 Gb of flash memory, and a rechargeable battery were used [41].

In a body-area network for a wearable art installation targeted at raising users' awareness about physiological sensing, an undergarment with a large pocket situated between the wearer's shoulder blades was created. The pocket contained electronic components, such as an Arduino UNO, wireless communication devices (XBee), a pulse sensor, and batteries. Biofeedback was projected using colored circles, and the heartbeat data were collected from a pulse sensor attached to the wearer earlobe [8].

Thus, when assembling these components altogether, in addition to meeting functional requirements, the system must ensure quality factors as well. For the swimming scenario, watertightness was required and ensured by shrink-wrapping the device in plastic foil, and isolating LED contacts using transparent silicone [41]. The weight and form factor of the wearable computers are important too [42], mainly because the wearable is worn for long periods; thus its weight and form factor should both be comfortable for the wearer. By enclosing the majority of hardware in a small area, the sensors (such as electrodes) can be worn underneath the device (such as an armband), ensuring that the interface is small and easy to use too [35].

For wearable technologies to be comfortable, their packaging housing the electronics should be small and lightweight. Considering that the wearer's dimensions are fixed, the device overhead needs to be minimized respecting both volume and weight restrictions [23].

To address this issue, the processing requirements may be delegated to other devices. For instance, when monitoring farming activities, Fukatsu and Nanseki [43] ensured that all the detected data from the wearable device were analyzed at a remote site instead of using an internal computer embedded in the wearable. By separating this function, the wearable device became a simple, small, and lightweight unit with high performance [43].

Besides striving for minimalistic design and ensuring that wearers can fasten the device to properly fit their dimensions, due to their close and continuous contact with the user skin, the hardware of a wearable should also be tested and validated to avoid safety issues caused either by excessive heat or allergenic materials [1]. To further assist in the development of comfortable wearable computers, designers should consult with anthropometry experts to ensure that the belts and headpieces have an appropriate length and diameter to comfortably fit most of the user population [19]. The texture of the device should be tested to ensure the user wears it comfortably.

To ensure proper fit and suit users with different wrist dimensions, bracelets, such as the iBand, can be adjustable in design [32]. Armbands such as the GE Fusion have an elastic strap, also to allow wearers to securely fasten the device to the their wrists [35]. If the device does not fit well in the user, data collection will be compromised, lowering accuracy and hindering also the wearer experience [38]. Issues with lack of sturdiness also hinder the user experience, especially if the device breaks down or fall apart too often [44]. Because the device dimensions should be kept to the viable minimum, all the decisions concerning electronic components should strive to employ their smallest available option [1].

Based on the analysis of existing wearable applications, seven components are common in their implementation. They are defined as follows:

- **User Interface**: It provides the communication channel with end users, be it passive (implicit interaction), active (explicit interaction), or hybrid (both). Although user interfaces vary largely depending on the form factor, device purpose and interaction modalities chosen; graphic displays are the most commonly employed for interaction with wearable technologies, including LED lights that are tiny and discreet, and more advanced displays in high resolution and full color. To combine multiple modalities, vibration is often embedded in the device for output responses, alert messages, whereas buttons and switches are often integrated in the equipment body and case for input entry.
- **Sensors**: As described in Sect. 1.4, sensors are often tiny electronic components whose placement depends on the data to be sensed and the level of accuracy required by the application. While skin sensors (such as electrodermal activity and

galvanic skin response) must be in close contact with the user skin, other sensors collecting environmental data can be placed facing the user's surroundings.

- **Actuators**: They are used to communicate output responses and provide feedback to the users, including audio actuators and vibrotactile actuators, which should be placed in close contact to the human skin to ensure the vibration is noticeable.
- **Processing Unit**: It is responsible to gather and integrate data collected with the sensors, treat and interpret it, in order to provide functionality, services and resources to end users. The level of complexity in the processing algorithms depends on the scale of the device; in other words, the more sensors and features available, the more complex the operations to treat and handle the data collected will be. The processing unit will also handle and communicate to users the device status, concerning energy levels, storage space, and connectivity. The wearable should provide scalable computational performance to support applications with varying requirements. The assessment of the processing performance of a wearable technology enables to monitor and control energy consumption as well as heat dissipation [1].
- **Power Unit**: It is responsible to collect and distribute power to the electronic components of the device. While battery holders allow for autonomy and stand-alone usage, power ports enable wearers to recharge their devices on demand. Proprietary chargers are available depending on the devices brand, models, and releases. In terms of power consumption, different algorithms influence the power requirements of a device [1]. The power consumption also depends on the complexity of the device features, number of sensors, data collected and their frequency, and interaction approach for input entry and output responses [27]. The battery and recharge remain as grand challenges in the user adoption [27], even when an external battery can be employed for long-term operation [1], energy efficiency still hinders the user experience [45].
- **Storage Unit**: Depending on the needs of the application to maintain data on the device, a storage unit, such as a memory card, is often necessary. The memory unit can store data locally and allow transfer of information across devices. Sufficient memory (normally volatile RAM) for application-specific processing must be available [1]. The storage enables to record sensor readings, user profiles as well as processing results. Memory should be nonvolatile, widely scalable, and also easily exchangeable by the user [1]. A slot for a MiniSD storage card can be used to extend built-in FLASH memory of the processor in use, to store, for instance, user and sensor data or additional application software [1].
- **Network and Communication Module**: To extend the processing power of the device, wearables are commonly used in connection to smartphones, or peripheric devices (such as headsets) in a body-area network. The communication protocols employed allow data sharing and transmission, information access, or even periodic upgrades. To share information with the appropriate personnel, data can be transmitted either wirelessly, via a short-range communication with another device, or over a long-range channel to central monitoring stations [17]. To address connectivity requirements, the system has to be equipped with wired and/or wireless interfaces [1].

A firmware facilitates the integration of hardware aspects in a wearable system. For an EOG goggle application for eye tracking, for example, a three-layer firmware was defined. It includes Hardware Abstraction Layer (HAL), a Device Layer (DEL), and a Task Layer (TAL). To access the hardware, the HAL provides interfaces to the upper layers, hiding all low-level hardware access. The device layer (DEL) provides functionality for external components, such as the Bluetooth module. The core functionality of the firmware is provided by five tasks which form the Task Layer (TAL). A separate Library (LIB) contains functionality commonly shared by these tasks [38], such as the CRC routines.

From a technical perspective, the main limitations of monitoring technologies are related to processing and storage capabilities. Monitoring devices include sensors to measure physiological signals and convert them into machine-readable data. Some wearable devices include dedicated resources to process the information; however, they are sparse and limited [34].

2.2.2   Software, Systems, and Applications

One of the most important characteristic of a wearable technology for end users is its utility. Unless wearers clearly understand the benefit and usefulness of the device, it is very unlikely they will accept, adopt it, and sustain their engagement with the technology. For Buenaflor and Kim [3], the perceived usefulness is defined as "the degree to which an individual believes that using a particular system will enhance their performance when completing of a certain task."

As described next, algorithms used in wearable applications serve multiple different purposes, including data collection, curation, fusion, classification, and controlling interventions as well as feedback responses. Thus, besides building the wearable device, stakeholders must address the procedures for data analysis, including methods dedicated to remove outliers, smoothing data and improving the reliability of the system results by either consulting domain experts, or verifying ground truth and baseline measurements [11].

For Ha et al. [10], concerning ECG signals, the integrity of the data needs to be verified throughout all the data flow from the acquisition of raw signals, through wireless communication and data transmission, until the feature management level. Concerning ubiquitous computing, the signals should be measured anytime and anywhere regardless of the activities the user is conducting [10].

Adaptive filtering can be used to treat the data collected with artifact reduction, whereas to reduce or eliminate noise, lowpass filter can be used [38] in combination with Butterworth filter [41]. To eliminate aberrant errors due to communication issues, the signals collected with IMU concerning user movement should pass through a lowpass filter. In this process, 15 Hz is set as the cut-off frequency to extract features from each segment [26]. For noise reduction, wavelet decomposition can be used as well. For artifact reduction, adaptive linear filtering can be used with an optional artifact-correlated signal [1].

Dedicated algorithms are required to efficiently cope with signal artifacts caused by physical activity from users. Without noise reduction and filtering, artifacts may dominate the signal (data collected) rendering desired detection unfeasible, for instance, for eye movements. This is particularly important for long-term user interaction, extensive data collection, with wearers executing a wide range of activities that constantly change during the day, requiring thus more advanced algorithms to curate data [38]. For segmentation and classification of human activities, such as attitude and gestures, data fusion algorithms can be employed to help detecting the user context. To merge sensor signals, data fusion algorithms are used; for activity and attitude recognition, algorithms and models employed include Bayesian, Kalman, and Hidden Markov Models [1].

In the context of EOG goggles for eye tracking, the processing steps required to analyze the data collected include five algorithms aimed at blink detection, saccade detection, blink removal, eye gesture recognition, and artifact compensation of signals induced by walking [38]. For EOG, besides detection of saccades, online algorithms can also help detecting fixations, blinks, smooth pursuit, and VOR from mobile eye-tracking data. VOR, or Vestibulo-Ocular Reflex, is a movement that refers to the user's visual reflex to keep a precise point insight while moving his or her head [39].

Concerning chest belts for monitoring physiological signals, the EQ01 provides limited information processing capabilities, including filtering and low-level knowledge extraction. The device is able to detect a few postures (e.g., standing, lying) from the analysis of the measured acceleration or extract the R-R interval for electrocardiogram analysis [34].

The analysis of data collected with sensors for physiological monitoring of oxygenation and pulse, using multiple algorithms, enables the automatic detection of respiratory issues, such as sleep apnea events [13].

Artificial neural networks (ANN) can be employed to map sensor data measured from human shoulder motion in order to position commands for input control. Using a sensor controller module, the position command is generated from sensor data. The inputs to the ANN can be data from sensors, whereas the outputs from the ANN are coordinates in the workspace. Although only direction information can be used to control 2-DOF motion, such directions are useful as input. The ANN must be the inverse model of the "fiber sensors" module and the weights of the ANN are learned by the ANN using a multilayered perceptron, for instance, using one hidden layer with six neurons [31].

Machine learning algorithms are able to extract useful information from signals collected from wearable sensors [35], for instance, to recognize sport-related activities, such as walking, jogging, running, sprinting, jumping, jump shot, layup shot, and pivot. In the activity recognition process, a support vector machine (SVM) classifier can be employed [26].

Several wearable applications have explored the suitability of different algorithms, methods, and devices to enable the automatic recognition of human activities. The approaches adopted range from estimating low-abstraction activities (such as chewing or sitting) to estimating complex activities, such as whether the person is leaving for work later than usual [46]. Initial work also focused on activities related to user mobility, using accelerometer data to infer whether a person is standing, sitting, or walking. Algorithms focused on counting steps and estimating calories burned aided to create applications for the fitness-tracking industry; however, recent efforts have focused especially on behavior recognition [46].

In head-mounted devices for brain–computer interfaces, algorithms help to recognize the user's intentions using a feature vector that characterizes the brain activity. Either regression or classification algorithms can be used to achieve this goal [47].

To recognize farming operations and detect patterns in the sensed data, estimation algorithms, such as pattern matching, Bayesian estimation, principal component analysis, and support vector machines, were used to classify the data in groups of farming operation with supervised learning [43].

Among the requirements for supervised learning, an extensive set of labeled data is needed. Thus, to address this issue and generate a dataset with training data for physical activity, Munoz et al. [36] recruited human subjects (research participants) to execute basic movements (e.g., knee extension exercise). The signals were annotated through a manual approach. Once tagged, the dataset was analyzed using the Weka machine learning software tool, generating an algorithm to classify the gesture transitions, such as a leg lift [36].

Even though annotations are helpful for learning algorithms and classification, insufficient labeling in complex contexts makes inherent artifacts of the data collected difficult to discern through automated approaches that may employ artificial intelligence algorithms [48].

To classify features from eye-tracking data and discriminate eye movements according to a feature set, Vidal et al. [39] ran a k-nearest neighbor (kNN) algorithm. The kNN was chosen because it is lightweight and fast, and enable real-time responses. To achieve a fivefold cross-validation, after shuffling and standardizing the data, it was separated in five segments with 20% of the saccades, 20% of the smooth pursuits, and 20% of the VORs [39].

Other aspects of software that must be carefully considered in the design phases include its responsiveness, accuracy, context-sensitivity, and accessibility. Those considerations are defined as follows.

- **Responsiveness**: The wearer interaction is short; thus, users become impatient if the device does not provide them with immediate responses. Glanceable interfaces and intuitive interaction design also facilitate to reduce the time needed for users to complete a task. Concerning the system, the required responsiveness to external events depends strongly on the type and method of sensor attachment, but in general, the time resolution is expected to be in the range of milliseconds [1]. Such requirement is particularly important when emergency response systems are at stake.
- **Accuracy**: When data is collected and presented to end users, wearers tend to trust that the values informed to them are correct. When calibration is needed to compensate for potential algorithmic or acquisition errors, users should not only be made aware of it, but also allowed to set their configurations accordingly.

- **Context-sensitivity**: Because wearables are widespread, the interaction model of such devices should respect the social norms and conventions of the users' contexts of use through an intelligent approach.
- **Accessibility**: There is a large range of users' profiles interacting with wearables; thus the devices should be designed for users with diverse needs, accommodating the requirements in the interface, interaction, and features of a wearable technology aiming to reach a large number of users, regardless of their limitation. For Khakurel [4], wearable devices should be designed to be inclusive regardless of the user impairment or disability [4].

In a wearable application, the software implementation varies depending on the device purpose. Still, when sensors are embedded in the device, the data collected can be applied to recognize different user activities, for instance, the number of steps in a fitness tracker with pedometer features. To that end, the signals must be properly interpreted after data collection, which is commonly done using machine learning techniques [42]. For wearable computing, the research on activity recognition faces challenges due to limited (or nonexistent) ground truth (e.g., lack of open repositories with labeled data), wicked problems, and ambiguity in the interpretations. The lack of precision also makes activity recognition a task- and domain-specific solution that does not serve for general purposes [42].

As researchers and engineers increasingly explore wearables, they also face challenges when developing and testing custom hardware prototypes. A key challenge in wearable computing involves knowing intimately the chip's architecture and the board's layout. There is an increased demand for platforms that allow engineers and researchers to quickly prototype and evaluate new wearables. To address this need and facilitate prototyping wearable devices, Graham and Zhou [49] proposed an open-source platform. Besides a main board, the platform proposed included four modules: a Bluetooth module, an LCD module, a sensing module, and a battery module. The platform can be built and assembled by researchers without depending on an expensive manufacturer, besides also enabling easy programming and debugging. Three examples of prototypes for wearable devices created with such a platform include a step counter, an environmental monitoring smartwatch, and an infrared-based localization system [49].

Although ground truth is essential to validate and evaluate algorithms as well as to train supervised models, for activity recognition it is not always easy to obtain high-quality, labeled data, with a sufficient number of examples. Thus, in an example of detection of muscle movement in a knee injury context, ideally, investigators would use myoelectric sensors and directly measure muscle activity. However, these sensors are invasive to the wearer because they must be placed directly on the user the skin in a recently injured joint [36]. Instead, to define ground truth in an experiment, investigators asked a physical therapist to manually classify leg lifts analyzing videos of patients exercising [36]. Such an approach is time-consuming, but tends to be more reliable and largely employed for classification.

To gather naturalistic ground truth data from eye movements using wearable eye trackers, a user study with EOG was conducted. The eye movements collected were analyzed by extracting basic signal features from them. In the experiment conducted, the feature analysis showed promise to help characterizing different eye movements [39].

For a swimming monitoring wearable application, to assess the reliability of the algorithm for automatic parameter extraction, the positions of the detected events were compared to manual annotations done in real time [41]. More specifically, the algorithms implemented were able to extract swimming parameters, such as the swim velocity, the arm strokes, the distance per arm stroke, the body balance, and the body rotation. The sensor angle measurement was validated, and the body balance measurement of the system was able to differentiate between good and bad balances. By analyzing the rotation amplitude and comparing the amplitudes of upper and lower body parts, the longitudinal body rotation measurement aided to quantify the body rotation of the swimmer. The results of the stroke efficiency evaluation were consistent with the visual observations [41].

In the case of classification algorithms, it is up to the stakeholders involved in the development of the wearable to identify and apply safety thresholds concerning false positives. This process is normally based on domain knowledge experts (such as physicians) and aim at minimizing eventual harm for end users, besides also enhancing the user experience for wearers.

In the case of output response, the feedback to users, be it audio, visual, or haptic, can be implemented using microcontrollers that command the actuators [41].

Even if current devices come from the factory with pre-programmed configurations, wearers should be able to calibrate, or customize, their devices according to their specific needs and profiles. Such calibrations serve, for instance, to improve the accuracy of classification of user gestures and activities (e.g., steps) as well as voice commands. To that end, in a manual approach requiring explicit interaction from users, the application should provide them with options for settings. This feature enables wearers to configure their devices and applications according to their specific needs.

In an automated approach, the algorithms should consider diverse users' profiles, and walking patterns, for example, vary in step parameters per individual. To detect and treat variations in walking styles for different subjects, Bulling et al. [38] implemented an algorithm. Such algorithm adapts itself to different persons, by calculating the walking step length on the basis of three consecutive movements executed separately by the left and the right legs [38]. Another aspect highlighted as important in the reading quality of EOG signals is the difference in head shape across participants. Adjusting the device fit in these contexts is crucial to increase the accuracy of an eye-tracking algorithm [38].

For an upper garment to control the user input with shoulder movements, whenever the subject wears the master device, the position of the device on the body changes. Since the amount of bending in a human shoulder is small, a change in the position of the device can cause a dramatic change in the coordinates of the position command. Beginning with a calibration process in this context is essential when the user wears the device [31].

Wearable technologies are not always enough powerful to enable complex information processing and advanced visualizations; therefore, the network and communication are relevant to transfer data to external devices enabling advanced analysis, large-scale repositories, and visualization.

When designing a bracelet to record events for cyclist, a smartphone application was used to enable wearers to include additional information when recording an event. The wearer benefits from a phone to take a picture, still the capture is triggered by a wearable personal device. In this case, the mobile phone extends thus the functionality of the wearable, allowing users to manually type sentences to be associated to an event registered with the camera [33].

In the PhysioDroid project, a remote persistent storage system is used to manage the data collected by the wearable monitoring device. The transmission of data occurs through a mobile app to a remote storage component that manages local persistence processes. In this project, the package functionalities were built on SQLite, a database engine suited for memory-constrained systems, like mobile devices. Its advantages include running in minimal stack space and requiring very little heap. SQLite defines a compact in-process library that implements a stripped version of SQL [34].

To monitor kids' health with a wearable sensor, a mobile application was also used. This app played an important role to the system by receiving physiological data from the wearable device, processing the data received, and alerting other users when a critical situation was detected [11].

2.2.3 Network and Connectivity

Due to the limitations in processing, resources, power and storage, oftentimes wearable technologies are neither self-contained nor stand-alone. To address such limitations, wearables often rely on external devices, equipment, and resources be it to access information or to request additional services.

In this context, a wearable technology must support flexible communication interfaces and enable application-specific adaptations for input and output requirements. For various applications, the interfaces to a scalable number of sensors worn on the human body should be made available. The communication channels currently employed vary, including wired interfaces (such as a serial connection cable), physical interfaces (such as USB ports), or wireless links (such as Bluetooth, or RFID).

The interface bandwidth must be adaptable to support body-area network topologies with distributed local sensor networks. These networks have different communication bandwidth needs when attached to a central wearable computer, at least when compared to direct interface to sensors [1]. Wireless communication with mobile devices can also serve to share a display, to provide wide-area communication or to support data exchange [1].

Wearables, such as head-mounted devices, rely on external sources of power and contents. Wrist-worn wearables often rely on smartphones and mobile applications to access resources and share data. To combine multiple sensors and leverage on the benefits of different form factors for input entry and output responses, body-area networks (BAN) integrating multiple devices are implemented. The physical connections between devices can be made available through USB ports and readers, or wired through cables. Wireless connections may be more convenient for users; however, they require synchronization (pairing) and physical proximity between devices. If a plug, port, or socket option is selected, this approach also adds mechanical issues and may imply in larger, or more expensive hardware. Wireless connection, such as Bluetooth, WiFi, or Infrared transmissions, on the other hand requires also a much larger power budget [23]. Alternatively, RFID tags, when attached to relevant objects (e.g., materials, facilities, and machinery) can facilitate activity recognition without any additional energy consumption requirement [43].

From a user experience perspective, it is more practical to connect different garment pieces wirelessly [1]. For a wearable system that collects and processes data (e.g., from respiratory sensors or ECG electrodes in a healthcare scenario), a wireless connection can be employed for transmitting the processed data. Also, an extractable memory card can be used for storage. With such an approach, wearers can still be constantly monitored while wearing the device, but without the hassle of being "hard-wired" to their patient beds in a somehow fixed position. Depending on further transmission and sharing protocols and tools, home care applications become also suitable for medical applications [23].

For virtual connections (wireless), the protocols commonly employed include BLE (Bluetooth Low Energy), WiFi, Zigbee, RFID, ANT+, and NFC (Near-Field Communication). For physical connections, USB C (Universal Serial Bus) and memory card readers are commonly used, as well as jumper wires (illustrated in Fig. 2.3). The Universal Serial Bus (USB) is an extension interface popularly employed, thanks to its well-supported, reliable standard.

For connectivity to provide storage, or additional processing services, cloud computing is a maturing paradigm in which flexible and extensible computing power is provided on demand over networks [47]. Through such paradigm, wearables can grant access to cloud functionalities for high-performance computation, large capac-

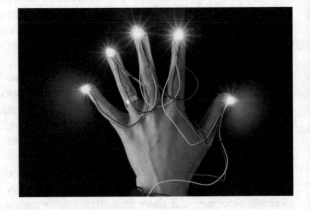

Fig. 2.3 Physical connections, with wires and cables, can be used to integrate multiple electronic components, such as sensors and actuators. In the LED manicure project, Sophy Wong uses LED lights on wearers' nails to adorn the body. Jumper wires connect the LEDs to the user bracelet. Credit: Sophy Wong. At https://sophywong.com

ity storage, and data analytics as well [34]. Concerning physical solutions for applications requiring additional storage space, a MiniSD card, or a flash disk attached to the USB (i.e., USB memory stick) can be used. Numerous USB peripheral devices are available to extend the device capabilities [1]. Additional communication interfaces include WLAN, BAN, and Zigbee, which can be used to facilitate wireless interoperability among sensors [3]. Six approaches for connectivity commonly employed in wearables are defined as follows:

- **ANT+**: It is an interoperable wireless transfer network protocol employed to collect, transfer, and store sensor data.
- **Bluetooth**: It is a wireless sensor interface that serves to link sensors, sensor networks, or a remote base station computer for management or downloading data from a wearable computer [1]. With a Bluetooth connection, data can be sent over a network in close proximity to the device [34].
- **RFID**: Inexpensive passive RFID tags can be used to identify people, places, and things [7].
- **NFC**: Near-Field Communication is a set of network protocols that permit to connect two devices that are within a 4 cm range.
- **Zigbee**: When more than seven sensor nodes are needed or when extreme low power is required, a digital radio is used based on the IEEE 802.15.4 standard physical layer protocol [7].
- **WiFi**: It is an IEEE 802.11x standard wireless technology used for network and Internet connection.

By transferring data collected with wearable sensors to external computers, further analysis, processing, fusion, and visualization are enabled [1]. In the HealthGear project, for instance, physiological sensors were wirelessly connected via Bluetooth to a Bluetooth-enabled cell phone. Bluetooth advantages include its pervasiveness in the devices, availability on cell phones and other mobile devices, and relatively low power consumption. Still, as the investigators remark, any other short-range wireless communication protocol could have been used too [13].

For the BSK board for basketball monitoring, data download was possible through a USB connection (i.e., without removing any pieces of the device) [26]. For ECG monitoring, Ha et al. [10] state that a wireless network, such as wireless personal area network (WPAN) or wireless local area network (WLAN), can be employed. In designing an ECG monitoring device, they employed Zigbee, because it is a low-cost, low-power, wireless mesh networking standard [10].

The choice of communication protocol and network for data transmission depends on several factors, including requirements related to time, security, volume of data, as well as effort to synchronize and connect devices and systems, financial costs associated, and physical space needs, including both the distance between devices and the assembly of electronic components required.

Besides extending the device capabilities, another advantage of enabling device connectivity is the potential for collaboration among users. Although most wearables involve a single user, the data collected can serve people in other remote locations.

Allowing users to communicate with people and computers in other locations fosters collaborative work [19].

Concerning energy consumption (discussed in the next section), connectivity is a critical feature. Oftentimes when a device does not have much power, it is only able to send a packet once every couple of seconds, or even, only when the energy on board is sufficient. NFC communication is preferred to exploit the energy transmitted from external readers, allowing for synchronization and exchange of data on user's demand without any energy expenditure on the device [27].

2.2.4 Energy and Power Sources

The major challenge that limits the vision of wearable technologies applied across domains is certainly the lack of autonomy of the wearable devices. The energy source in the latest generation devices still requires regular recharges, the batteries last a day or a few days only, forcing the users to stop wearing the device, which interrupts both the data collection and normal usage [27].

Due to their continuous and varied data collection, smartwatches, sleep-tracking wristbands, smart glasses, and smart badges require much more power because of their much richer sensing capabilities and functions [27].

The power management can be designed to optimize energy consumption by ensuring that the operations occur when there is enough energy available to successfully complete them, and as such, opportunistically activating the system to avoid state loss. Also, when performing extreme duty cycling, a self-sustainable system can be achieved by placing the device in ultra-deep sleep mode that saves energy, for instance, during the night when data acquisition may be not needed [27].

To address energy-efficiency issues, a comprehensive approach tackling both hardware and software is needed. Concerning software-related decisions, the device should periodically and opportunistically acquire information from the sensors according to the available energy, and an aggressive power management should be implemented to save battery. Concerning hardware-related decisions, novel ambient energy harvesting circuits, and low-power design should be integrated to employ an ad hoc low-power multisensory strategy [27].

The battery consumption should be optimized, so that wearers can use the devices with minimal interruption. Most devices still require a recharge every few days, or even hours, falling short on the wearers' expectations for a satisfactory experience [27]. Although the energy requirements often oblige wearers to remove their devices for recharging the battery, design decisions of data collection, stand-by mode, and energy preserving can optimize the energy usage. For Siewiorek [51], "there is more to gain on reducing power demand than increasing the power source" [51].

2.3 Contexts of Use

Unlike legacy systems operated from Desktop computers, and stationary settings, where environmental conditions remain stable over time, and users perform only one task at a time, wearable applications are strongly impacted by transient requirements, dynamic conditions from users' contexts, and multitasking behaviors from wearers. Users of wearable devices are in motion when they wear and interact with their devices [50]. Users naturally move to perform daily activities, be it at home doing chores, at work, exercising, or during social activities [3].

Wearers interact when they are walking, driving, moving from one place to another, making and receiving calls, reading and sending text messages [50], swimming [41], or even while sleeping [13]. To have a full understanding about how an attached load of a wearable technology affects perceptions of movement, it is crucial to understand what movement users are performing (e.g., walking, jogging, bending, sitting down) [30]. Previous work on pedestrians' behaviors, for instance, reported that during wearable interaction there is an increased task load and reduced walking speed [18].

Context-awareness involves more than considering merely physical activities of the user [38]. Also, the work environment where the device is used should be characterized, and then, the context of its use should be identified as well [4]. If the conditions change when users are moving, so does their environment, the complexity of the tasks they are completing, and their physical and cognitive abilities [42]. Aspects like user attention and intentionality are both important [38]. The understanding of contextual information inform the design aspects that must be changed to improve the users' comfort with appropriate design modifications [30].

Because small-scale, stand-alone wearables are often used continuously, their design should account for transient contexts of use. The case and cover of devices should be made out of a strong material, for instance, scratch-resistant plastic for a belt buckle [1]. Smartwatches and fitness trackers should be water-resistant to stand humidity. These devices should also be robust and sturdy to stand ordinary shocks [23].

The design of interfaces for wearable devices continuously worn must also consider that wearers switch locations; therefore, light, noise, and privacy levels vary accordingly. Designers should consider that the user interaction is short and requires divided attention, since most users focus on their main activities while interacting with wearable devices. When applications that augment (instead of replacing) the user experience are created, designers should strive to allow the user to focus on the physical world, besides also reducing the time needed to provide responses [51].

When users are running and trying to interact with a wearable, there is potential for disturbance. In HCI research, usually, interactive tasks are evaluated by assessing the interaction exclusively, for instance, in a controlled environment where external factors do not disturb the user. However, task load and walking speed should be considered as well. The end user evaluations in controlled spaces provide insights into the user interaction, but for running they neglect a specific pattern of movement that is constantly repeated by the runner, with coordinated movements of both legs and both arms. "Since interactions with wearables typically require movements of body parts (e.g. to touch a button), these device interactions can interfere with the running movement" [18].

The contexts of use where the user interaction takes place are transient for wrist-worn devices, such as smartwatches and fitness trackers. Head-mounted devices on the other hand are often wired to computing stations (e.g., Desktop computers) and used in more controlled environments, such as a living room or a bedroom. Because headsets for entertainment (gaming with VR and AR) are used indoors, the environment where the user interaction takes place is often more stable concerning light, noise, and user location. Head-mounted devices for augmented reality can be used either indoor or in outdoor environments, superposing information to the real world. Outdoor environments, such as museums or stores, require additional tests in the implementation process to ensure the user interaction is effective in specific settings.

Clothing is an essential element of human life; therefore, for the integration of computational technologies into clothing to be successful, it must first address the culture and tradition of the wearers [9]. Because culture has an important influence on users' behaviors, beliefs, and decisions, it also influences the user acceptance and use of wearable technology [3]. In the evaluation of the iBand, a bracelet for exchanging contact information, the effects of contextual differences were noticed, as they affected the way in which the wearable was accepted and used in cross-cultural settings [32].

To sense the users' context, badges and jackets have been explored [52]. More specifically, a wearable sensor badge was built with (hard) electronic components to sense ambulatory activities and enable context-aware applications. Also, a wearable sensor jacket was built using advanced knitting techniques to form (soft) fabric stretch sensors to measure upper limb and body movement. The goal of such applications was to recognize the user activity with unobtrusive sensors, detecting the posture and movements of the wearer with knitted stretch sensors and knitted conductive tracking [52]. In the context of swimming, data collected with body-worn systems for context and activity awareness facilitates data tracking for swimmers. An automated approach for tracking activity prevents manual efforts from wearers to press buttons to count the lanes completed and to stop the timer [41].

One approach to gather valuable information about the wearers' activity and contexts is the analysis of their eye motions. Eye gestures can be performed by the user to intentionally and inconspicuously provide contextual information [38].

Data collected through wearable sensors are beneficial to provide situational awareness to a wearable computer. In this context, "the interface between the wearable computer and the wearer can be sympathetic to the user's activities," and therefore useful to mediate the user interaction with wearable applications [52]. Concerning the implementation structure, in context-sensitive design decisions not only is the interaction between user and wearable computer important, but so is the interaction between the computer and the sensors within the infrastructure system [17].

2.4 Tasks

To properly characterize the contexts of use when implementing a wearable application, the stakeholders should consider which activities and tasks the wearers need to execute. Modeling user tasks stands out as one of the most challenging activities in the design of wearable computers [53]; however, a thorough task analysis helps informing design decisions concerning the appropriate user interface and interaction mechanism [17]. Hence, task analysis should precede any implementation steps.

The tasks that users execute in a wearable context vary in category depending on the level of interaction between the wearer and the technology. Three basic categories of independent tasks were identified by Burgy [17]: (i) primary task, (ii) support task, and (iii) control task [17]. Additionally, four composite tasks can be built by combining tasks from basic categories. The three task categories are defined as follows:

1. **Primary Task (PT)**: It does not require a direct interaction with the technology, being thus passively sensed in an implicit approach.
2. **Support Task (ST)**: It requires a unique and atomic interaction from the wearer with the technology; in this task category, the wearable device supports the user in either providing information or accepting input entries.
3. **Control Task (CT)**: It refers to a unique interaction of the wearer with the technology; this task category concerns the user navigation in the wearable application.

The tasks wearers execute vary in nature, duration, and requirements. Concerning the user interaction specifically, there are several occasions in which users can benefit from a wearable device for input control. Examples of control tasks include accepting calls, closing reminders, switching music, changing views, selecting running modes, or monitoring parameters when tracking exercise routines [18].

2.5 Wearer

Besides understanding the contexts of use where the interaction with wearables takes place and also the main tasks performed by wearers, also their profile must be characterized when implementing or evaluating a wearable technology. The potential beneficiaries of wearable applications vary per user profile, concerning specific age groups, background, and needs.

Although the profiles of wearers vary, the potential for long-term continuous monitoring of physiological signals makes wearables particularly promising for users with diverse needs and vulnerable populations, including babies and children, those with cardiovascular diseases, patients with chronic conditions, and older adults [4]. Wearables also stand out for athletes and fitness enthusiasts who enjoy quantifying and analyzing their performance [29].

Age and life stage issues impact the uptake potential of a wearable [54]. Concerning age, wearables have been explored in monitoring babies [73], kids [56], and older adults [3].

Babies can be monitored using instrumented socks. Such socks serve for physiological monitoring of heart rate and oxygenation. In the commercial market, Owlet socks[1] are available. They aim at preventing sudden death of infants. From scientific research, to monitor newborn babies, a sock was also evaluated; it was instrumented with EDA, temperature, and motion sensors [55].

Wearable electronics hold great potential for monitoring kids. For childcare, wearables can improve and automate activities related to the children security and safety, besides also informing caregivers, nurses, and practitioners in a healthcare context. Using smart clothes, a single garment can keep information about a child, including the name of the child and his/her parents, age, allergies, etc. This information enables nurses to have an easy access to the kid's profile and vital information associated [56]. Wearable health-monitoring systems have been developed to track, log, and communicate body temperature and heart rate for caregivers, important vital signs of children that allow parents to monitor their kids' health remotely [11].

For older adults with hearing impairments, hearing aids are traditionally used as assistive technologies. Also, concerning memory impairments, head-mounted devices can aid to augment cognitive functions [57]. For Buenaflor and Kim [3], independence is valuable to elderly people; hence, they would wear a system "if it is deemed useful, reliable, and provides obvious benefits to their independent life" [3]. On the other hand, concerning self-efficacy, older adults may not be used to technology; thus, computer systems can be hard for them to understand [3] and require training [57]. Also, age-related impairments, including visual, motor, and cognitive ones, should be carefully considered in technology design.

Concerning the level of expertise, backgrounds, and individual motivations, for athletes, both novices and experts enjoy a community of practice. For novices, peers help to maintain motivation and sustain a healthy fitness program, whereas for experts, peers formed communities to spend time together in either physical or social activities [54].

Across domains, lay users as well as experts can both benefit from wearable technologies. It is worthy noting though that users with more technical experience may be more confident and are also expected to be more willing to use wearables than those with less technical experience [3]. In the healthcare sector, for instance, patients, practitioners, and caregivers can all benefit from wearable solutions. In summary, there is not a single user profile that defines the standard wearer, but several different users' profiles. Their individual differences, be it in age, gender, culture, or technology experience, impact their acceptance of technology [3] and should therefore be considered carefully throughout the design phases.

Concerning their gender, for Munoz et al. [36], certain garments and accessories are less likely be worn by men (e.g., leggings), because this limits the number of potential users, when designing wearable technology, they opted for more generic

---

[1] www.owletcare.com.

(gender-neutral) form factors, such as a knee brace [36]. The usage of smart jewelry also varies depending on social conventions [58].

Although the application of wearables is diverse and extensive, in general, the market of commercial wearables has its own niche users, led by early adopters of novel technologies. Concerning its potential, there are promising and vast opportunities for wearable technologies to monitor more vulnerable users, such as elders and children [11]. Still, the wearable market is disproportionally driven and dominated by a young adult, tech-savvy, predominantly male population of early adopters of technology, with a consumer sample pertaining to a middle to upper socioeconomic class. With the exception of dedicated devices, or those that serve as assistive technologies and are adopted by wearers with diverse needs seeking to replace, augment, or restore human senses. Such technologies are targeted at visual, hearing, motor, cognitive, or situational impairments [59]. In health care, certain inclusion criteria also hold true, for instance, devices for patients with diabetes who use glucometers and insulin pumps as wearables. Matassa et al. [33] expect that the end user customization of devices enables manufacturers to reach a wider user population for wearable technologies. When creating a bracelet, they suggested that crafting Lilypad boxes to garnish everyday objects could help to extend the adoption of a wearable system to a wider population [33].

Concerning the user experience, the sense of ownership, or self-identification, toward the device feedback is one of the main characteristics that users perceive and acquire when using body-centered technologies. "Through this data appropriation and interaction, the body is iteratively transforming and developing" [8]. Thus, regardless of user profile, the user involvement in the design stages—since early phases, iteratively and closely—is fundamental.

For Siewiorek [51], designers have to work directly with end users of wearables to understand their needs, context, profiles as well as the opportunities in which wearable technology can assist them [51]. In involving users in the design process, Forlizzi and McCormack [54] recommend to create profiles of potential users, such as personas, as a good approach to communicate findings from user studies to the research and development teams. The users' profiles should include varied types of demographic, lifestyle, and attitudinal information [54]. For Nunez and Loke [8], a body-centered approach aids to design wearable technologies emphasizing the dynamic interplay between visibility and transparency of body. They also envision wearable technologies as a critical resource for learning and self-development [8].

When designing the wearable technology, there are several wearers' perceptions that are relevant. For [60], wearers' internal contexts include their motivations (intrinsic and extrinsic), perceptions, cognitive effort, and learning behaviors [4]. Self-awareness, for instance, is an important resource for interactive experiences that are grounded in the user body [8].

Due to social conventions, the perception of utility and wearer comfort, as well as the thoughts and feelings associated to wearing a garment will vary per individual user. Still, those concepts are key in the wearer decisions to either reject a technology, or to accept, adopt, and sustain engagement with it. Examples of negative feelings that can be involved in the wearer experience include embarrassment, shame, discomfort, awkwardness, stigma, and safety [3, 61]. In previous research studies, participants reported feeling awkward when the device affected their movement [62].

Concerning the physical aspects of a wearable device, excessive size and weight can cause embarrassment to the wearer in a social context [58], besides also negatively impacting his/her movements. Technologies that are uncomfortable, too large, or too heavy eventually cause pain to the user, whether direct (due to friction, knocking, or heat) or indirect (e.g., due to muscle fatigue) [30].

Concerning safety, the materials should be hypoallergenic and the temperature should be appropriate for prolonged touch. In a context of soldiers assessing a body-area wearable system, the evaluation of the device showed that wearing it caused skin irritation. More specific examples of negative impacts of a device include itching of the skin, redness, sensitivity or abrasion, and skin irritation. Additional complaints can include prickly heat, extreme sweating, acne, or muscle cramps [63].

Concerning social aspects, including potential stigmas and user acceptance, a wristband alarm device that appears to be a technical aid may be considered stigmatizing for certain users, whereas a panic alarm system that is smaller, less obtrusive, and discreet can be preferred among wearers [3]. Concerning heat, to analyze a possible inconvenience for the user, temperature should be assessed prior to device deployment, while the system is running under heavy load, for instance, in a bench-mark test. The device case can help to dissipate heat, depending on the materials employed. Still, the hottest components should not be placed in direct contact with the wearer skin but isolated, for instance, with a plastic housing of high thermal resistance manufactured with thin walls to ensure it is lightweight [1].

The user acceptance of a wearable technology is affected by technological and human factors. Six human factors that play important roles in the acceptance of wearables are: fundamental needs, cognitive activity, physical aspect, social aspect, demographic characteristics, and technical experience [3]. They are summarized as follows:

- **Fundamental needs**: Wearables should fulfill basic human needs to increase acceptance rates;
- **Cognitive activity**: Wearables are accepted or rejected depending on the user's perception on its learning curve, usefulness, and ease of use;
- **Social aspect**: The effect of wearing a device on the social interaction of the individual, i.e., in public contexts, influences his or her acceptance;
- **Physical aspect**: Comfort, safety, appearance, and mobility are also influential, especially for technologies used in long term;
- **Demographic characteristics**: Needs, preferences, perceptions, and the ability to adopt new technologies are influenced by age, gender, and expertise of the wearer.

The attention levels of the wearers are also relevant when creating wearable interfaces. While desktop user interfaces assume that users are purely concentrating on digital tasks, when designing user interfaces for wearable computers, this is atypical. Hence, understanding the limitations and abilities related to human attention is crucial. Particularly, understanding how many tasks or what types of tasks users can successfully accomplish at once is important [42].

The level of attention and fatigue will vary not only per individual wearer, his/her age, occupation, and affective state, but also depending how long the interaction lasts. Attention and fatigue are known to influence the user interaction with technology and are dependent on the time of the day, day of the week or other environmental circumstances and events that can cause situational impairments for end users.

Concerning human factors and the user interaction, three characteristics that stand out when designing the wearable interface include the following [42]:

1. **Visual attention**: It refers to the need of users to focus on the wearable interface when interacting with it, a low demand for visual attention can be obtained when the user interface is glanceable, and multimodal responses are provided in a meaningful and intuitive way, for instance, combining audio output and vibration in addition to graphics.
2. **Physical demand**: It refers to the effort required from users to interact with the technology, concerning motor, and physical aspects, including the need, duration and frequency of button presses, touch, swiping, scrolling, gestures (finger, hand, head), and speech.
3. **Cognitive demand**: It refers to the workload users place in completing a task, the mental requirements to recall information, process it, and respond accordingly in the interaction process.

2.6 Universal Design and Customization

To accommodate the needs of diverse users, a unique solution of hardware and software is not suitable. Therefore, design aspects concerning device and application should enable end user customization and personalization to adjust the technology to specific user's needs.

As most devices are not custom-made for an individual user, to adjust the fit and the device dimensions, in a wrist-worn or head-mounted device, the straps should allow regulation so that wearers can decide on a comfortable fit. Comfort is affected by the size, shape, temperature, and weight of the technology and how it affects natural body movements [3], and users' safety. Fastening straps are commonly employed in head-mounted displays, such as VR headsets, and wrist-worn wearables, such as smartwatches and fitness trackers. Custom-made devices are built to precisely fit the dimensions of a single user; however, besides being more expensive, they tend to serve specialized purposes, like for prosthetic devices. Other wearable devices are not customizable at all regarding their dimensions; however, they may be pinned or plugged into wearers' clothes and garments, for instance, Sun Sprite (UV monitor) or pedometers.

Concerning the customization of applications, smartwatches are popular due to their flexibility, since in addition to their default applications, they also allow users to choose and install modular applications (apps), adapting thus the device to the users' preferences. These apps are available in online markets for download and installation and have become a core driver of device utility and adoption among wearers [21].

Regarding calibration at the software level, headsets enable users to adjust input controls, for instance, through eye gestures for tracking [38]. Other calibrations concern the image rendering according to the depth of perception of wearers, volume settings, contrast levels, font size, and brightness levels. Additional configurations may also be available within the device features, like widgets for alarms and reminders that can be tailored to specific users' needs. For voice recognition, the wearer can take time to train a wearable system to recognize his or her voice and as such achieve a higher accuracy in the interpretation of voice commands [19].

For output responses using vibration to calm users, the authors of a wearable study believe that anxiolytic effects can be observed to a range of heart-like vibrotactile stimulation frequencies and that the "ideal" frequency varies per individual. In designing the armband, they ensured that users could select the vibrating frequency that corresponds better with their state and possibly the one that could be the most efficient to meet their individual needs and lifestyles [28].

For athletes, they considered the ability to obtain context-sensitive, personalized information about their bodies to be a very compelling feature of wearable technologies and for them tailoring information to their personal needs is useful to avoid potential overload with generic content and recommendations [54].

At the software level, even everyday activities that are trivial for "able-bodied" users could pose risks for individuals with particular diseases, quickly threatening their health. For patients with diabetes, for instance, some changes in their level of physical activities, nutritional habits, or dietary patterns can be life-threatening [11].

In a wearable health system to monitor kids, the threshold for each measure is defined manually or automatically based on the user age, gender, and weight. Also, the user should be able to choose the modalities and approaches for alerts, such as an SMS or e-mail for alarms [11].

Concerning the PhysioDroid, a system for monitoring vital signs of a wearer, a notable feature is its ability to detect risky conditions. In the application, some vital sign measures are easy to interpret, using thresholds, as they reach critical or extreme values (e.g., no respiration, too low or high skin temperature, or heart rate collapse). However, the interpretation of these signals in ordinary situations will largely vary for each individual. Heart rate measurements differ depending on gender, age, weight, height, and pre-existing conditions, among others. Physicians are able to correctly interpret vital signs per patient. For the system to be tailored to a patient, the medical knowledge should be incorporated by the specialist to the system to customize the setting for "normality" and "abnormality", adapting the alerts and notices accordingly. To ensure urgent responses and appropriate care, an automatic emergency call or message may be set to inform the closest clinical center [34].

End users benefit from personalizing the form factor of their wearable accessories [33]. To that end, several studies have focused on universal design guidelines and principles to enable personalization of wearable technologies [4]. However, it is still challenging to design wearable devices that are personalizable to accommodate diverse needs from individuals, and as such successfully meet user requirements.

The influence of demographic aspects of end users (such as age and culture) have not been extensively investigated on prior research on wearables [4].

To be more accepted by wearers, personalized notifications should allow for user control. To set when and how the delivery of notifications occurs, configuration options should be available. For output responses, text, audio, graphic, tactile, and haptic are alternative modalities for the delivery of personalized information, data about daily user behavior, and the environmental context of use. Multimodal alerts on the device screen influence the accessibility of the information, resources, and services. For older adults and users with diverse needs, the configurations and settings should be made available in detail and presented during initial interaction steps [64].

2.7 Design Challenges

While recent advances in technology expanded the potential of wearable devices, numerous inherent limitations still challenge the design of wearable interfaces. The shortcomings in the domain cut across multiple concerns, including issues regarding usability, implementation, power, sensors, networks, privacy, and safety of wearable technologies. These shortcomings must be addressed in the design phases to ensure that next-generation wearable technologies can be accepted, and adopted, and wearers sustain their engagement with the technology. While wearables have been increasingly adopted recently, their form factors still pose challenges to designers and often such devices fail to achieve sustained user engagement [21].

Existing interaction paradigms, guidelines, models, and best practices from desktop computers are not always suitable for wearable technologies [17], and current approaches to facilitate the implementation of wearable technologies are still limited. Compared to desktop systems, wearable technologies have restricted capabilities [50], especially regarding input and output alternatives, processing power, and storage.

For Virkki and Aggarwall [56], 16 challenges on wearable electronics stand out. They were categorized regarding hardware, physical, and application aspects as listed in Table 2.1.

Table 2.1 List of 16 challenges for wearable electronics according to Virkki and Aggarwall [56]

Hardware	Physical	Application
Unobtrusiveness	Error resilience	Security
Sensitivity	Reliability	Privacy
Calibration	Interoperability	User-friendliness
Energy	Bandwidth	Ease of deployment
Data acquisition		Scalability
Efficiency		Mobility

2.7.1 Usability and Wearability

For end users, because the traditional interaction paradigms from conventional mobile phones and Desktop computers are no longer applicable in the wearable landscape, interacting with novel wearable technologies poses additional challenges. Also, social barriers might dissuade wearers from using wearable devices that stand out, such as a head-mounted display (HMD), in public spaces [3].

Concerning the user activity, such as walking and running, displays used in wearable computing are limited in size and resolution making readability of text more difficult [42]. Such constraints require a new design of interface components [42] as well as new ways to conceptualize and work with wearable technologies [2].

For designers, the novelty of wearable computing as a discipline limits the standard approaches in which the user interacts with wearable computers. When compared to desktop computers, for which a keyboard and mouse are standard peripheral devices for input entry, wearable devices available are diverse in their form factors, interaction modalities, and paradigms [65].

Concerning the wearers, few anthropometric studies have been conducted, hindering the ability to create devices of heterogeneous form factors that are well suited to fit wearers of different dimensions [66]. For Griffin et al. [67], ensuring effective fit of wearables to the body dimensions of a diverse population is complex [67]. For Siewiorek [51], knowing when and how a wearable should interrupt the end user remains an open question [51].

In addition to that, the design of input entry can be complex on wearables since there is no space to integrate a full keyboard and a mouse. While several handheld technologies require users to use a stylus to write on a touch screen, this approach is not feasible once the wearer is moving, not only the correct positioning becomes extremely difficult to achieve but also the wearer is required to use both hands [50]. Because of their reduced screen dimension and limited interaction techniques, wearable computers face input and output problems [50]. New interaction techniques and user interface (UI) patterns are needed [68]. The existing interaction model for Desktop has to be extended to consider activities that are not purely interaction with the machine, but still influence the wearer interaction [17]. For example, the location and the nature of the activity significantly affect the level and type of support needed by users [17]. When moving, users tend to focus their visual attention on navigating in their environments, which makes graphic user interfaces that are visually demanding unsuitable and hard to operate in a wearable context [50].

Moreover, the contextual changes of the user interaction on the go and the limited processing capabilities of wearable devices require interactive solutions that are even more simplified and intuitive, with reduced time for completion, minimum number of tasks, and low cognitive load on wearers.

Another aspect that may also influence the system performance is the social wearability of the technology, which also impacts the wearer decision to either adopt or reject a wearable. The social wearability affects also the emotional comfort of the wearer [69].

One of the key acceptance challenges for wearables that stand out is the device ergonomics. To be practical, a wearable must be small and light enough to fit inside clothing, to be attached into a belt [1] or other accessory, or to be worn directly like a watch or glasses [22].

Also, to ensure the wearer's comfort, designers must pad all hard components, to protect the wearer and prevent harm [5]. The development of musculoskeletal disorders attributable to wearing wearable computers that are heavy, large, and uncomfortable for extended periods of time is a possibility [30]. Thus, their evaluation, followed by redesign and refinements, should be thorough.

The reduced dimensions of devices limit the physical space available as interactive surfaces, be it to display content, notify wearers, or receive user input. Wearable systems suffer from limitations in their processing capabilities, memory, battery, and storage. Besides this, wearable interfaces must be efficient and intuitive, providing immediate responses and quick feedback for end users.

Wearable users often interact with their devices in dynamic contexts of use, in which the characteristics, constraints, and requirements are transient, frequently and continuously changing. Finally, most users are already familiarized with Desktop PCs and mobile devices, whose interaction paradigms do not transfer directly to wearables, given that the user interaction takes place in stable or static environments, the resources available are less limited, and conventional solutions for input (keyboard, mouse, gestures) and output (graphic and auditory user interfaces) are convenient.

While smart garments tend to be more convenient for wearers to access and interact with, unfortunately, many challenges remain to fully exploit their potential and make them popular. While the cloth may be washable, the attached circuit boards are not; hence, to address this challenge, it will take time before wearers begin to treat wearables as their ordinary clothing [5].

The inherent challenges in the design of wearables span across cross-cutting concerns, including device, system, and user interfaces, that must account for both the contexts of use and users' profiles—mental models, abilities, background, impairments. For Nunez and Loke [8], important questions to address when designing the user interaction for wearable technologies include the following [8]:

1. What happens to the body, or its self-awareness, while interacting with wearable technology that aims at self-exploration and learning?
2. When does the body become present or transparent in interacting with technology?
3. How can we proactively use body awareness as a primary resource for self-use and self-development in wearable technology design?

2.7.2   *Implementation*

Well-known usability constraints and user interface development libraries available
for desktop and mobile applications are not always suitable for the design of wearables [42]. A wearable computer used, for instance, for maintenance, where hands-free interaction is needed, makes any keyboard impractical to use [42].

Due to changes in the interaction paradigms, designers need new interface
metaphors to facilitate the implementation of the wearer interaction [5]. Existing
support that is relevant is scattered across sources, making it hard for stakeholders,
including designers, developers, and investigators, to find unified support that guides
them in taking the right design decisions for wearable applications in an efficient
way. Also, individually designed interfaces validated for past applications have the
drawback that they are too specific and not always easily reusable in different configurations [42]. The bulky form factors summed with an overall low usage coefficient
are also major drawbacks on wearable computing. If users have to wear uncomfortable equipment, the appliances tend to be used scarcely, for very brief periods,
resulting in high abandonment rates [1].

The integration of electronic components also leads to numerous design challenges, especially when stakeholders strive to minimize the dimension of the technology during assembly, aiming at a device that is comfortable to wear, and avoid
physical burden and disturbance for wearers [3]. The integration of electronic components is a challenging process that involves combining a set of interactive pieces,
power, processing units in a small device and configuring them to effectively operate
together in an energy-efficient way [42].

Lastly, proprietary architectures of commercial devices may hinder the integration
with external systems and networks, especially when multiple devices of different
brands, models, or versions are used in conjunction and compatibility issues arise
[70].

2.7.3   *Power*

Ideally, wearers expect their battery lives to last for days in a row. However, as a
rule of thumb, a stand-alone power supply is expected to last at least 15 h, or one
working day, without requiring recharge. If the application consumes only low power,
a primary battery is suited for stand-alone devices. Otherwise, a secondary battery, for
instance, in the form of a rechargeable accumulator, is necessary as well. In addition
to the adoption of low-power components, the duty cycle of the equipment should be
configured to optimize the power consumption of devices that remain continuously
operating [23].

In what regards battery life, the data collection should strive for optimization to
extend the system run time. Still, it is challenging, or even unfeasible, to precisely
predict an event of interest and then equip the user to record an event of interest [71].

Design decisions that facilitate the optimization of energy consumption involve the duration of the operations, the number of cycles, the frequency of readings from sensors (sampling rates), the time of activation, and duration of idle periods [1].

Concerning power consumption, while it is trivial to provide energy for short-term data collection, for long-term operations, energy must be either brought to the system, harvested or captured from other resources or equipment [17]. Today, wearables are typically battery-powered, and their limited lifetime is a critical drawback for wearers using the applications as well as stakeholders implementing those [27].

2.7.4 Network and Sensors

Concerning connectivity, wearable devices need to access external services and resources from other equipment to extend their capabilities and overcome inherent limitations in processing power, memory, functionality, and battery requirements. Oftentimes, integration between stationary devices or services and a wearable solution that is self-contained and stands alone becomes necessary [71].

Concerning network and communication, issues with synchronization and data transmission can occur. Crosstalk problems between nearby devices was noted when using IR to connect iBand bracelets [32]. Bluetooth connections may require less power, but can also become unstable besides having a limited spatial range for reachability.

Concerning sensors, one of the biggest challenges stakeholders face concerns their design complexity. Also, not always low cost, portable, and user-friendly sensors are available for usage in wearable technologies and alternative designs must be sought [35]. To precisely and correctly collect, analyze, and interpret data from wearable sensors, numerous challenges are involved [11].

Concerning EMG specifically, the challenges include the separability and reproducibility of measurements, and achieving good skin contact with electrodes to read signals with high quality [35]. EOG electrodes arranged around the left eye of a wearer can be mounted on flat springs to achieve a good skin contact [38]. IR (infrared) sensors, although less subject to light changes, tend to be fixed or cumbersome to move [35].

In wearable health, in order for multiple wearable sensors combined to provide real-time interventions to a patient, the data collected must be rapidly processed and communicated to external computers (such as a mobile phone) so that the sensor data is subject to event classification using a pattern recognition approach or a machine-learning algorithm. To provide real-time interventions, such as alert messages to the user, or a text message to a remote caregiver, the communication process needs to be stable and reliable [7], besides also preserving the privacy of the user, and preventing unauthorized access and use of his or her data.

2.7.5 Safety

When devices are used for health care, during extensive periods, developers also face challenges related to safety. Medical validation, certification, or legal approval is often limited for wearable technologies [72]. For a robust implementation, the device case and components should be shockproof. Also, the materials employed should be biocompatible when directly exposed to the user skin to ensure safety [23].

Safety issues in the workplace could be caused by input devices that demand too much attention from users. The consequences of a poor interaction design could cause catastrophic problems on certain workplaces, especially when users are subject to stressful events [19].

For specific domains, the commercial systems currently available not always satisfy strict requirements for safety-critical and healthcare applications. Even if the systems offer relevant data, their format is based on proprietary algorithms, which cannot be properly reviewed and validated [70]. According to Oliver and Flores-Manga [13], "proprietary data formats prevent users from consolidating and correlating health monitoring data from different devices" [13]. Also, the connections for data transmission and device synchronization may be insecure and power demanding.

2.7.6 Privacy

Concerning continuous data collection, captured through wearable sensors, open questions remain to be addressed regarding surveillance, privacy, and control [71]. For assistive wearables to enhance social communication, the conversation between the end user and his or her peers is analyzed. Such use creates an important tension between social inclusion and privacy [73].

By allowing the continuous collection of detailed information about the user's life, including health, location, movement, and daily activities, wearable devices lead to a privacy invasion [74]. In this context, data leakage while collecting and processing data with wearable technologies has been identified as a major issue that should be promptly addressed [75].

For Kirkham and Greenhalgh [73], the four main privacy risks on wearable technologies for assistance include the following:

1. Accidental publication of data contained within the system;
2. Deliberate misuse of data collected;
3. Use of personal data without individuals' consent;
4. Unfair, or unlawful, usage of data; and
5. Infringement of the privacy of any individuals with whom the user interacts.

Seeking to reduce the privacy flaws caused by ad hoc and do-it-yourself systems, proactive, rather than retroactive, efforts are needed. "Best practice" frameworks and approaches have yet to be defined to facilitate the implementation of wearable systems that appropriately consider end users' and data privacy controls [73].

Summary Although wearable devices have already proven to be successful in many application domains and contexts of use, their problem space is wide and their design space is broad and still largely unexplored relative to their potential [76]. Making appropriate design decisions in a broad landscape can be challenging and therefore many design considerations need to be thoroughly taken into account. This chapter begins introducing the several different disciplines whose domain knowledge contributes to establish the field of wearable computing. Then, we also list, define, and discuss a number of design considerations and cross-cutting concerns that stakeholders, including designers, developers, and investigators, must take into account when creating the wearable interaction or when interacting with wearable computers.

The cross-cutting concerns that must be considered in the design of wearable technologies include user interfaces and interactive approaches, network and communication, storage and sensing units, energy modules, and processing power. More specifically, we define and exemplify (a) hardware aspects, and its electronic components, including sensors and actuators, processing boards, and communication ports; (b) software aspects, as well as systems and applications that process users' data and provide them information, services, and relevant resources on-demand; (c) network and connectivity that allow for data transfer and information exchange among devices and service providers; and (d) energy aspects that allow powering the device, collecting and processing data, as well as providing users with output responses and feedback when needed.

Due to the fact that wearables are used on the go, the contexts of use vary as well as the tasks that users execute when interacting with their devices. Also, the users' profiles are heterogeneous, and their similarities and differences should be considered in the design of software and hardware aspects.

While substantial progress is noted in the domain, wearables have inherent limitations concerning their interaction surfaces, processing power, and connectivity. Hence, when defining the interaction space, such limitations must be carefully considered to address inherent trade-offs between conflicting requirements, and to ensure wearers have intuitive solutions that are effective for them to accept, adopt, and sustain their engagement. The chapter ends with a list of design challenges that stakeholders face in the design of technology, covering usability and wearability, implementation and power, network and sensors, users' safety, and privacy aspects.

References

1. Amft O, Lauffer M, Ossevoort S, Macaluso F, Lukowicz P, Troster G. Design of the QBIC wearable computing platform. In Proceedings. In: 15th IEEE international conference on application-specific systems, architectures and processors, 2004 Sep 27 (pp. 398–410). IEEE
2. Cranny-Francis A, Hawkins C (2008) Wearable technology. Visual Commun 7(3):267–270
3. Buenaflor C, Kim H (2013) Six human factors to acceptability of wearable computers. Int J Multimed Ubiquitous Eng 8(3):103–114
4. Khakurel J. Enhancing the Adoption of Quantified Self-Tracking Devices. (Doctoral dissertation, University of Technology, Lappeenranta, Finland) ISBN 978-952-335-318-3
5. Billinghurst M, Starner T (1999) Wearable devices: new ways to manage information. Computer 32(1):57–64
6. Rhodes BJ (1997) The wearable remembrance agent: a system for augmented memory. Personal Technol 1(4):218–24
7. Fletcher RR, Ming-Zher Poh RR, Eydgahi H (2010) Wearable sensors: opportunities and challenges for low-cost health care. In: Proceedings of the 2010 annual international conference of the IEEE engineering in medicine and biology society, pp 1763–1766
8. Nunez-Pacheco C, Loke L, Crafting the body-tool: a body-centred perspective on wearable technology. In: Proceedings of the 2014 conference on designing interactive systems 2014 Jun 21 (pp. 553–566). ACM
9. Toney A, Dunne L, Thomas BH, Ashdown SP (2003) A shoulder pad insert vibrotactile display. IEEE; 2003 Oct 21
10. Ha K, Kim Y, Jung J, Lee J (2008) Experimental evaluations of wearable ECG monitor. In: 2008 30th Annual international conference of the IEEE engineering in medicine and biology society 2008 Aug 20 (pp. 791–794). IEEE
11. Jalaliniya S, Pederson T (2012) A wearable kids' health monitoring system on smartphone. In: Proceedings of the 7th Nordic conference on human-computer interaction: making sense through design, 2012 Oct 14 (pp. 791–792). ACM
12. Zheng Y, Leung B, Sy S, Zhang Y, Poon CC (2012) A clip-free eyeglasses-based wearable monitoring device for measuring photoplethysmograhic signals. In: 2012 Annual international conference of the IEEE engineering in medicine and biology society, 2012 Aug (pp. 5022–5025). IEEE
13. Oliver N, Flores-Mangas F (2006) HealthGear: a real-time wearable system for monitoring and analyzing physiological signals. In: International workshop on wearable and implantable body sensor networks (BSN'06) 2006 Apr 3 (pp. 4-pp). IEEE
14. Abbosh AI, Babiceanu RF, Al-Rizzo H, Abushamleh S, Khaleel HR (2013) Flexible Yagi-Uda antenna for wearable electronic devices. In: 2013 IEEE antennas and propagation society international symposium (APSURSI) 2013 Jul 7 (pp. 1200–1201). IEEE
15. Dunne LE, Brady S, Tynan R, Lau K, Smyth B, Diamond D, O'Hare GM (2006) Garment-based body sensing using foam sensors. In: Proceedings of the 7th Australasian user interface conference-volume 50 2006 Jan 1 (pp. 165–171). Australian Computer Society, Inc
16. Gioberto G, Dunne LE (2012) Garment positioning and drift in garment-integrated wearable sensing. In: 2012 16th International symposium on wearable computers, 2012 Jun 18 (pp. 64–71). IEEE
17. Burgy C, Garrett JH (2002) Wearable computers: an interface between humans and smart infrastructure systems. Vdi Berichte 1668:385–98
18. Seuter M, Pfeiffer M, Bauer G, Zentgraf K, Kray C (2017) Running with technology: evaluating the impact of interacting with wearable devices on running movement. Proc ACM Interact Mobile Wearable Ubiquitous Technol 1(3):101
19. Gobert D (2002) Designing wearable performance support: Insights from the early literature. Techn Commun 49(4):444–8
20. Reich J, Wall C, Dunne LE (2015) Design and implementation of a textile-based wearable balance belt. J Med Dev 9(2):020919

21. Dibia V (2015) An affective, normative and functional approach to designing user experiences for wearables. Normative and Functional Approach to Designing User Experiences for Wearables (July 14, 2015)

22. Roy L (2003) Next-generation wearable networks. IEEE Comput Pract, 31–39

23. Scheffler M, Hirt E (2004) Wearable devices for emerging healthcare applications. In: The 26th annual international conference of the IEEE engineering in medicine and biology society, 2004 Sep 1 (Vol. 2, pp. 3301–3304). IEEE

24. Goyal R, Dragoni N, Spognardi A (2016) Mind the tracker you wear: a security analysis of wearable health trackers. In: Proceedings of the 31st annual ACM symposium on applied computing–SAC'16, pp 131–136. https://doi.org/10.1145/2851613.2851685

25. Strohrmann C, Harms H, Troster G, Hensler S, Muller R (2011) Out of the lab and into the woods: kinematic analysis in running using wearable sensors. In: Proceedings of the 13th international conference on Ubiquitous computing, 2011 Sep 17 (pp. 119–122). ACM

26. Nguyen LN, Rodriguez-Martin D, Catala A, Perez-Lopez C, Sama A, Cavallaro A (2015) Basketball activity recognition using wearable inertial measurement units. In: Proceedings of the XVI international conference on Human Computer Interaction 2015 Sep 7 (p. 60). ACM

27. Magno M, Brunelli D, Sigrist L, Andri R, Cavigelli L, Gomez A, Benini L (2016) InfiniTime: multi-sensor wearable bracelet with human body harvesting. Sustain Comput: Inf Syst 1(11):38–49

28. Azevedo RT, Bennett N, Bilicki A, Hooper J, Markopoulou F, Tsakiris M (2017) The calming effect of a new wearable device during the anticipation of public speech. Sci Rep 7(1):2285

29. Peng M, Wang T, Hu G, Zhang H (2012) A wearable heart rate belt for ambulant ECG monitoring. In: 2012 IEEE 14th international conference on e-health networking, applications and services (Healthcom) 2012 Oct 10 (pp. 371–374). IEEE

30. Knight JF, Baber C (2005) A tool to assess the comfort of wearable computers. Human Fact 47(1):77–91

31. Lee K, Kwon DS (2000) Wearable master device for spinal injured persons as a control device for motorized wheelchairs. Artif Life Robot 4(4):182–7

32. Kanis M, Winters N, Agamanolis S, Gavin A, Cullinan C. Toward wearable social networking with iBand. InCHI'05 extended abstracts on Human factors in computing systems 2005 Apr 2 (pp. 1521–1524). ACM

33. Matassa A, Rapp A, Simeoni R. Wearable accessories for cycling: tracking memories in urban spaces. In: Atelier of smart garments and accessories, held in conjunction with 2013 ACM international joint conference on pervasive and ubiquitous computing (UbiComp 2013) 2013 (pp. 415–424). ACM

34. Banos O, Villalonga C, Damas M, Gloesekoetter P, Pomares H, Rojas I (2014) Physiodroid: combining wearable health sensors and mobile devices for a ubiquitous, continuous, and personal monitoring. Sci World J 2014

35. Cannan J, Hu H (2012) A wearable sensor fusion armband for simple motion control and selection for disabled and non-disabled users. In: 2012 4th computer science and electronic engineering conference (CEEC) 2012 Sep 12 (pp. 216–219). IEEE

36. Munoz D, Pruett A, Williams G. Knee: an everyday wearable goniometer for monitoring physical therapy adherence. In: CHI'14 extended abstracts on human factors in computing systems 2014 Apr 26 (pp. 209–214). ACM

37. Tikander M, Harma A, Karjalainen M. Binaural positioning system for wearable augmented reality audio. In: 2003 IEEE workshop on applications of signal processing to audio and acoustics (IEEE Cat. No. 03TH8684) 2003 Oct 19 (pp. 153–156). IEEE

38. Bulling A, Roggen D, Troster G. It's in your eyes: towards context-awareness and mobile HCI using wearable EOG goggles. In: Proceedings of the 10th international conference on Ubiquitous computing 2008 Sep 21 (pp. 84–93). ACM

39. Vidal M, Bulling A, Gellersen H (2011) Analysing EOG signal features for the discrimination of eye movements with wearable devices. In: Proceedings of the 1st international workshop on pervasive eye tracking & mobile eye-based interaction 2011 Sep 18 (pp. 15–20). ACM

40. MacLean D, Roseway A, Czerwinski M. MoodWings: a wearable biofeedback device for real-time stress intervention. In: Proceedings of the 6th international conference on PErvasive technologies related to assistive environments 2013 May 29 (p. 66). ACM
41. Bachlin M, Forster K, Troster G. SwimMaster: a wearable assistant for swimmer. In: Proceedings of the 11th international conference on Ubiquitous computing 2009 Sep 30 (pp. 215–224). ACM
42. Witt H (2007) Human-computer interfaces for wearable computers. PhD thesis
43. Fukatsu T, Nanseki T (2009) Monitoring system for farming operations with wearable devices utilized sensor networks. Sensors 9(8):6171–84
44. Motti VG, Caine K (2016) Smart wearables or dumb wearables?: understanding how context impacts the UX in wrist worn interaction. In: Proceedings of the 34th ACM international conference on the design of communication 2016 Sep 23 (p. 10). ACM
45. Motti VG, Caine K (2014) Human factors considerations in the design of wearable devices. In: Proceedings of the human factors and ergonomics society annual meeting 2014 Sep (Vol. 58, No. 1, pp. 1820–1824). Sage CA: Los Angeles, CA: SAGE Publications
46. Favela J (2017, October) Inferring human behavior using mobile and wearable devices. In: Proceedings of the 23rd Brazillian symposium on multimedia and the web (pp. 11–13). ACM
47. Powell C, Munetomo M, Schlueter M, Mizukoshi M (2013) Towards thought control of next-generation wearable computing devices. In: International conference on brain and health informatics, vol 29. Springer, Cham, pp 427–438
48. Healey JA. Wearable and automotive systems for affect recognition from physiology (Doctoral dissertation, Massachusetts Institute of Technology)
49. Graham D, Zhou G (2016) Prototyping wearables: a code-first approach to the design of embedded systems. IEEE Int Things J 3(5):806–15
50. Brewster S, Lumsden J, Bell M, Hall M, Tasker S (2003) Multimodal eyes-free interaction techniques for wearable devices. In: Proceedings of the SIGCHI conference on Human factors in computing systems 2003 Apr 5 (pp. 473–480). ACM
51. Siewiorek D (2017) Wearable computing: retrospectives on the first decade. GetMobile: Mobile Comput Commun 21(1):5–10
52. Farringdon J, Moore AJ, Tilbury N, Church J, Biemond PD (1999) Wearable sensor badge & sensor jacket for context awareness. In: The proceedings of the third international symposium on wearable computers. San Francisco, CA, Oct. 18–19, 1999
53. Smailagic A, Siewiorek D (2002) Application design for wearable and context-aware computers. IEEE Pervasive Comput 1(4):20–9
54. Forlizzi J, McCormack M (2000) Case study: User research to inform the design and development of integrated wearable computers and web-based services. In: Proceedings of the 3rd conference on Designing interactive systems: processes, practices, methods, and techniques 2000 Aug 1 (pp. 275–279). ACM
55. Fletcher R, Dobson K (2010) iCalm: wearable sensor and network architecture for wirelessly communicating and logging autonomic activity. IEEE Trans Inf Technol Biomed 14(2):215–223
56. Virkki J, Aggarwal R (2014) Privacy of wearable electronics in the healthcare and childcare sectors: a survey of personal perspectives from Finland and the United Kingdom. J Inf Secur 5(02):46
57. Steinert A, Haesner M (2017) Google glass for older adults—a field test evaluation. Innov Aging 1(Suppl 1):1194
58. Rantala I, Colley A, Hakkila J (2018) Smart jewelry: augmenting traditional wearable self-expression displays. In: Proceedings of the 7th ACM international symposium on pervasive displays 2018 Jun (p. 22). ACM
59. Motti VG (2019) Assistive wearables: opportunities and challenges. In: Proceedings of the 2019 ACM international joint conference on pervasive and ubiquitous computing and proceedings of the 2019 ACM international symposium on wearable computers (pp. 1040–1043). ACM
60. Khakurel J (2018) Enhancing the Adoption of Quantified Self-Tracking Devices, Lappeenranta University of Technology

61. Dunne LE, Profita H, Zeagler C, Clawson J, Gilliland S, Do EY, Budd J (2014) The social comfort of wearable technology and gestural interaction. In: 2014 36th annual international conference of the IEEE engineering in medicine and biology society 2014 Aug 26 (pp. 4159–4162). IEEE

62. Weller P, Rakhmetova L, Ma Q, Mandersloot G (2010) Evaluation of a wearable computer system for telemonitoring in a critical environment. Personal Ubiquitous Comput 14(1):73–81

63. Tharion WJ, Buller MJ, Karis AJ, Mullen SP. Acceptability of a wearable vital sign detection system. In: Proceedings of the human factors and ergonomics society annual meeting 2007 Oct (Vol. 51, No. 17, pp. 1006–1010). Sage CA: Los Angeles, CA: SAGE Publications

64. Khakurel J, Knutas A, Melkas H, Penzenstadler B, Porras J (2018) Crafting usable quantified self-wearable technologies for older adult. International conference on applied human factors and ergonomics. Springer, Cham, pp 75–87

65. Zucco JE, Thomas BH (2016) Design guidelines for wearable pointing devices. Front ICT 27(3):13

66. Erickson K, McMahon M, Dunne LE, Larsen C, Olmstead B, Hipp J (2016) Design and analysis of a sensor-enabled in-ear device for physiological monitoring. J Med Dev 10(2):020966

67. Griffin L, Compton C, Dunne LE (2016) An analysis of the variability of anatomical body references within ready-to-wear garment sizes. In: Proceedings of the 2016 ACM international symposium on wearable computers 2016 Sep 12 (pp. 84–91). ACM

68. Rawassizadeh R, Price BA, Petre M (2015) Wearables: has the age of smartwatches finally arrived? Commun ACM 58(1):45–7

69. Carton A, Dunne LE (2013) Tactile distance feedback for firefighters: design and preliminary evaluation of a sensory augmentation glove. In: Proceedings of the 4th augmented human international conference 2013 Mar 7 (pp. 58–64). ACM

70. Friedl KE (2018) Military applications of soldier physiological monitoring. J Sci Med Ssport 21(11):1147–53

71. Hayes GR, Truong KN (2005) Autism, environmental buffers, and wearable servers. IEEE Pervasive Comput 4(2):14–7

72. Torous BJ, Gualtieri L (2016) Knowns and Unknowns. Psychiatric Times, Wearable Devices for Mental Health, pp 4–7

73. Kirkham R, Greenhalgh C (2015) Social access vs. privacy in wearable computing: a case study of autism. IEEE Pervasive Comput 14(1):26–33

74. Motti VG, Caine K (2015) Users' privacy concerns about wearables. International conference on financial cryptography and data security. Springer, Berlin, Heidelberg, pp 231–244

75. Cho JY, Ko D, Lee BG (2018) Strategic approach to privacy calculus of wearable device user regarding information disclosure and continuance intention. KSII Trans Int Inf Syst 12(7)

76. Suhonen K, Muller S, Rantala J, Vaananen-Vainio-Mattila K, Raisamo R, Lantz V. Haptically augmented remote speech communication: a study of user practices and experiences. In: Proceedings of the 7th Nordic conference on human-computer interaction: making sense through design 2012 Oct 14 (pp. 361–369). ACM

Chapter 3
Wearable Interaction

Abstract This chapter describes multimodal interfaces and interactive solutions for input entry and output responses for wearable technologies. Focusing on the design of wearable interaction for different form factors, this chapter discusses the suitability, benefits, and drawbacks of each modality. Multimodal interfaces are presented, from popular head-mounted displays and wrist-worn wearables, to customized smart textiles and alternative form factors. This chapter describes the interaction design process, covering five interaction modalities and highlighting their benefits and drawbacks for the user interaction depending on the user context, application domain, and form factor. The multiple modalities discussed are graphics, tactile, gesture, audio (voice-based interaction), and brain–computer interfaces. This chapter provides examples of user interaction with illustrations of wrist-worn devices, head-mounted devices, smart clothes, and alternative form factors, such as back-mounted devices and chest-mounted devices.

3.1 Wearable Interaction

Chapter 2 presents a number of considerations that help to inform design decisions for wearable technologies and that must be carefully taken into account in the implementation process. One of the considerations that stands out and impacts the user experience is the usability of the device and its underlying application. To shed light in to design considerations for wearable interfaces, this chapter covers essential aspects of interface and interaction design. Multiple modalities for input entry and output responses are discussed, helping designers to take more informed decisions when considering those in the implementation and evaluation process.

Wearable devices have already proven to be successful in a variety of domains, however their problem space is wide and their design space besides being broad is also largely underexplored [1]. When compared to stationary technologies, the design of wearables should consider an additional set of user requirements [2]. Additionally, as discussed in the previous chapter, wearable computers involve several aspects related to human factors, including safety, ergonomics, anthropometry, and ease of use [3]. Those can be challenging to prioritize when conflicting requirements arise.

© Springer Nature Switzerland AG 2020
V. G. Motti, *Wearable Interaction*, Human–Computer Interaction Series,
https://doi.org/10.1007/978-3-030-27111-4_3

Concerning human factors, the main challenges in the design of wearable interfaces include open questions, such as how to properly fit the computer to the human in terms of interface, cognitive model, contextual awareness, and adaptation to tasks being performed? These are aspects that certainly deserve further research and development [4].

The role of the human body in interactive experiences with wearables is critical, however it has received limited attention thus far [5]. Also, the design of wearable interfaces cannot rely on existing interaction paradigms, previously established, as simply shrinking down existing computing tools does not take full advantage of the opportunities given by employing the human body as an interactive platform where a new context of use emerges [6].

In this novel scenario, the application of conventional principles of UI design (such as the traditional direct manipulation [7]) is no longer valid. Dedicated devices for input entry and output responses used for wearer interaction or presentation in wearable computing include head-mounted displays and gloves. Such devices vary from conventional devices used in desktop or mobile computing where the WIMP (Windows Icons Menus Pointing) paradigm dominates [8].

The nature of next-generation wearables indicates that the usability issues faced today by conventional devices will become even more challenging in the future. Inputting information into small portable devices, such as smartphones, is difficult and time-consuming due to their small form factors. With devices such as smartwatches, manipulation becomes more difficult. Furthermore, voice commands still pose many challenges to be fully and effectively exploited in daily life [9].

Contrary to a Desktop PC, in a wearable context, the user interaction cannot always rely on traditional interactive modalities, using graphic user interfaces and "point-and-click" interfaces. In this new context, input and output approaches must be reimagined and redesigned as well. Wearable computers often have very limited screen space, and their input devices are often used with a single hand. The displays are not always reachable in the user's view, and may even be placed with an arbitrary orientation. In such interaction scenarios, pointing devices are unsuitable [7].

The design alternatives for wearables are more limited concerning the device dimensions and the interaction contexts. Environments are more varied and dynamic, for instance, when users are on the move. User profiles are characterized by specific target audiences, including older adults, children, and adolescents. Additionally, the improvements in network connections and bandwidth available to wearable technologies, summed with the consequent increase in the number of services, demand new interaction techniques, so that wearers can have access to services while switching locations [10]. In dynamic contexts of use, the design of the wearable interaction should strive for controls that are quick to find, and simple and easy to operate [11]. The wearer interaction should be so intuitive that a user manual and training become unnecessary [11].

Three interaction mechanisms have been defined concerning output responses, and how the device communicates with the user, and input entry, concerning the way in which the device captures information about the user, or how the user instructs the device on what to do and how. According to Khahurel (2016), the three interaction mechanisms that characterize the user interface are [12] as follows:

(1) **Input and Navigation Mechanisms**: Button, text elements, navigation and visualization items, contrast levels, icons, and interaction technique (including gestures and audio) and
(2) **Output Mechanisms**: Screen, display, colors, and interaction techniques (including visual, auditory, and haptic approaches).

To provide input entry solutions for wearers, without excessive burden on them, implicit interaction is recommended. Examples of implicit interaction include adapting the input settings to the users' needs and contexts of use, optimizing the need for user input (relying on passive sensing whenever possible), and limiting the selection space to ensure rapid user interaction [8].

When interacting with wearables, users tend to have limited attention levels [13], being often moving and multitasking. Other limitations inherent to the wearable interaction are: it occurs in a short duration in an unplanned way, users have only one free hand available to input commands and control the interface, and the environment is subject to continuous changes (e.g., indoor and outdoors).

To overcome such limitations, previous studies employed a trial-and-error approach seeking to identify corresponding design guidelines [4, 6], understanding and characterizing the end users' perspectives [1] and experiences [14, 15], besides also evaluating wearable applications [16]. While it is possible to find extensive work on the practicalities of wearable applications, there is no consolidated support to guide stakeholders on how to properly consider human factors and their qualitative aspects during the design phases.

Research and development conducted in the early stages of wearable technologies have primarily focused on technical issues [17]. By focusing on the feasibility of an individual approach, the usability and wearability often become neglected. By excluding the users' perspective during the design phase, the devices' acceptance is likely to be compromised, especially when the resulting device is bulky, invasive, or cumbersome [18], and especially if recordings must be continuously made in their natural environments [19]. The acceptability of the wearable design is also related to the perceived control that the user has over a device [20].

Other factor that also affects user acceptance is the perceived risks that a wearable computer poses to the user [21], be it due to safety issues or ergonomic aspects. End users may feel disappointed with the physical size of a wearable system, if it is considered to be bulky, cumbersome, or uncomfortable, or it has a nonconventional form factor. Prior work has shown that wrist-mounted keyboards tend to be unpopular after evaluation with end users [22]. Wearable technologies can only enhance human abilities significantly, if the target users are deeply involved in the design and evaluation cycles [23].

Another limitation concerns the number and dissemination of research findings that can effectively aid designers to enhance the acceptability of wearables. Such findings are still limited and tend to be highly specific regarding the wearer population, a form factor or application domain [24]. Besides this, there is a lack of systematic knowledge that allows reuse by stakeholders, be it guidelines to inform the design process or methodological approaches to support the design and evaluation of a device [25].

From an industrial perspective, it has been noted that more than half of the U.S. consumers who have owned an activity tracker (such as a wristband, bracelet, or a smartwatch), no longer use it [26]. Also, a third of U.S. consumers who have owned a tracker stopped using the device within 6 months of receiving it. From a scientific perspective, the abandonment of wearables has also been studied and related to poor usability levels, i.e., the devices not always meet users' needs, they collect data that is not found relevant or useful, and their maintenance becomes unmanageable [27]. Also, users loose interest, do not find enough value in use, and misplace either the device or the charger [28]. Adopting a strategy oriented to human factors is the key to long-term success to ensure acceptance of wearable devices [26], especially when their benefits are clear, and their applications are considered useful by the end users [27].

For wearable devices and smart clothing to effectively interact with users, we must consider human aspects [29] and adopt a wearability-driven design approach [30]. The multiple sensory engagements of human users are directly applicable to wearables, with their multiple sensory, cultural, social, and affective appeals [31]. Concerning the users' demographics, younger and older adults perceive "external contexts" differently, more specifically there is a clear distinction between certain aspects of the device usability, such as font size, touch-screen interaction, interaction technique, and applications installed [12].

To consider human factors during design phases, from a human-centered perspective, several principles have been defined [32]. Six principles have been identified for product design in an enterprise context to address issues in wearable computing. Also, 20 principles have been identified in a scientific research context (see Sects. 4.2.1, 4.2.2 and 4.2.3) [15, 32, 33]. These principles inform designers during the design phase. Design principles meet a general-purpose requirement, since they are applicable regardless of domain or use case scenario. They also enable designers to effectively consider human factors during the wearable application design in the earliest stages, providing guidance for both the design phase and the evaluation phase as well.

3.2   Interaction Design

The design of interfaces for wearables relies mostly on four interaction modalities. When combined, such modalities provide feedback for wearers (output responses) as well as alternatives for input entry. Using speakers, headsets, earplugs, audio actuators, or piezoelectric beepers, audio signals are frequently used for alerts and for voice-enabled communication. By integrating microphones in the device and voice recognition algorithms in the application, audio can be used for input entry.

Microphones are placed mainly near the wearer's head (for instance, in a wire of an earplug) or are portable, embedded in a wrist-worn device. Vibration (using vibro-tactile actuators) is mostly used for brief notifications or to call the wearer's attention. Vibrotactile settings are adjusted in magnitude, duration, and pattern to ensure the vibration is noticeable by the wearer and to facilitate meaningful interpretation of the feedback provided.

Graphics present and display images, texts, and videos for wearers, in devices with projection or screens, or using light emitting diodes (LEDs). Touch is used for selection of menu items, in touch-enabled screens, touch pads, or through finger press in physical buttons. Gestures can be detected through different approaches, for instance, with touch recognition in a capacitive screen or using IMU sensors embedded in a device and coupled with classification algorithms. Eye gestures can also be detected using EOG.

To facilitate the design decisions, Burgy [34] proposed the interaction constraints model. Such model informs the interface design by mapping potential constraints for different work scenarios and situations, matching those to user interfaces [34]. Still, calibration is necessary to ensure feedback effectiveness.

For Seuter et al. [35], the interaction approach interferes with the user activities and thus need to be carefully decided to minimize distraction and optimize user interaction [35]. For Smailagic and Siewiorek [32], computer systems distract a user in both explicit and implicit ways, reducing the user's effectiveness. If the technology also overwhelms wearers with data, it might cause information overload [32]. Mid-air gestures, for instance, might substantially reduce interference if designed well. Voice interaction is also an option but may be subject to interference with breathing. Additionally, people might be reluctant to use voice interaction in public settings where might overhear private conversations bystanders [35].

While speech and handwriting recognition are common inputs for wearables, advances in position sensing, eye tracking, stereographic audio, and visual output coupled with three-dimensional virtual reality information are promising interaction paradigms, expected to become more prevalent in future wearable applications [32].

For Zucco and Thomas [36], voice and gesturing inputs tend to be restricted to a limited set of commands, which are often not usable, unless the application is specifically tailored, and calibrated, to a specific user profile [36].

The brightness of LED lights for feedback should be checked, so that they are strong enough to be perceived by wearers but without dazzling them. Also, vibrations produced by the vibration motor must be strong enough to be noticeable, even if the device (such as a wristlet) is only slightly tightened. Beep sound cannot be effectively perceived with the device mounted at the user wrist or used in a noisy environment. Even mounting the beeper close to the ear on the head may not be sufficient for all users to effectively perceive it, for instance, in a swimming context [37]. Therefore, evaluation in the field and with actual users is necessary.

Concerning the adaptation of the user to a wearable device, Nunez and Loke [5] divide the human perception of feedback responses during the interaction with a wearable in five cyclic phases [5] as follows:

1. The placement of wearable technology on the body: raising user awareness toward the body and evoking the technology.
2. Feedback recognition and understanding: The technology is operational and draws the user attention.
3. Feedback ownership and interaction: The wearer recognizes and accepts the information the device provides him or her, as part of body. There is a sense of ownership the user experiences from the device feedback. The interaction is conscious.
4. Observation on device for changes in display: The cycle begins again once the technology responds and draws attention to itself.
5. Feedback ownership and interaction: The relationship between ownership toward the data, interaction, bodily feedback, and observation becomes cyclical.

The wearer interaction ends when the technology is no longer operational and the device stops functioning. At this moment, the user awareness is redirected to his or her surroundings [5].

3.3   Interaction Modalities

Wearable interfaces are expected to combine several modalities (e.g., gesture and speech) to provide wearers with more natural ways of communicating [38]. When compared to a single modality, multidimensional auditory and gestural techniques enable richer and more advanced interactions with wearable technologies and their respective applications, especially when wearers are moving [10].

The combination and settings of the desired modalities for both input entry and output responses depend mainly on the nature of the task and the information to be managed [7]. Human abilities and limitations of the target wearer population also affect how users perceive feedback and provide input commands. Most wearable devices combine multiple approaches for the wearer interaction, using conventionally graphic displays [39], and lights, for output responses, and touch and button press for input entry. Wearable user interfaces benefit from wearers' visual, audio, and tactile senses. Thus, graphic user interfaces are built on how the visual stimulus is constructed considering cognitive limitations of the human brain [8].

Vibration is often used to call wearer's attention. An "idle alert" on a fitness tracker can address inactivity by vibrating when wearers are still for too long [40]. Haptic interfaces that use temperature are less common, but have already been explored in conceptual research. Wearable computing may use audio or haptic interfaces because the possibility to provide users with unobtrusive tactile feedback may overcome challenges and limitations inherent to graphic and audio interfaces [8].

To ensure that feedback is noticeable, the output configurations and settings must be tailored according to the context of use, wearer profile, and optimized for battery efficiency. For instance, when the wearer is attending a meeting and should not be disturbed, a low-level ambient output would be most appropriate. However, if the wearable computer is used in an emergency to locate disaster victims, an augmented reality overlay of tracking information on the real world would be more suitable [7]. For a swimming scenario, to gather users' feedback on output responses, three actuator devices were implemented, providing audio, visual, and haptic feedback during swimming [37]. While the visual and the haptic feedback showed high potential to be used during swimming, the audio feedback was almost not perceived during the evaluation experiments [37].

Regardless of the context in which the wearer interaction occurs, to facilitate the feeling of ownership to the displayed data, the representation of the data needs to be convincing for the wearer. Also, reliable feedback is necessary regardless of the modality employed [5].

The design decisions on the interaction modality are dependent on the system's requirement and numerous trade-offs exist concerning privacy, ease of use, energy consumption, wearer's comfort, and sensor accuracy [41]. For Cho et al. [42], the effects of feedback type and presentation mode should be further and carefully explored considering also credibility, trustworthiness, quality, usefulness, and intention to use related to the output responses [42].

For Seuter et al. [35], "when faced with the choice of placing a device in a location where it is easy to see but harder to reach, prioritizing reachability over visibility might be advisable." However, a risk analysis to identify boundary conditions should be considered, especially concerning continuous user movement, e.g., if runners cannot focus on their way in the direction they are running in for too long, accidents can happen [35].

While haptic feedback is discrete, it may be not suitable for sensitive conditions, for instance, for users with impairments or medical conditions. In case a vibration motor is not suitable to provide feedback for users (for instance, due to potential harm caused to a sensitive joint), a single LED light can be employed to indicate when the brace is switched on or off. Two bi-color light emitting diodes (LEDs) in red and green can also be employed to provide users with visual feedback [37]. An auditory beeper can be used to inform the wearer when the repetitions of an exercise are completed. When compared to LED lights, a vibration motor adds more bulkiness to a wearable [43].

Also, fatigue can be associated with input entry of different modalities. Controlling eye movements intentionally, for instance, is considered to be tiring if the interaction lasts more than a few minutes. In fact, fatigue is an intrinsic problem not exclusive of eye gestures, but common to other input modalities including speech or hand gestures, and especially concerning when the gestures must be executed for long periods. Eye gestures outperform these modalities in circumstances in which the wearer's hands cannot be used, i.e., due to situational impairments due to manual work (e.g., driving, operating machines, typing, etc.) and also when speech input is not possible (e.g., for privacy reasons, in very silent or very noisy surroundings) [44].

Even though commercial toolkits facilitated the implementation of multimodal interaction designs for wearable technologies, identifying effective interaction modalities for wearable computers remains as one of the most important challenges in designing wearable systems [32]. For Zucco and Thomas [36], despite being extensively researched areas, input modalities and interaction techniques suitable for wearable computers are challenging to define, especially regarding decisions on how to seamlessly and appropriately interact with a wearable computer. This is a multi-faceted problem that requires careful attention from designers [36].

Another important challenge for human–computer interaction design on wearable computers concerns advancing interactive technologies while preserving human attention, especially striving to avoid cognitive overload of wearers due to information saturation [32].

Although interacting with a wearable computer poses challenges not relevant to its desktop counterpart, the requirements to enter data and control the device to provide input entries remain the same. With desktop systems, a keyboard and a mouse are typically available, thus for wearable devices the main challenge involves identifying input modalities and interaction techniques that suit end users' needs [36].

For Zucco and Thomas [36], although the input modalities presented thus far for wearables are compelling in their application contexts, they typically require specialized hardware and software to function. "The modalities mostly provide discrete input that may be directly mapped to a specific action." Another issue is that some form factors are specifically tailored to suit a unique task. Without the ability to implement specialized hardware and software, wearers often turn their attention to commercial devices to find a suitable wearable interaction [36].

3.3.1 Graphics

Despite the fact that graphics require high energy consumption, graphic user interfaces are the most frequently employed in wearable technologies. The two main reasons for that include (i) the fact that users are more familiar with graphic displays and (ii) advanced renderings in graphic user interfaces facilitate to convey information to wearers in a more intuitive way. The complexity of the graphic renderings varies, ranging from simple LED lights, as illustrated in Fig. 3.1, used to communicate the device state or an event status for users to more advanced multimedia that presents interactive videos in head-mounted displays used for gaming.

As illustrations, in EOG goggles, four LEDs can be employed to provide a simple output response interface [44]. Another example of light usage to convey feedback is the iBand, a bracelet created to exchange contact information, in which a green light was used to indicate whether a data exchange was successful [45].

Despite being more intuitive, depending on their complexity levels, graphic interfaces may require more power and higher visual attention from wearers. Energy consumption is especially higher for high resolution, extensive usage of colors, and intermittent display operation. However, low energy requirements are needed when visual feedback is provided by an e-paper display [46].

While LCD or OLED technologies consume more energy, e-paper displays consume power only during display updates. E-paper displays do not consume any power for image retention being able to hold an image for days without requiring a power

Fig. 3.1 LED lights serve as
a visual actuator to
communicate output
responses to end users during
their interaction. Credit:
Sophy Wong. Available at:
https://sophywong.com

supply, and also they do not need any background light because they reflect light similar to traditional paper, which makes them readable even under direct sunlight [46].

Graphic user interfaces may be easier for wearers to read due to more intuitive contents; however, they often have very limited amounts of screen space in wearable devices, and thus visual displays can easily become cluttered with information and widgets [10]. Also, the wearer interaction is limited on time, so glanceable interfaces—with icons or short commands—are recommended for wrist-worn devices.

It is challenging to design visual interfaces that operate properly when users are moving and performing additional tasks, and thus have limited attention and situational impairments [10]. Although a wearable device to display information of exercise status is valuable for athletes, they also need to have their hands free while accessing the display content so that to avoid taking time out from their workouts [47].

Design decisions for graphics involve color, icons, text (font size, typeface, spacing, alignment, layouts), resolution, and navigation path. Their adaption to the context of use include changing fonts (typeface, size, contrast), changing brightness (adjusting contrast based on light levels of the environment), and contrast changes (to adjust contents and background lights) [8].

Adaptations to the users' contexts are also dependent on the application domain. In a healthcare context, for instance, Cho et al. [42] investigated information presentation and found that comparative and textual format is more effective to encourage healthy practices in participants, promoting participants' willingness to take preventive healthcare measures, in comparison with identical information presented in a non-comparative and image format. Because text format is more analytic and systematic, users may perceive textual feedback as more credible and trustworthy than feedback sent with images, even if text contents may take longer to interpret [42].

3.3.2   Tactile

Haptic devices deliver feedback to the user skin, including a sense of touch that varies in intensity, magnitude, pressure, duration, and pattern. Prior work has evaluated tactile pressure in therapeutic suits for children with autism [48] and in a bracelet to calm users down [49]. Haptic feedback is often limited to a vibration function since there is no other approach to provide haptic feedback that can be implemented with a small and inexpensive device [50].

Vibrotactile stimuli have been explored to communicate feedback to end users [49, 51], for instance, sending wearers a single haptic vibratory buzz to notify them once a leg lift was completed using a wearable knee brace [43] or notifying them about their heartbeat rates using a double heartbeat-like rhythm tactile sensation [49]. The Lumo sensor for posture monitoring, for instance, fastens upon one's lapel or brassiere strap, recording and correcting the wearer posture with vibration [40]. As Schull [40] states, the application is customizable, allowing users to control when they are notified and how [40].

A finger-mounted wearable haptic display was proposed to present the weight sensation of a virtual object to the wearer. The feedback provided was based on the fact that the stresses applied on fingerpads due to the weight of an object generate a sensation for users even when the proprioceptive sensation on the user wrist or arm is absent. Such a wearable serves as an haptic display to present a gravity sensation of a virtual object using dual motors and a strap. By wearing the device on the index finger and thumb, a user perceives grip force, gravity, and inertia of a virtual object [50].

For assistive technologies, tactile output has been used to enhance audio communication. A belt was created to assist children with profound hearing impairments so that they could perceive sounds through vibrotactile feedback [52].

The sense of touch is promising as an effective channel of communication in wearable computing [51]. Not only because it has potential for a low social weight in the human computer interaction, but also because the benefits of tactile interfaces include providing a more intimate and private experience for wearers [51]. Tactile input is also discreet, delivering feedback to the wearer through an unobtrusive channel, and presenting information with low cognitive load [51]. Tactile interfaces built into personal accessories, such as jewelry, are promising to deliver discreet feedback if done abstractly [53].

In a bracelet, named doppel, an on-demand, discrete, user-controlled, heartbeat-like vibration was delivered through the wristband. The wristband is connected via Bluetooth to a smartphone application so that the users can measure their resting heart rate and choose their preferred speed and intensity of tactile stimulation in relation to their own heart rate [49].

Although the touch screen interaction paradigm is currently dominant in mobile devices, it is challenging to fit it into very small wearable devices, such as wrist-worn wearables [39]. When dedicated devices are created, the design decisions for tactile interaction involve vibration (intensity, duration, pattern), pressure, and stroking [51]. Vibrotactile stimulators can be built using solenoids, speakers, piezoelectric stimulators, and electromagnetic motors [51].

Haptic devices are also called tactile devices because both focus on stimulating the user skin [8]. The benefits of tactile output devices are that they are discreet, unobtrusive, private, and small [8]. Also, because tactile devices stimulate the skin, they do not interfere with visual or audio displays [8]. The main drawback of tactile responses is that users are not used to communicate naturally using it, thus conveying intuitive responses becomes challenging for designers.

For input entry, touch-based interfaces include physical buttons for control through finger press, text entry in keyboard commands, or typing in virtual keyboards (combining graphic user interfaces for output display, and gesture recognition for input commands). For an EOG goggle for eye tracking, two physical buttons were integrated to allow the user to access the basic functionalities of the device [44].

Concerning its limitations, tactile-based systems tend to be impractical for most users with disabilities [54]. More specifically, users with vision impairments are not always able to use a touch screen, however they might have higher sensitivity to perceive tactile feedback from output responses.

3.3.3 Gesture

Even though there has been little use of physical hand and body gestures for input on the move, gestures are beneficial for interaction since wearers are not required to look at a display to interact with it (as necessary when users click in a button on a screen) [10]. Gestures are convenient for wearable communication as users can perform them while moving [8]. Also, when compared to direct manipulation techniques, gestures require lower visual attention thanks to kinesthetic feedback and proprioception [8].

Natural gestures may be used for input entry in several different situations. To use head gestures as an interaction technique, for example, head movements including nods or shakes can enable item selections in the audio menu space, in touch-screen interfaces, wearers can use their fingers (or a stylus) to make 2D gestures. Lastly, a tracker integrated on a device can ensure it is also used for pointing or gesturing [10].

Although the use of subtle expressions and micro-gestures is interesting, gestural interaction may be also seen as too unnatural as users are not always used to communicate through gestures (with exception of sign languages) [9].

Gestural input can be either passive or active. In a passive mode, the device simply "listens" for movements that can trigger a function without conscious intention of the wearer. In an active mode, the wearer actively and intentionally executes a movement to give instructions to the technology [55]. Gesture is used for input entry, be it executed through finger gestures on capacitive screens on smartwatches or head gestures detected with inertial measurement units (such as accelerometers and gyroscopes) embedded in head-mounted devices. Gestures that are distinct from everyday actions are less likely to be misinterpreted as an input gesture [55].

Gestures can also be executed with users' eyes, to control input entry with eye gaze and saccade. To investigate the use of explicit eye gestures, Bulling et al. [44] created an EOG goggle. The eye movements of the wearer were parsed and processed from EOG signals and used for game controls in experiments [44].

To study specific design guidelines for input entry and cursor command, Zucco and Thomas [36] selected four wearable devices for gesture interaction. The devices included: a trackball, a touchpad, a gyroscopic mouse, and a Twiddler mouse. They provided the user with the ability to perform general cursor movement, object selection, and object drag and drop [36]. As described in the Sect. 4.3.2, the effectiveness of the input approach depends on whether the user is stationary or moving.

3.3.4   Audio

Audio responses stimulate the auditory system of the wearers in order to provide them information and alerts [8]. Acoustic feedback can be provided as an auditory icon, with a brief and distinct sound [8]. Particular sounds can make the human interaction meaningful, beyond the specific narrative and the specific user [31]. The quality of a sound (pitch and loudness) depends on the properties of the sound wave called frequency and amplitude [8] and may be adjusted according to the user profile, application features, and context of use, striving to balance notice rates and user satisfaction.

Devices used mainly for auditory feedback differ on their form factors, speakers, and integrated intelligence to optimize sound quality. Auditory feedback devices, such as earpieces, headsets, and head phones, are small and portable, when compared to desktop sound systems for audio output. They also have the advantage of cancelling environmental noise if necessary, and combining multiple audio sources with different positions in the physical space around the user, enabling interactions to occur [10]. By enabling wearers to maintain their visual attention on navigating the world around them and allowing information to be presented to the users' ears, nonspeech audio tends to be very effective at improving interaction on mobile devices [10].

To employ auditory feedback in a wearable system, two approaches are used. In a speech-based audio interface either a computer-generated voice or a recorded natural human voice presents information to a user. In a nonspeech audio interface, audio tones are used to call user attention and alert him/her. Auditory feedback is key for hands-free interaction, and can be implemented via bone conduction, for instance, to allow the mapping of gestures to control an application [36]. Other benefits associated to auditory interaction include the following:

- reducing the cognitive load on the wearer visual system;
- reducing the need and the information load of a graphic display;
- reducing demands for visual attention;
- enabling hands-free interaction; and
- calling the wearer attention.

Voice-based input, if used for long periods, can cause fatigue though. Therefore, the recommendation is to let the computer to automatically perform as many user tasks as possible aiming to reduce the number of voice input from the wearer and as such minimize the potential strain on the user's voice [3].

Among the disadvantages of using sound, we can highlight the lack of accuracy in some speech-based recognition systems for input (especially when users are non-native speakers of the language, and long and complex commands, as well as open sentences are involved), lack of privacy, as bystanders can overhear the interaction, cognitive overload if the interaction space is broad and hierarchical, and fatigue if the interaction lasts more than a few minutes. Auditory interaction is also ephemeral (as wearers rely on short-term memory to recall the information), and non-intuitive (when beeps and alert sounds are not natural in the users' communication, requiring training and imposing a steep learning curve for wearers).

Also, some users may prefer to not talk to their devices [9]. Concerning the user context, speech recognition is not well suited if the wearer interaction is carried out in noisy environments [10]. For voice commands, noisy areas are problematic adding another human–computer interaction (HCI) challenge for wearable devices, concerning physical interactivity and social acceptance [9].

Concerning responsiveness, voice-based input approaches tend to have slow response times, particularly for motion control [54]. Lastly, it is crucial for designers and developers to balance the timing, frequency, and tone of the audio feedback, ensuring that wearers are able to notice it, but are not overwhelmed with auditory responses that occur too frequently or are too loud. Assessing the annoyance of the audio feedback is recommended, to test with wearers any potential issues caused by using sound in the wearable interface [10].

For input, speech recognition is the most natural way for wearers to provide control commands [8], since no previous training is required, and thus the learning efforts necessary are lower when compared with interaction techniques. Also, speech interaction, besides being the most natural way for human communication, neither requires visual feedback nor occupies the user's hands [8]. Although available speech recognition algorithms have overcome many technical problems with the sentence interpretation, the accuracy of the recognition algorithms for voice commands is not always perfect [8].

The hands-free nature of speech interaction enables users to use their hands and as such optimize task performance. Also, speech interaction is well suited for complex primary tasks and when task performance is important. Speech interaction allows users to maintain visual focus on the primary task without a significant impact on manual activities. Speech interaction is recommended when the primary task is manual work and requires visual attention or physical demands to be executed correctly [8].

3.3.5   Brain–Computer Interfaces

Thoughts are gathered through brain–computer interfaces (BCIs), which sense information from brain signals and translate it to electrical signals. They employ machine learning to classify patterns in brain signals following five consecutive stages: signal acquisition, preprocessing or signal enhancement, feature extraction, classification, and control interfacing [9].

Three popular BCI devices are commercially available today, Emotiv EPOC,[1] Neurosky Mindwave,[2] and Interaxon Muse.[3] All devices are lightweight headbands with several EEG sensors that measure brain signals and brain waves [9].

The biggest challenge in BCI is that brain signals are hard to isolate, as they are mixed with other signals coming from several brain activities [9]. For Roh et al. [56], the scalp EEG is polluted by noise and artifacts such as eye movement, user's movement, and heartbeat. Therefore, the signals collected from the wearer's scalp are a combination of brain active potentials with some other artifacts passing through soft tissue and bone [56].

Thought-controlled computing is in its infancy; however, substantial progress has been made and there is a promising potential on accessible technologies for wearers with motor impairments. Only by overcoming key challenges in BCI, thought control will be fully exploited in next-generation wearable computing devices. Recent achievements of current technologies summed with ongoing developments are promising to further advance BCI technology, and as such enable practical thought control for next-generation wearable devices in the future [9].

3.4   Wrist-Worn Devices

Intelligent watches have been available for a long time; however, continued miniaturization of technology summed with advanced connectivity and touch screens paved the way for watches to compete with smartphones. Smartwatches provide live access

---

[1] https://www.emotiv.com/epoc/.

[2] https://store.neurosky.com/.

[3] https://choosemuse.com/.

Fig. 3.2 The interaction with smartwatches is primarily driven by graphic user interfaces (GUIs), and tactile approaches, including touch-based and button-press interaction for input entry. Vibration and audio are also employed for output responses, to call wearer attention and to communicate events with short commands

to information and intelligent features [9]. Thanks to its conventional look, smartwatches have a higher market penetration and adoption rate than other wearable devices [33].

Wrist-mounted displays (WMD) are equipped with technologies that allow a display to be mounted on the wearer body. Wrist-mounted displays are traditionally attached to the forearm or to the wrist of the wearer [8]. When compared to a smart glass, the watch is considered to be more flexible with respect to moving into the field of view when users are running [35]. Although this form factor is familiar to end users due to conventional wrist watches, wrist-worn wearables (as illustrated in Fig. 3.2) have some constraints that are specific to their solution space, more specifically their interaction surface is limited, and the screen size (when a display is available) is also reduced.

In addition to that, there are limitations in terms of processing power and trade-offs with responsiveness, data collection, and battery efficiency. Although WMDs might be easier to use in the beginning, they also have drawbacks, first by not supporting hands-free operation all the time and second by requiring full user attention to check graphic displays [8]. Overall commercial devices rely on a combination of multimodalities, using vibration to draw users' attention, graphics to present information, touch as input entry, and button press as selection approach. User interaction tends to be short, less than a minute, or a few minutes. For Khakurel (2018), predominant usability issues related to smartwatches, their user interfaces, and interaction aspects, include font size and interaction techniques, such as notification, button location, and tap detection, as well as hardware (concerning mainly the screen size) [12].

As wearable computers are often used to support real-world tasks [8], with wearables, the user interaction with the real world becomes the primary task [7] and the interaction with the wearable computer becomes a secondary task. As secondary task, the wearable interaction needs to be supported with minimal user effort and cognitive load [8], allowing the attention of the wearer to be divided among tasks of various kinds, including driving, swimming, or running.

3.5 Head-Mounted Devices

A head-mounted display (HMD) is a headset placed on the user's head and adjusted around it with a strap for proper fit. HMD requires sophisticated engineering techniques to integrate seamlessly electronics, optics, and mechanical components into a lightweight system that renders advanced graphics and multimedia contents [8]. Head-mounted devices are characterized by virtual reality headsets (as illustrated in Fig. 3.3) that take into account the wearers' motions using the sensors embedded in the goggle, and display renderings for end users.

The renderings of VR are mainly centered on the immersion of the virtual environment, used to simulate real places and situations for end users [57]. Multiple modalities are also combined, and go beyond multimedia graphics, but consider also gesture-based and voice-based input. Text, sounds, 3D models, images, and 360 environments may all be uploaded to design VR contents, as well as interactive contents [57].

Fig. 3.3 Virtual reality headsets immerse users in a computer-generated view of the world. The wearer interaction with virtual reality headsets focuses on three-dimensional graphic user interfaces (GUIs), audio for output responses, and head gestures for input entry

Other categories of head-mounted devices include augmented reality headsets that combine physical objects from real world with computer-generated contents to augment the user experience, as well as earpieces, which are usually tiny and used to sense users' signals (including pulse and oximeter) continuously to provide audio features in the inner ear or through bone conduction.

When comparing VR with AR headsets, the degree of acceptable occlusion for a head-mounted system is decided based on potential risks of the environment in which the user interacts with the device [3].

Recent advances in virtual reality (VR) and head-mounted displays have enabled a wide range of applications, including those created for therapeutic purposes. Although research and development have increased to create products in this field, little is known about wearable immersive virtual reality applied to therapeutic purposes [57]. Also, the nature of interaction with head-worn displays and interactive glasses remains as an unsolved research problem, leaving open questions such as how input should be provided to head-worn displays and glasses, and what are the appropriate and suitable interaction metaphors for head-mounted displays [36].

To create interactive contents for VR and games, several technologies and frameworks exist. A-frame is a VR framework that can be used in integration with HTML (for entities and to design the VR scene), JavaScript (used for the game engine, to change scenes according to users' behavior, movements, and choices) [57].

In an augmented reality (AR) experience, headsets can also be used to integrate a pair of microphone with in-ear headphones, seeking to provide signals from the binaural microphones directly to the headphones so that the user is exposed to a modified representation of the real acoustic environment [58]. A commercially available see-through display for AR is the Microsoft Hololens, an untethered, binocular head-worn device that uses gaze to move the cursor, gesture for interaction and voice commands for input control. The device also provides a handheld clicker for use during extended sessions, which provides selection, scrolling, holding, and double-click interaction [36].

For input purposes, head-mounted displays use tactile interaction. The Moverio BT-200, a head-worn display, enables user interaction via a touchpad placed on the top of the controller along with function keys, including home, menu, and back [36].

Other purpose common to head-mounted devices is to serve as a brain–computer interface (BCI), for example, with the Emotiv headset which is also considered as HMD. BCI devices employ electroencephalography (EEG) technology to read brain signals from users and control applications [59]. Brain–computer interfaces (BCI) are advancing rapidly and noninvasive BCIs begin to be used in games and in health care. Thought control of wearables is an intriguing vision that would facilitate more intuitive HCI; however, to achieve control, BCI requires strong processing power that is not available on mobile devices [9]. In this context, HCI modalities that are compact and compatible with wearables have become more critical. Thought control of wearable devices is inevitable, fostered by the need for convenient and intuitive HCI modalities [9].

A headband was also proposed to monitor users' mental health. The system integrates EEG and HRV signals, allowing the visualization and recording of users' mental state drawn from raw signals from the user brain. The recorded data set can be transmitted to experts, including psychiatrists for diagnosis and analysis [56]. Headband enables hands-free interaction, so that wearers can still move their arms during the measurements [56].

While in virtual reality (VR), the wearer interacts with a virtual world, in augmented reality (AR), the real world is enhanced with useful information, services, and resources. The augmentation is typically achieved by overlaying graphic images from the real world with computer generated information [8]. Despite having a promising potential across domains, the overlaying process is costly in terms of processing power, computational vision, and energy consumption.

Electrooculography (EOG) is a measurement technique for head-mounted eye tracking that allows the recognition of the user activity and attention using, for instance, goggles with dry electrodes, integrated into a frame, and connected to a small pocket-worn component with a DSP for real-time EOG signal processing [44].

The interaction paradigms for VR and AR are known as non-see-through and see-through displays, ranging from completely immersive devices (with which users are blindfolded to the world) to projection of information in real-world settings (with which users see and navigate in actual physical spaces).

Head-mounted devices have considerably evolved in the past decades, with improved resolution on graphics, higher response rates, reduced prices, lightweighted devices, and an increasing number of applications for gaming, training, and videos. Although safety issues have been addressed in past years, depending on their applications, calibration to the user, and duration of usage, head-mounted devices can still cause nausea, dizziness, eye strain, fatigue, or headache in wearers [3]. In an evaluation of three form factors for runners, the glasses' display was considered by study participants as distracting; also the targeting input with glasses was considered difficult; lastly, the smartglasses had a stronger impact on the running movement [35].

In another study, with head-mounted displays, concerning effects on vision, participants reported: irritation in the eyes, visual fatigue, and headache [22]. Such effects are of important considerations when designing head-mounted displays, to identify and address, to the extent as possible, potential causes, be those related to the technology, tasks, or users' context. In previous studies, the study participant commented that he "felt slight headache, which may be related to other reasons such as general tiredness of a long week and the lack of sleep."

Another concern with head-mounted devices is related to visual impairments, for scalability with a variety of users and graphic interfaces, goggles, and head-mounted displays should still allow wearers who use glasses to interact with the devices [44].

Concerning the interaction design, the multiple different interaction techniques used in head-mounted devices commercially available provide discrete input that is directly mapped to a specific action. As a result, current input techniques do not provide general-purpose input and are tied to one specific device and application [36].

With the growing availability of wearable glasses-based displays that are smaller, less obtrusive, and targeted at the consumer market, research addressing the user interaction with head-mounted devices is crucial, especially to ensure input entry and output responses that are suitable, subtle, and socially acceptable [36].

3.6   Smart Clothing

Electronic textiles can be seamlessly integrated in clothes, ensuring they become "smart" or "intelligent". Smart clothes also called e-clothes due to their added electronic components [60] empower the wearer with a smart device for personal use that is continuously available [38]. Smart clothes are defined as an "apparel with unobtrusively built-in electronic functions". Electronic textiles include, for instance, conductive yarn, copper meshes, conductive textiles, and paint. Embedded in garments, these electronics provide wearers with additional functionality that is able to sense and communicate data, harvest energy, or even augment memory, intellect, creativity, communication, and physical senses of the users [60].

To ensure that electronic textile materials can be washed and worn regularly, treatment methods are necessary. Conductive yarns and threads are used to connect electronic pieces. Although conductive thread helps connecting the wearable components to each other, these connections tend to be fragile depending on their assembly approach and context of use [43]. In which case, the wires for the sensors can be fed up a channel and sewn directly into the fabric (e.g., arm of a shirt) [61].

Although the availability of e-sewable kits increased in the market, enabling investigators and hobbyists to implemented customized prototypes, in the commercial market, few pieces that can be considered as smart garments are available for sale. The Levi Jacquard Jacket by Google [4] is an exception. It is a denim jacket that allows wearers to control other devices, handling calls, controlling music players, access alert, and navigation combining earphones and a core controller. A jacket to support shopping was also proposed using positioning sensors to alert consumers when they pass by a store of interest [62]. Another jacket focused on sensing users' context, and movements, for activity recognition [38].

The advantages of fabric sensors, or e-textiles, are that they can be [38]

- integrated to smart clothes unobtrusively;
- produced through standard garment industrial techniques; and
- washed and ironed (unlike hardware-enhanced clothing).

Figure 3.4 illustrates a temperature-sensitive skirt.[5] Designed to sense the environment temperature, the skirt contains LED lights that change color according to the temperature of its surroundings. For easy laundering of the skirt, the LED circuit can be removed.

---

[4]https://atap.google.com/jacquard/.

[5]https://sophywong.com.

Fig. 3.4 Smart clothing varies on their form factor, benefitting from e-textiles as well as conductive threads to integrate components in the garment. In the temperature-sensitive skirt, Sophy Wong integrated LED lights that change color based on the temperature of the environment. To facilitate laundry, the LED circuit is completely removable. Credit: Sophy Wong. At: https://sophywong.com

3.7 Alternative Form Factors

In addition to wrist-worn devices (such as bracelets and armbands) and head-mounted devices, wearable sensors have been successfully integrated into clothing garments as well as fashion accessories, such as hats, socks, shoes, and eyeglasses [63]. Although alternative form factors also exist, including belts [64], badges [38], caps [37], knee braces [43], customized T-shirts [61], scarves, necklaces, and vests [48], they are less popular, and traditionally built as conceptual prototypes for scientific research, or customized to address specific user needs. Still, due to the potential opportunities and inherent limitations of technology, wearables of alternative form factors also employ the same four modalities for the users' interaction, be it for input, output, or both.

Gloves have been explored to support gesture interaction, using sensors to recognize hand postures and gestures. A limitation with data gloves that employ accelerometers concerns the usage of the earth's gravity as a fixed reference frame since in wearable applications' users risk losing their orientation when performing physical tasks in the real world [8]. Also, although gloves prevent the user from holding a physical device, having extra material surrounding the hand of the user may hinder the execution of his or her tasks, besides also reducing tactile feeling, and interfering with reaching into tight spaces [36].

Belts also leveraged technology advances, integrating a complex computing system in a small buckle. They can be employed in medical aiding and supervising systems, mobile worker, and maintenance assistance as well as security and rescue applications [30]. As an accessory, belts are not subject to typical cleaning procedures of regular garments, and thus washability is not a major issue. Besides this, they can be worn for functional and aesthetic reasons as well [30]. By integrating the main electronics in the buckle of a belt, the belt itself can be used as an extension bus providing also mechanical support for additional components [30]. The belt itself houses batteries, cables, and connectors, illustrating possible design synergies between the core functionality of clothing and wearable electronics [65]. Another design exploration for belts was the belt-mounted mouse, focusing on supporting the user interaction, it employed an isometric joystick device, mounted on top of the battery pack attached to the belt [66].

Contact Lenses have been conceptually explored, including nanometer thin layers of metal along with light emitting diodes (LED) to sense data and provide information. Prototype lenses with an embedded spherical curved LCD can show simple patterns. More recent prototypes of telescopic contact lenses show some progress in the domain, even though challenges remain concerning safety, battery, sensing and transmission capabilities [9].

A forearm-mounted keyboard was also explored to support the end user interaction with text entry by typing on the forearm keyboard. The device was strapped to the subjects non-preferred forearm using elasticized Velcro straps. The back of the keyboard was slightly curved in order to make it fit comfortably on the wearer arm, and the keys were rubberized with white characters [66].

For wearables in the insole of a shoe, sensors and electronics can be used to measure the skin conductance. The device is embedded in the heel of a shoe and a wire runs through the shoe to attach the sensors to conductive snaps held in the insole with the electrodes. Snap in insoles with disposable electrodes allows electrode replacement to be easy and inexpensive [67].

For undergarments, respiration sensors can be embedded in a bra. These sensors detect respiration by measuring the chest cavity expansion, with two magnets embedded in an elastic tube that when pulled apart generates an electric current which is measured by an ADX sensor [67].

A body-area network including cap, goggle, and back-mounted devices was explored to monitor swimming activities. While the swim goggle includes a visual actuator (LED lights), a controller board was placed underneath the bathing cap [37].

To explore the problem of tracking compliance and to aid patients during the rehabilitation process, a fully functional wearable knee brace was created. It passively senses and also records exercise routines, augmenting the existing relationship between patients recovering from knee injuries and their physical therapists [43].

3.8 Final Remarks

Moving beyond a conventional desktop interface makes the design process of wearable technologies more complex [15], mainly because the environments from which the wearer interacts with the technology vary and the interaction requirements are transient, changing dynamically depending on external constraints from the user environment as well as the situational impairments it imposes for the wearer. These changes impose constraints that existing design guidelines fail to cover in a comprehensive manner. Also, existing interaction paradigms are unable to fully address such constraints.

In practice, simply shrinking down computational tools from the desktop to smaller dimensions will result in miniaturized computers, dismissing the vast opportunities of exploiting a new context and the human body as a platform [6].

Considerations that strongly affect the user's intention to use, acceptance, and adoption include wearability, privacy concerns, social influence, and individual attitude [12]. For stakeholders creating novel devices, the assembly of electronic components in a small, lightweight form factor is a challenge, especially when novel form factors are at stake.

Ideally, a wearable interface should become a "natural" extension of the wearer, neither requiring continuous attention to control it [8], nor inhibiting users main activities, tasks, and movements [61].

From a usability and a design perspective, effective user interfaces and approaches for delivering information must be developed to inform and educate users [42], allowing high learnability and easy of use with intuitive interaction approaches.

Appropriately and effectively interacting with a wearable is a documented issue that still challenges the design of wearable computers. Even though research undertaken in this area is extensive, the design of the user interaction remains as an unsolved problem that is vital to wearable computing [36].

Interacting in a wearable context brings with it challenges, including the decisions about appropriate interaction modalities, when and how to communicate with wearers regarding approaches for input entry and output responses. Important challenges also involve balancing the attention users need to interact with a wearable while executing primary tasks simultaneously, besides deciding on the device dimensions, weight, unobtrusiveness, responsiveness, usefulness, and the social implications associated to the technology when used in public spaces [36].

Among those challenges recognizing the user's context in an accurate way and adapting to it accordingly stands out. The *intelligence* of a device lies on properly understanding the user's space, so that both input and output are optimized to fit in seamlessly, addressing potential user requirements.

While it is not feasible to find answers in the current literature, with solutions that fit specific form factors, user profiles, and context of use, HCI provides methods and tools that help to better understand users' needs and as such bridge the gap between design decisions for interactive technologies and users' expectations about it.

Summary

This chapter discusses the interaction aspects that should be considered when designing user interfaces for wearable computers. We focus on five modalities for input entry and output responses, namely, graphics, tactile, gesture, audio, and brain–computer interfaces. Although graphic displays are largely used in wrist-worn and head-mounted devices, they are often combined with tactile interaction to notify users with vibrations, and beeps to communicate information. Vibrotactile interfaces are also often combined with visual and audio displays. Overall, by combining multiple modalities, designers help to ensure that users are able to effectively notice the feedback and responses coming from wearable devices when alerts, messages, and notifications are sent.

Concerning the interaction modalities, there are several trade-offs that require consideration when taking design decisions. Thus, we also discuss the benefits and drawbacks associated with each modality, for instance, concerning ease of use, privacy, and energy consumption. While some modalities are more intuitive for wearers to interact with (e.g., graphics and touch), they may also lead to higher energy consumption or present privacy issues. Such trade-offs, despite challenging, must be carefully considered in design phases.

The interaction with wearables varies depending on the form factor of the device; in other words, wrist-worn wearables provide users different affordances than head-mounted devices or smart clothes. We explain the potential opportunities for interaction design across form factors, providing examples from industry and academia as well as a critical discussion on potential design decisions.

This chapter covers head-mounted devices and wrist-worn wearables, expanding also on examples of nonconventional form factors, such as belts, contact lenses, bras, vests, and smart clothes.

References

1. Suhonen K, Muller S, Rantala J, Vaananen-Vainio-Mattila K, Raisamo R, Lantz V (2012) Haptically augmented remote speech communication: a study of user practices and experiences. In: Proceedings of the 7th Nordic conference on human-computer interaction: making sense through design 2012 Oct 14 (pp. 361–369). ACM
2. Scheffler M, Hirt E (2004) Wearable devices for emerging healthcare applications. In: The 26th annual international conference of the IEEE engineering in medicine and biology society 2004 Sep 1 (Vol. 2, pp. 3301–3304). IEEE
3. Gobert D (2002) Designing wearable performance support: Insights from the early literature. Techn Commun 49(4):444–8

4. Siewiorek D, Smailagic A, Starner T (2008) Application design for wearable computing. Syn Lect Mobile Pervasive Comput 3(1):1–66
5. Nunez-Pacheco C, Loke L (2014) Crafting the body-tool: a body-centred perspective on wearable technology. In: Proceedings of the 2014 conference on designing interactive systems 2014 Jun 21 (pp. 553–566). ACM
6. Gemperle F, Kasabach C, Stivoric J, Bauer M, Martin R (1998) Design for wearability. In digest of papers. Second international symposium on wearable computers (cat. No. 98EX215) 1998 Oct 19 (pp. 116–122). IEEE
7. Billinghurst M, Starner T (1999) Wearable devices: new ways to manage information. Computer 32(1):57–64
8. Witt H (2007) Human-computer interfaces for wearable computers. PhD thesis
9. Powell C, Munetomo M, Schlueter M, Mizukoshi M (2013) Towards thought control of next-generation wearable computing devices. In: International conference on brain and health informatics. Springer, Cham, pp 427–438
10. Brewster S, Lumsden J, Bell M, Hall M, Tasker S (2003) Multimodal eyes-free interaction techniques for wearable devices. In: Proceedings of the SIGCHI conference on Human factors in computing systems 2003 Apr 5 (pp. 473–480). ACM
11. Siewiorek D (2017) Wearable computing: retrospectives on the first decade. GetMobile: Mobile Comput Commun 21(1):5–10
12. Khakurel J. Enhancing the Adoption of Quantified Self-Tracking Devices. (Doctoral dissertation, University of Technology, Lappeenranta, Finland) ISBN 978-952-335-318-3
13. Starner T (2001) The challenges of wearable computing: part 2. IEEE Micro 21(4):54–67
14. Troshynski E, Lee C, Dourish P (2011) Accountabilities of presence: reframing location-based systems. Droit et cultures. Revue internationale interdisciplinaire 1(61):171–93
15. Motti VG, Caine K (2014) Human factors considerations in the design of wearable devices. In: Proceedings of the human factors and ergonomics society annual meeting 2014 Sep (Vol. 58, No. 1, pp. 1820–1824). Sage CA: Los Angeles, CA: SAGE Publications
16. Koch S, Marschollek M, Wolf KH, Plischke M, Haux R (2009) On health-enabling and ambient-assistive technologies. Methods Inf Med 48(01):29–37
17. Cho JY, Ko D, Lee BG (2018) Strategic approach to privacy calculus of wearable device user regarding information disclosure and continuance intention. KSII Trans Int Inf Syst 12(7)
18. Angelini L, Caon M, Carrino S, Bergeron L, Nyffeler N, Jean-Mairet M, Mugellini E (2013) Designing a desirable smart bracelet for older adults. In: Proceedings of the 2013 ACM conference on Pervasive and ubiquitous computing adjunct publication 2013 Sep 8 (pp. 425–434). ACM
19. Kidmose P, Looney D, Jochumsen L, Mandic DP (2013) Ear-EEG from generic earpieces: a feasibility study. In: 2013 35th annual international conference of the IEEE engineering in medicine and biology society (EMBC) 2013 Jul 3 (pp. 543–546). IEEE
20. Garabet A, Mann S, Fung J (2002) Exploring design through wearable computing art (ifacts). In: CHI'02 extended abstracts on human factors in computing systems 2002 Apr 20 (pp. 634–635). ACM
21. Buenaflor C, Kim H (2013) Six human factors to acceptability of wearable computers. Int J Multimed Ubiquitous Eng 8(3):103–114
22. Weller P, Rakhmetova L, Ma Q, Mandersloot G (2010) Evaluation of a wearable computer system for telemonitoring in a critical environment. Personal Ubiquitous Comput 14(1):73–81
23. Norman D (2013) The paradox of wearable technologies. Technol Rev 116(5):101–3
24. Tharion WJ, Buller MJ, Karis AJ, Mullen SP (2007) Acceptability of a wearable vital sign detection system. In: Proceedings of the human factors and ergonomics society annual meeting 2007 Oct (Vol. 51, No. 17, pp. 1006–1010). Sage CA: Los Angeles, CA: SAGE Publications
25. Karahanoglu A, Erbug C (2011) Perceived qualities of smart wearables: determinants of user acceptance. In: Proceedings of the 2011 conference on designing pleasurable products and interfaces 2011 Jun 22 (p. 26). ACM
26. Ledger D, McCaffrey D (2014) Inside wearables: How the science of human behavior change offers the secret to long-term engagement. Endeavour Partners 200(93):1

27. Lazar, Amanda, Christian Koehler, Joshua TanenbauLazar A, Koehler C, Tanenbaum J, Nguyen DH (2015) Why we use and abandon smart devices. In: Proceedings of the 2015 ACM international joint conference on pervasive and ubiquitous computing 2015 Sep 7 (pp. 635–646). ACM

28. Torous BJ, Gualtieri L (2016) Knowns and Unknowns. Psychiatric Times, Wearable Devices for Mental Health, pp 4–7

29. Cho G (2009 Dec 23) Smart clothing: technology and applications. CRC Press

30. Amft O, Lauffer M, Ossevoort S, Macaluso F, Lukowicz P, Troster G (2004) Design of the QBIC wearable computing platform. In: Proceedings 15th IEEE international conference on application-specific systems, architectures and processors, 2004. 2004 Sep 27 (pp. 398–410). IEEE

31. Cranny-Francis A, Hawkins C (2008) Wearable technology. Vis Commun 7(3):267–270

32. Smailagic A, Siewiorek D (2002) Application design for wearable and context-aware computers. IEEE Pervasive Comput 1(4):20–9

33. Dibia V (2015) An affective, normative and functional approach to designing user experiences for wearables. Normative and Functional Approach to Designing User Experiences for Wearables (July 14, 2015)

34. Burgy C, Garrett JH (2002) Wearable computers: an interface between humans and smart infrastructure systems. Vdi Berichte 1668:385–98

35. Seuter M, Pfeiffer M, Bauer G, Zentgraf K, Kray C (2017) Running with technology: evaluating the impact of interacting with wearable devices on running movement. Proc ACM Interact Mobile Wearable Ubiquitous Technol 1(3):101

36. Zucco JE, Thomas BH (2016) Design guidelines for wearable pointing devices. Front ICT 27(3):13

37. Bachlin M, Forster K, Troster G (2009) SwimMaster: a wearable assistant for swimmer. In: Proceedings of the 11th international conference on Ubiquitous computing 2009 Sep 30 (pp. 215–224). ACM

38. Farringdon J, Moore AJ, Tilbury N, Church J, Biemond PD (1999) Wearable sensor badge & sensor jacket for context awareness. In: The proceedings of the third international symposium on wearable computers. San Francisco, CA, Oct. 18–19, 1999

39. Oakley I, Lee D (2014) Interaction on the edge: offset sensing for small devices. In: Proceedings of the SIGCHI conference on human factors in computing systems 2014 Apr 26 (pp. 169–178). ACM

40. Schull ND (2016) Data for life: Wearable technology and the design of self-care. BioSocieties 1–17. https://doi.org/10.1057/biosoc.2015.47

41. Dunne L (2010) Beyond the second skin: an experimental approach to addressing garment style and fit variables in the design of sensing garments. Int J Fashion Des Technol Educ 3(3):109–17

42. Cho H, Yoon H, Kim KJ, Shin DH (2015) Wearable health information: Effects of comparative feedback and presentation mode. In: Proceedings of the 33rd annual ACM conference extended abstracts on human factors in computing systems 2015 Apr 18 (pp. 2073–2078). ACM

43. Munoz D, Pruett A, Williams G. Knee: an everyday wearable goniometer for monitoring physical therapy adherence. In: CHI'14 extended abstracts on human factors in computing systems 2014 Apr 26 (pp. 209–214). ACM

44. Bulling A, Roggen D, Troster G (2008) It's in your eyes: towards context-awareness and mobile HCI using wearable EOG goggles. In: Proceedings of the 10th international conference on Ubiquitous computing 2008 Sep 21 (pp. 84–93). ACM

45. Kanis M, Winters N, Agamanolis S, Gavin A, Cullinan C (2005) Toward wearable social networking with iBand. In: CHI'05 extended abstracts on Human factors in computing systems 2005 Apr 2 (pp. 1521–1524). ACM

46. Magno M, Brunelli D, Sigrist L, Andri R, Cavigelli L, Gomez A, Benini L (2016) InfiniTime: multi-sensor wearable bracelet with human body harvesting. Sustain Comput: In Syst 1(11):38–49

47. Forlizzi J, McCormack M (2000) Case study: user research to inform the design and development of integrated wearable computers and web-based services. In: Proceedings of the 3rd conference on Designing interactive systems: processes, practices, methods, and techniques 2000 Aug 1 (pp. 275–279). ACM
48. Duvall JC, Dunne LE, Schleif N, Holschuh B (2016) Active hugging vest for deep touch pressure therapy. In: Proceedings of the 2016 ACM international joint conference on pervasive and ubiquitous computing: adjunct 2016 Sep 12 (pp. 458–463). ACM
49. Azevedo RT, Bennett N, Bilicki A, Hooper J, Markopoulou F, Tsakiris M (2017) The calming effect of a new wearable device during the anticipation of public speech. Sci Reports 7(1):2285
50. Minamizawa K, Fukamachi S, Kajimoto H, Kawakami N, Tachi S (2007) Gravity grabber: wearable haptic display to present virtual mass sensation. In: ACM SIGGRAPH 2007 emerging technologies 2007 Aug 5 (p. 8). ACM
51. Toney A, Dunne L, Thomas BH, Ashdown SP (2003) A shoulder pad insert vibrotactile display. IEEE; 2003 Oct 21
52. Saunders FA, Hill WA, Franklin B (1981) A wearable tactile sensory aid for profoundly deaf children. J Med Syst 5(4):265–70
53. MacLean D, Roseway A, Czerwinski M (2013) MoodWings: a wearable biofeedback device for real-time stress intervention. In: Proceedings of the 6th international conference on PErvasive technologies related to assistive environments 2013 May 29 (p. 66). ACM
54. Cannan J, Hu H. A wearable sensor fusion armband for simple motion control and selection for disabled and non-disabled users. In: 2012 4th computer science and electronic engineering conference (CEEC) 2012 Sep 12 (pp. 216–219). IEEE
55. Dunne LE, Profita H, Zeagler C, Clawson J, Gilliland S, Do EY, Budd J (2014) The social comfort of wearable technology and gestural interaction. In: 2014 36th annual international conference of the IEEE engineering in medicine and biology society 2014 Aug 26 (pp. 4159–4162). IEEE
56. Roh T, Bong K, Hong S, Cho H, Yoo HJ (2012) Wearable mental-health monitoring platform with independent component analysis and nonlinear chaotic analysis. In: 2012 annual international conference of the IEEE engineering in medicine and biology society 2012 Aug 28 (pp. 4541–4544). IEEE
57. Etchart M, Caprarelli A (2018) A wearable immersive web-virtual reality approach to remote neurodevelopmental disorder therapy. In: Proceedings of the 2018 international conference on advanced visual interfaces 2018 May 29 (p. 61). ACM
58. Tikander M, Harma A, Karjalainen M (2003) Binaural positioning system for wearable augmented reality audio. In: 2003 IEEE workshop on applications of signal processing to audio and acoustics (IEEE Cat. No. 03TH8684) 2003 Oct 19 (pp. 153–156). IEEE
59. Shrestha P, Saxena N (2017) An offensive and defensive exposition of wearable computing. ACM Comput Surv 50(6):1–39. https://doi.org/10.1145/3133837
60. Virkki J, Aggarwal R (2014) Privacy of wearable electronics in the healthcare and childcare sectors: a survey of personal perspectives from Finland and the United Kingdom. J Inf Secur 5(02):46
61. Knight JF, Baber C (2005) A tool to assess the comfort of wearable computers. Human Fact 47(1):77–91
62. Randell C, Muller H (2000) The shopping jacket: wearable computing for the consumer. Personal Technol 4(4):241–244. https://doi.org/10.1007/BF02391567
63. Fletcher RR, Ming-Zher Poh RR, Eydgahi H (2010) Wearable sensors: opportunities and challenges for low-cost health care. In: Proceedings of the 2010 annual international conference of the IEEE engineering in medicine and biology society. pp 1763–1766
64. Reich J, Wall C, Dunne LE (2015) Design and implementation of a textile-based wearable balance belt. J Med Dev 9(2):020919

65. Lukowicz P (2008) Wearable computing and artificial intelligence for healthcare applications. Artif Intell Med 42(2):95–98. https://doi.org/10.1016/j.artmed.2007.12.002
66. Thomas B, Tyerman S, Grimmer K (1997) Evaluation of three input mechanisms for wearable computers. In: Digest of papers. First international symposium on wearable computers Oct 13 (pp. 2–9). IEEE
67. Healey JA. Wearable and automotive systems for affect recognition from physiology (Doctoral dissertation, Massachusetts Institute of Technology)

Chapter 4
Design Guidelines and Evaluation

Abstract This chapter focuses on quality factors, design principles, and guidelines that must be taken into account when stakeholders are creating or evaluating wearable solutions. The patterns and interaction paradigms described were extracted from the scientific literature and industrial domains as well. By explaining what approaches can be employed to evaluate wearable technologies, using different methods for data collection and different criteria for assessment, this chapter provides readers with a comprehensive list of design principles that can inform decisions from designers, developers, and investigators when creating novel wearable technologies or evaluating existing ones. While some of the design principles are targeted at industry experts, others focus on scientific research. Concerning evaluation, this chapter also provides readers with examples of scales, questionnaires, metrics, and questions that can be employed when assessing technology to better understand the user perspective and experience when interacting with a device. Theoretical definitions as well as illustrative examples are presented. This chapter concludes with design challenges and considerations that must be taken into account during the interaction design and evaluation.

4.1 Quality Factors

Depending on the focus of a wearable technology, there are multiple criteria that can be employed to evaluate it. In the evaluation phases, most scientific research is driven by the effectiveness of the solution proposed, through feasibility tests. However, to achieve high levels of acceptance, adoption, and sustained engagement among wearers, several different quality aspects must be taken into account, in an iterative way, in the design, development, and evaluation phases. For Knight et al. [1], besides assessing cognitive components, such as emotion and anxiety, the focus of design and evaluation should be placed also on physical factors of the wearable technology, including size, weight, weight distribution, format, location of device on the body, and its method of attachment [1].

The key criterion for design evaluation of a wearable is wearability. Wearability is defined as the willingness of wearers to use a wearable technology [2], or in other

© Springer Nature Switzerland AG 2020
V. G. Motti, *Wearable Interaction*, Human–Computer Interaction Series,
https://doi.org/10.1007/978-3-030-27111-4_4

words, the factors that affect the degree of comfort the wearer experiences while wearing a device [3]. Wearability includes several multidimensional factors—the physical, cognitive, psychological, social and emotional state of the wearer. Positive wearability characteristics include the softness, pliability, and washability of the wearable technology [4].

Most importantly, wearers are more likely to purchase and use a device when there is a clear benefit for them. In other words, the usefulness and utility of the device are key for users to adopt it. Then, the human factors also play an important role, as users need devices that are easy to interact with, comfortable to wear, and designed with the users' contexts and needs in mind. Lastly, the costs of wearing the device are also crucial for end users, be those financial or to overall efforts to maintain, wear or use the device.

To determine to which extent a wearable interface is effective, efficient, and satisfactory in the evaluation, qualitative and quantitative data should be collected during the evaluation session. Effectiveness and efficiency can be objectively measured through the accuracy and operational speed with which a wearer performs a task [5]. By asking the wearer about his or her opinion about a device, subjective assessment can be gathered. Examining interaction data automatically collected, the satisfaction of the user with the interface cannot be effectively determined. Thus, it is crucial to ask wearers to express their opinions concerning comfort and acceptability of the technology [5].

There is an extensive number of quality factors of multiple dimensions that influence the wearability of a technology. Knight and Barber [6] identified 92 terms associated to it [6]. Among those, comfort stands out as one of the most important aspects for users to accept a wearable technology; however, comfort should not be measured simply with a one-dimensional construct [1]. Still, for the sake of feasibility, simplification of the multidimensional factors is needed, and thus based on the initial list of 92 constructs an investigation was conducted to reduce the terms and reach a practical set of six constructs. In practice, comfort is strongly influenced in the wearer's experience with the technology considering six dimensions: emotion, attachment, harm, perceived change, movement, and anxiety [6].

4.2   Design Principles

Over the last decades, seeking to improve the design of wearable interaction, scientific research in academia, and development in industry defined several principles, interaction styles, interface components, and guidelines for interfaces design [5]. Principles have a broad applicability, and can help to analyze and compare design alternatives for different implementations [5]. For wearable computing, the design principles for user interfaces and wearer interaction were identified to support, guide, and inform the design, development, and evaluation of wearable technologies. Such principles cut across different concerns of the wearable design, including hardware and software aspects, human factors and quality factors. The wearable principles defined thus far come either from product design or from scientific research studies.

4.2.1 Principles to Address Issues in Wearable Computing

Driven by the fact that wearables should minimize distraction, reduce cognitive overload, and strive to preserve user attention; Smailagic and Siewiorek [7] defined four principles for the design of wearable technologies [7].

Principle 1: User Interface Models

An appropriate set of metaphors should be employed to provide wearers with access to information. Because the correct metaphors are not always available, since they take time to develop, extensive experimentation with close involvement of end users is required to define and refine appropriate models for the user interface.

Principle 2: Input and Output Modalities

Input and output across several modalities, along with the capabilities of the human brain, have been extensively investigated by cognitive and computer sciences. Still, current interaction approaches require extensive training to achieve high accuracy and ease of use. Inaccuracies cause frustration on users. Also, most advanced modalities require extensive computing resources which are not always available in lightweight, low-power wearable computers. New, easy-to-use input devices are needed.

Principle 3: Matched Capability with Application Requirements

Although several mobile systems integrate in a small package as much capacity and performance as possible, not all capabilities are essential for end users. Enhancements, such as 3-D graphics in high resolution, require substantial resources, drain the device battery, and may actually compromise ease of use by overloading the user with information. Interface design and evaluation should focus thus on the most effective means for information access, with a minimalist but effective design.

Principle 4: Quick Interface Evaluation Methodology

Although existing techniques to evaluate a human–computer interface require complex procedures, such an evaluation is long and thus not suitable to inform the interface design. The evaluation techniques for wearables should focus on decreasing human errors and reducing frustration.

4.2.2 Wearable Principles for Product Design

Based on a design competition from industry and social norms combined with utility accrual perspective, Dibia et al. [54] propose six principles to guide the design of smartwatches for enterprises and individuals [8].

Principle 1: Sensor-Based Interaction

The limited interaction surface of wearable devices should be extended by leveraging the sensors embedded in the technology. For example, advanced touch gestures (such as tap, swipe, pinch, and zoom), motion, and voice can be leveraged for input entry commands while vibration can be leveraged for personalized feedback.

Principle 2: Visual Normative Adherence

User interfaces should be designed to conform to expectations of both wearable technologies and fashion items. For example, watch face apps for smartwatches should be designed such that they are both meaningful and elegant, wearers are comfortable using it in public spaces, and do not feel embarrassed, uncomfortable, or ashamed by the design decisions of hardware or software.

Principle 3: Isolated Functionality

Each application of a wearable device should be clearly developed to meet a given and well-specified user need as opposed to generic apps with multiple functions. Where possible, apps should be tied to specific outcomes and dedicated, so that they are meaningful to a specific user population.

Principle 4: Complementary or Incremental Value

The value of a wearable application is tied to how well it performs its focal task when compared to similar applications on other devices, including platforms such as smartphones and tablets. This performance-based value may be realized from application to specific contexts or by software filtering. For example, a wearable device dedicated to track exercise routines is "handier" to use in the gym when compared to a smartphone. Similarly, a wearable device can provide value by automatically delivering notifications only from contacts that are important for end users, including family members and friends.

Principle 5: Glanceability and Actionability

The notifications and alerts of a wearable application, regardless of the interaction modalities combined, should be designed in such a way that they are easy to read (legible), to assimilate within a simple glance and be responded to with simple user actions (efficiently).

Principle 6: Computational Offloading

Due to the inherent constraints of wearables, complex or resource intensive tasks should be transferred to other devices with higher processing capabilities to the extent possible or applicable. For example, a wearable device may perform resource-intensive operations like audio sampling, geocoding, or data processing on a connected smartphone or tablet and display the final results to the end user.

4.2.3 Wearable Principles for Scientific Research

Twenty design principles were identified in an extensive review of the scientific literature. These principles inform the design of wearable technologies, especially concerning their interaction aspects [9]. They are defined as follows:

Aesthetics Concerns aspects related to the form and function of any wearable object [10], mainly those associated with its attractiveness level. An attractive design, rather than a medical one, tends to improve the desirability of a device [11]. Aesthetics is perceived by the wearer and by external viewers as well [3].

Affordance Concerns how intuitive the physical aspects of a device are, regarding their interpretations, possibilities for interaction, and respective functionalities [12]. A wearable with good affordances respects the shape of the human body and its anatomical constraints.

Comfort Concerns the freedom from discomfort and pain [13]. Users feeling enough comfort, no longer sense the device after some time wearing it. Comfort involves an acceptable temperature, texture, shape, weight, and tightness [14]. Comfortable devices fit users, enabling their natural movements, without imposing additional burden and any constraints—be those physical or psychological ones. Flexible and elastic materials are well suited to permit normal joint movements from wearers [15]. Smaller form factors and more convenient sensor locations on the body can also aid to ensure users' comfort [16]. Six categories of affect influence comfort levels: emotion, attachment, harm, perceived change, movement, and anxiety [17, 18].

Contextual awareness Concerns the scenarios where the wearable device will be used, as well as the constraints and opportunities involved. Context-sensitive applications are capable of clearly understanding the requirements of platforms in use (regarding the capabilities and limitations of a device), the users (their profiles, abilities, characteristics, and eventual impairments) and environments. Also, contextual information drives the design process and the adaptations of a wearable application. Context-aware user interfaces use information gathered by sensors worn on the user's body to adapt the interfaces, their presentations, modalities, navigation, and contents, to ensure that the input and output of the wearable device address user requirements in different contexts of use [5]. The comfort perceived by users is strongly affected by the device purposes [19], varying significantly depending on social contexts. Understanding well the context is a key factor in the design process, as several device's properties can be affected, for instance, by cultural differences [20]. Such differences are essential criteria to consider and to reach users' acceptance.

Customization Anthropometric measures considerably vary in human users' shape, size, and dimension. Users also vary in their individual preferences, interests, and wishes. To engage users, the look and feel of the wearable devices should enable customization, considering diverse aspects, as the users' sensitivities, wishes, and interests [21]. Customization in size, color, and appearance aids users to feel more comfortable wearing the device and to integrate it to their normal outfit [22]. Personalized options include the choices of colors, functions, weights, and sizes [11].

Ease of Use A straightforward, simple, and intuitive interface [19] enhances the usability levels of the device, aiding to increase the engagement levels of users. Both input and output interfaces should be easy to use [13].

Ergonomy Refers to the physical shape of the device, its ergonomic aspects regarding the respect to the body anatomy, its constraints, and how users perceive it [23, 24].

Fashion Strongly affects the perception of comfort and desirability of a wearable device [19]. It refers to how stylish the technology is, helping to make the device more (or less) ubiquitous, integrating it into a conventional landscape and respecting cultural norms.

Intuitiveness Concerns the immediate understanding of how the interaction occurs, e.g., regarding existing buttons, keys, commands, and features [19]. It applies the affordance concept to the cognitive aspects of the interaction.

Obtrusiveness Physiological sensors have various degrees of intrusiveness, where intrusion may involve using body tissue to diagnose a particular physiological state or condition. Devices considered to be non-intrusive are often obtrusive and cumbersome to some extent. Devices should be transparent [25], enabling natural body movements [15] and carefully considering anatomical characteristics and constraints of the human body.

Overload Differently than technology that has been facing a continuous miniaturization process, humans still have a finite and limited processing capacity. Thus, the number of concurrent activities they can perform at a given time is limited, posing a special challenge to designers of wearable devices. Mobile interfaces may hinder the user's primary task if they do not properly consider the human cognitive capabilities during the design process [19].

Privacy Refers to how subtle the interaction can be, i.e., how discreetly is possible to exchange information with wearers, for input and output, and mainly when users need confidentiality ensured [26]. Exclusive communication channels can ensure privacy and discretion in the interaction [27]. Users must be able to choose their desired level of privacy in parts of, or in all, collected data with respect to access by users' groups (e.g., relatives, friends, and practitioners) [25]. Users are sensitive toward sharing relevant information about them, especially if revealing such information could harm them somehow in a social sense [28].

Reliability Refers to the level of confidence and trust that users have on the device [13], considering hardware, software, and application aspects; it concerns safety (no harm to the user), precision (provide faithful, accurate data), and effectiveness (expected responses). In every day use situations, wearers will not rely on a technology that fails too frequently, thus a wearable should be electronically, mechanically, and computationally fail proof, and trustworthy as well [29].

Resistance Understanding the context in which the wearable device is used, aids practitioners to identify acceptable levels of resistance, specially considering: abrasion, impact, temperature, humidity, flexure, and laundering. Devices should resist impacts from washing and wearing [13], ensuring durability [14].

Responsiveness Users are less patient when they are on the move when seating still at a desktop, as such it is important to provide them feedback in near real time, ensuring high levels of system responsiveness [19]. Ensuring high responsiveness helps users to complete their tasks more efficiently and be more productive [13].

Satisfaction Concerns how the device is able to meet users' expectations, wishes, and requirements. It involves varied aspects, e.g., effectiveness, performance, and beauty. It measures the overall level of fulfillment of users emotionally and functionally [13].

Simplicity Refers to the ease of use, intuitiveness, and affordance of the device, i.e., by putting simple interaction options and by presenting the feedback needed in a simple manner, the user can interact in a straightforward way, with high efficiency [19]. It respects principles of a minimalist design by including only features and interaction options that are fundamental for wearers to accomplish their tasks.

Subtlety Refers to how transparent the communication is, e.g., notifications intended for the owner of the device, should not disturb other people nearby. Notifications should not impose any social burdens [22]. Users are often concerned with excessively attracting other people's attention [27]; a subtle approach ensures more privacy and discretion to users.

User-friendliness Respects the mental model of the end user, proposing options that facilitate the interaction, in an easy and intuitive approach. In case of errors, recovery should be made available [13].

Wearability Considers the physical shape of objects and their active relationship with the human form [19]. Wearability includes most of the principles previously defined [30], including comfort, affordance, and aesthetics. It is a key factor for the success of a device, in terms of user's engagement and satisfaction. "Dynamic wearability" occurs when the devices are worn with the body in motion [10].

For wearable technologies to be adopted and utilized continuously and in large scale, they must first gain acceptance from the intended users [28].

Nunez and Loke [31] question the transparency aspects of a wearable as dictated by ubiquitous computing and natural user interfaces. For them, the disappearance of self and technology seeking to achieve a transparent and skilful action "overlooks the potential of self-awareness as a critical resource for interactive experiences grounded in the body." If the technology and the user effectively disappear, the body and awareness of self are no longer the central points of interest in technology design [31].

4.3 Design Guidelines

Industry and academia have investigated extensively how to support and improve the user interaction with wrist-worn wearables. While companies such as Apple, Samsung, and Android proposed guidelines to aid designers in the definition of interfaces, the scientific literature reports work on prototyping, testing, and evaluating wearables for diverse purposes. Practical guidelines provide valuable help to address common design problems, preventing potential issues. Still, guidelines are also considered generic to serve specific purposes, and may have poor applicability depending on the device focus [5].

Guidelines from the scientific literature are often extracted from quantitative and qualitative evidence extracted from multiple user studies. Guidelines can be used by technology designers, application developers, and the research community when seeking to improve the design of novel wearable technologies [32]. Guidelines provide designers with a foundation upon which to begin their implementations and direct their design decisions. Equipped with the knowledge and insights from guidelines, designers need to select the guidelines that are effectively applicable to their context of use and the specific wearers' requirements [33]. Therefore, the guidelines presented next should be examined and appropriated in order to suit specific contexts of use as well as specific user's needs. When applying the guidelines, designers need to weigh the costs and benefits associated to them to select those that appropriately meet the users' requirements and fit into their contexts of use [33].

4.3.1 Industrial Guidelines

Companies that commercialize wrist-worn wearables, such as Apple, Samsung, and Android, provide sets of design guidelines to support the development of novel applications for the wearable devices that they commercialize. Such design guidelines are beneficial to support the creation of wearable applications, ensuring they comply with design standards for user interface and interaction. Still, design guidelines may be vague to suit different application domains, besides also serving mainly the company goals. By no means, such guidelines replace iterative evaluation with actual users. Lastly, little is known about their specification process.

Apple guidelines have been released to support the design of interfaces for the Apple Watch [34]. These guidelines focus on three specific topics: personal, holistic, and lightweight interaction. They concern, respectively, personal communications of the individual user, edge-to-edge UI design (to optimize the use of the screen space), and quick interactions. Ten UI elements are covered, including images, tables, and sliders, and also instructions about how to set icons and images are provided. The design process for the Apple Watch applications focuses on three main principles: simplicity, ease of use, and consistency.

Samsung provides user interface design guidelines for gear applications [35]. The guidelines include design principles, interaction, notifications, navigation, styles, and accessibility. They aim at minimal user input through natural and simple interaction approaches. The personalization, context-sensitiveness, and accessibility of the applications are also emphasized. Fifteen UI elements are covered, including header, bar, badge, button, grid, pop-ups, and list.

Android provides guidelines for wearable designers to create their own applications for wrist-worn devices that are commercially available. These guidelines focus on customized user interfaces, notifications, and watch faces [36]. Best practices for interaction are provided, for instance, regarding the design of solutions for effective navigation and user interfaces. Such practices cover responsive design, customized views, accessibility, and user input with control through touch gestures.

Industrial guidelines are effective to help designers throughout a design process, indicating how to design better interfaces. However, they are generic, serving high level purposes. They are neither exhaustive nor replace final evaluations with end users. In practice, little is known about their specification process, methods employed, target audience, and validation approaches. Hence, in addition to applying design guidelines, a thorough involvement of end users in the design and evaluation process is recommended to ensure applications that suit well their actual needs.

4.3.2 Scientific Research

Industrial guidelines for wearable systems are often generic, serving multiple platforms, user groups, or application domains. Guidelines from scientific research, on the other hand, tend to be more specific than industrial ones, aiming at a specific form factor or a unique interaction modality. Siewiorek [37] defines eight golden rules for wearable design regardless of form factor, including [37]

1. Avoid changing wearers' inherent behaviors due to the size, weight, and energy consumption of the technology.
2. Provide rapid responses.
3. Ensure systems are intuitive without requiring user manual.
4. Avoid information overload, in which a user may focus on the technology rather than the physical world.
5. Balance between wearer control and automation to avoid risks when the user looses initiative and follows technology instructions blindly.
6. Fit the system into existing procedures and current logistics.
7. Be aware of environmental influences and their impact on the system.
8. Optimize power consumption.

In the design of wearables, guidelines focus on wearability, which is defined according to the physical shape of a wearable technology in what regards its active relationship with the human form [38]. For Gemperle [10], the design of a wearable computer involves a great deal of compromise, which is both inherent and inevitable when one integrates human users and human–computer interaction with the constraints related to the technology and its context of use [10].

For gesture interaction and input entry, Zucco and Thomas [33] evaluated pointing devices commercially available. They conducted three comparative user studies, focusing on the devices' effectiveness for traditional computing tasks such as drag and drop, and menu selection tasks. Users were wearing a computer and a head-worn binocular display as well. From the qualitative and quantitative findings of these studies, the authors derived design guidelines and recommendations to provide guidance when designing pointing devices suitable for use with wearable computing systems [33].

The 15 design guidelines for gesture-based input entry and cursor control, proposed by Zucco and Thomas [33], are defined in Table 4.1.

Table 4.1 15 design recommendations and guidelines for input entry and cursor control by Zucco and Thomas [33]

Guideline 1	Allow or encourage interaction in a range of natural positions. Promote natural placement, comfortable to hold or to attach
Guideline 2	Ensure cursor stability while mobile. Movement of device should not cause unwanted interaction
Guideline 3	Minimize body movement required to manipulate the cursor
Guideline 4	Button presses should be easy and intuitive. Buttons should be suitably spaced to prevent accidental button presses. Avoid positioning buttons where the device is attached or contacts with the hand.
Guideline 5	Avoid the interplay between button press and cursor movement.
Guideline 6	Provide simple interactions to achieve complex functionality
Guideline 7	Encourage single handed use if appropriate Consider the effect of arm movements caused by use in motion (two handed use)
Guideline 8	Ensure the device can be stably attached to the user body or held in the hand Avoid the use of the other hand to stabilize the device
Guideline 9	Facilitate quick access and grasp time for a handheld device
Guideline 10	Promote unobtrusive pointing device with subtle use
Guideline 11	Ensure a compact size and lightweight device
Guideline 12	Encourage eyes-free interaction with simple design, operation, and functionality
Guideline 13	Provide a wireless pointing device
Guideline 14	Avoid the use of accelerometers for cursor control if mobile (e.g., users walking)
Guideline 15	Choose user interface components that suit coarse mouse movements

Concerning wrist-worn wearables specifically, differences exist in their form factors, designs, and functionalities. Bracelets and armbands are employed mostly for activity tracking while watches are frequently used as personal computers as well. Despite such heterogeneity, most research on wrist-worn wearables focuses on the design of smartwatches. More specifically, Rekimoto [39] focused on gesture recognition of hand and forearm movements to support the user interaction in office settings [39]. Angelini et al. [11] focused on the design of a smart bracelet for older adults serving as a personal assistant [11]. Oakley and Lee [40] investigated tactile interaction (touch) in alternative placements of the watch with the EdgeTouch prototype [40]. Xu and Lyons [41] explored the design space of smartwatches, using mainly visual notifications (light icons) for messaging, calls, calendar, and timer [41].

Ashbrook [42] focused on the design of micro interactions and gesture recognition [42]. Houben and Marquardt [43] provided a toolkit for prototyping smartwatch applications [43]. The toolkit focuses on cross-device interaction, defining an input space for smartwatches. This space consists of (i) *on* the watch interaction, when direct interaction with physical contact takes place; (ii) *above* the watch interaction, when gestures are performed in the tri-dimensional space above the watch; and (iii) *internal* sensing interaction, when sensors passively collect user's input data.

Aiming to enhance the wearability of a device, concerning its quality factors, a number of improvements can be considered:

1. **Concealing**. If a device results to be *embarrassing* for end users to wear, it should be made less conspicuous, and more discreet, for example, by reducing the size of the device, obscuring it from view of bystanders, or hiding it underneath clothing. Eventually, reducing the embarrassment factor will occur naturally as more people begin to use a device, and adoption rates increase, novel technologies become everyday clothing items.

2. **Familiarization**. If a wearer is *anxious* to use a technology, this can indicate discomfort related to safety, reliability, or insecurity. Reducing anxiety may involve a greater understanding of the device, mainly because the lack of knowledge makes novice users fear the unknown. Emotion and anxiety may be also improved with time and experience as the wearer becomes more used to the device.

Because certain devices are better suited to specific task(s) and mobility condition(s), guidelines are often specific as well, depending on the interaction modality or context of use.

For **gesture** recognition, specifically in EOG goggles with eye tracking, only large movements in the horizontal, vertical, and diagonal directions can be accurately classified. Gestures with smaller scales are more difficult to detect reliably. By optimizing the electrode placement and mounting, or by designing HCI interfaces which rely mainly on eye gestures executed on the horizontal axis, or with larger vertical eye movements, this limitation may be solved [44].

Joanne Zucco and her colleagues conducted two experiments with four commercially available input devices: a trackball, a touchpad, a gyroscopic mouse, and a Twiddler mouse. Study participants performed drag-and-drop tasks while wearing a head-mounted display and the investigators collected and assessed the time to complete a task, the task error rate, and the users' impressions about ease of use. In the first experiment, the users were stationary; in the second, they were walking. The effectiveness of the input device depends on whether the user will be stationary or moving, i.e., the gyroscopic mouse was the most effective device for stationary tasks but the least effective for walking tasks [45].

More specifically, for selection, a gyroscopic mouse is the fastest input approach, for drag-and-drop tasks, the gyroscopic mouse is not only the fastest but also the most accurate device while users remain stationary. Drag-and-drop operations are more complex than target selection, thus the interaction guidelines for drag and drop also apply for selection. The gyroscopic mouse is a suitable choice when both interaction models (selection and drag and drop) are required, and the wearer remains stationary when using the device. Conversely, when precise menu selection is needed, such as the steering necessary for a linear pop-up menu, the gyroscopic mouse is a less suitable choice. The gyroscopic mouse seems to favor coarse mouse movements and may be a suitable choice if used in conjunction with interface objects that allow for larger mouse movements [33].

For **vibrotactile** displays, the implications for design include (1) applying an even and adequate force to the stimulators; (2) respecting the curvature of the body and avoiding excessive weight; (3) considering wearer perception of distinct activation areas by ensuring the best possible contact with the body, even when additional garment layers are between the stimulator and the wearer skin; (4) design for optimal fit, to ensure perception of active motors; (5) make sure the wearer distinguishes the stimulated region by limiting the number of stimuli, ensuring close proximity to the wearer skin, and setting the magnitude of the vibration to noticeable levels [46].

For contexts of use where users are *running*, problems faced during the interaction with wearables are related to users' comfort, ease of use, familiarity, and interference with human motion [47].

- **Comfort**: concerns the device placement, fit, size, weight, stability, and how practical the device is to wear (fastening it, carrying it, attaching it to clothing, among others);
- **Ease of use**: refers to how easy it is for wearers to access information that is available in their field of view concerning mainly graphic or visual displays, also concerns how simple it is for wearers to provide input entries in input fields and their design in terms of size, affordances, and access options, and lastly, it refers to how fast the user interaction is, regarding both the responsiveness of the device and the interaction steps required; in practice, runners' complaints may involve input fields, e.g., "The targeting was difficult on the small input field of the smartglasses", whereas their compliments can refer to the accessibility of the technology, for example, "the watch was easy to reach and to move into the view field";
- **Familiarity**: includes references to previous user experiences, and how wearers are used to similar devices, and their interaction techniques, expressed through comments such as "Familiar use. I always run with my watch.";
- **Interference**: is related to additional movement required from wearers and their effects on the users' movements and their running rhythm; it also refers to challenges in handling the device, as well as visual, motor, or mental distractions, including comments such as: "I needed to interdigitate my arms so that the interaction broke my rhythm."

Usability guidelines facilitate the device implementation for manufacturers, researchers, and application developers as well. For *older adults* using wrist-worn wearables, such guidelines include improvements in hardware and software, regarding user interfaces and interaction design [48].

- **Enhancing Usability for Hardware**: focuses on the physical aspects of the technology as well as the connectivity and displays for output, specifically seeking to:
  - **Allow for Configure-to-Order (CTO) Products**: Aiming to reduce usability issues related to device and screen size, technology designers should ensure both are sized appropriately for the needs of older adults. Designers should consider CTO products with wide device and screen size measurement and shape variations, depending on individual preferences.

- **Consider Maximum Magnitude of Effect for Minimal Means**: Hardware design of smartwatches and pedometers should be comfortable to the body, ensuring wearability and improving the aesthetic experience of older adult users with minimalist and optimized designs. Removing unwanted hardware, such as the near-field communication (NFC) and radio frequency (RF) chips handling calls and texts, reduces the shape, size, and weight of smartwatches and pedometers enabling them to become lighter and more comfortable for end users.
- **Improve Sensor Precision**: Older adults may have difficulties trusting the reliability of notified sleep analysis data, such as wake after sleep onset (WASO), sleep efficiency (SE), and total sleep time (TST) with current smartwatches and pedometers. Therefore, technology designers and researchers should consider alternative techniques to improve notifications of sleep analysis data, for instance, by (i) identifying sleep stages: awake, light sleep, deep sleep, and rapid eye movement (REM); (ii) measuring skin temperature, light, and activity across days to detect internal circadian rhythms; (iii) capturing entire body movements, rather than focusing on one specific body part; and (iv) detecting the complete set of motion-related parameters.
- **Consider Culture when Designing the Devices**: Cultural norms influence how users perceive wearable technologies, for example, Finnish users place more importance on device and screen size than their U.S. counterparts. Designers should thus identify and address cross-cultural design requirements.

- **Enhancing Usability for User Interfaces (UIs)**: Older adults indicate that the user interfaces of devices, including characteristics such as typography, button location, and interaction techniques, affect their daily usage. Age, disabilities, and environmental context certainly influence the user experience.

    - **Consider Alternative UIs**: Interface manipulation contributes to positive user experiences, and one basic approach to improve the usability of technology consists in considering alternative user interfaces (AUI). User personalization should be supported for older adults. For example, calibrating the UI for the user age and any impairments in its first usage would allow devices to personalize the typographical variables automatically, modifying: font size, font color, and background color. Such changes reduce the demands placed on user accommodation (the eye's ability to change its optical power for a better focus) and vergence (eye movements to focus on near and far objects) [48].

4.4 Interaction Paradigms

When designing wearable technologies, it is essential to consider the user's information in addition to the users' work spaces. "The wearable computer must blend seamlessly with existing work environments, providing as little distraction as possible." Such a requirement replaces the conventional interaction paradigm from desktop computers, in which there is a fixed physical relationship between the user and the devices such as a keyboard and mouse [7].

4.4.1 Wrist-Worn Interaction

Despite its inherent challenges, the interaction with wearables, including wrist-worn devices, brings a number of benefits to end users. These devices are continuously collecting data about the users and their surroundings, raising awareness about daily habits, physical activity levels, and routines. Wearables also empower users with information that previously could not be easily collected and visualized. While self-reporting is time-consuming, and prone to human error (due to confusion or forgetfulness), data collection through wearables occurs pervasively, passively, and discreetly. The proximity of the device to the human body and continuous usage enable wrist-worn wearables to recognize users' activities and locations in a more comprehensive way [49].

Among several wearable devices, the wristwatch stands out as a piece of technology that is well understood by the population at large and that has gained an increasing interest in the wearable computing field as an interactive platform [42]. The wrist has proved to be an excellent location to place devices that need to be accessed quickly [42, 49], as just by glancing their eyes in their wrist, users can be notified about information of interest. A light blink, a beep, or a quick vibration can be noticeable and effective to quickly communicate information to end users, even when the device is located in the peripheral view of the user.

Although wrist-worn wearables provide several benefits for their users, designing their interfaces and interactive solutions is still challenging. Several reasons contribute to that, among which we can highlight: (i) the complexity of the UI must be properly simplified to fit to the constraints of the device; (ii) the amount, extent, and frequency of the interruptions must be optimized, context-sensitive, and minimalist; (iii) the activation of functionalities must be precise to avoid accidental inputs; and (iv) the data collection must be accurate, to prevent ambiguous recognition and interpretation of users' gestures.

Two common problems faced by wrist-worn users during their interaction and by UI designers during the development phases consist of fat fingers and midas gesture. As defined in [50], the former concerns the occlusion of the UI contents by the user finger during interaction, and the later concerns an accidental input, when the user triggers an unintended action.

For the design of interaction and evaluation purposes, it is worthy noting that wearers may be either left- or right-handed, which impacts the way they interact with a watch interface [51]. Such individual differences are important, and require proper accommodations in the design, evaluation, and deployment of a wrist-worn wearable.

Despite the benefits and increasing functionality of wrist-worn technologies, the academic work focused on wristwatch interfaces has had a narrow scope, being mainly limited to tackle either input or output methods, often concerning one unique modality or input/output approach. Open questions remain, especially regarding: how to create a usable interface on the wrist? [42], and how to create suitable interaction algorithms and UI patterns that optimize precision in small screen and low-resource contexts? [49].

4.4.2 Wrist-Worn Interaction Paradigm

When designing smartwatches, fitness trackers, and pedometers, technology designers must carefully consider the usage environment and wearability factors to ensure users' adoption and lead them toward more positive opinions and attitudes concerning their intention to use the device [32].

Two major obstacles emerge in the design of interactive solutions for wrist-worn wearables. The first concerns the physical limitations of wrist-worn devices, as those significantly reduce the interactive surfaces available for providing feedback and displaying output responses to end users. The second concerns the contexts of use in which the wrist-worn interaction takes place, as those impose important constraints to the user interaction, including, for instance, the task completion time, the resources used, and the choice on interaction modality for input entry and output response.

To address these two major obstacles, two interaction paradigms emerge: microinteractions and multidimensional graphical user interfaces [50]. These paradigms facilitate the design of and the user interaction with wrist-worn wearables seeking to overcome major design limitations in this field.

Microinteractions consist in user actions devoted to provide an input entry or to receive an output response. These actions compose the communication interface between end users and wearable devices. They are feasible regardless of application domain, purpose, and interaction modality; however, they are characterized by a really short life span: less than 4 s [42] and few requirements regarding users' attention levels (glanceability), cognitive load, user efforts, system processing, memory usage, and battery consumption. Microinteractions are the building blocks that enable a successful communication flow between users and wearables.

Multidimensional graphical user interfaces, as Fig. 4.1 illustrates, overcome the physical limitations of a wrist-worn display, by presenting users with a window of content at a time, which is extracted from an interaction continuum. The graphical user interfaces are connected through conventional logical sequences and navigated through three-dimensional linear schemes. Logical sequences can include data items sorted by name, relevance, or frequency of usage. The linear schemes can be contin-

Fig. 4.1 Multidimensional interfaces are structured in three axes, (x, y, and z), expanding the design space of wrist-worn devices with graphic displays. For touch-based interaction, wearers navigate horizontally by swiping (left or right) the screen and vertically by scrolling (up or down)

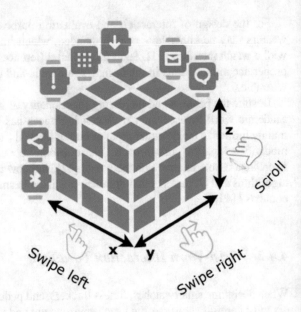

uum, by providing wearers with a circular list of options. Because just a single portion of the interface is rendered in the screen at a given time, the UI is no longer limited by the physical constraints of the device display. The microinteraction paradigm also takes into account restrictions of a brief time frame for completion (less than 3 s), low attention levels, and cognitive requirements from users during their interaction.

Microinteractions

Microinteractions occur when users are able to complete their tasks (e.g., access information, respond to an action, or receive a notification) in a short period of time, which lasts less than 3 s. The task completion has low demand of the wearer cognition, effort, and attention.

Microinteractions still enable users to complete their interaction goals; however, they simplify the main task of the user, breaking it in smaller chunks that maintain only essential UI elements in a minimalist layout that is not only simple but intuitive as well. Microinteractions enable the completion of both user input (with an entry command) and system output (with a feedback response) in different modalities.

Table 4.2 defines a taxonomy of categories for potential microinteractions in a wrist-worn wearable, based on [50]. The nature of the microinteractions depends on the system requirements, whereas their modalities depend on the device resources, especially the sensors and actuators available in the device, and the contexts of use where the user interaction occurs. The user profile and potential impairments also influence the choice of interaction approach.

Common examples of microinteraction in a wrist-worn wearable include, for output responses from the user interface and system: displaying the date, time, weather, an incoming call, number of steps, and heart rate; for output feedback from the

Table 4.2 Taxonomy of 20 microinteractions for users interacting with wrist-worn devices, including four different modalities: audio, graphics, gestures, and vibrotactile [50]

Audio	Beeps
Graphics	Blink, light, display
Gestures	
1D	Tap, touch, hold, press, release
2D	Slide, swipe, pinch, scroll
3D	Move, act
Vibrotactile	
Haptic	Drag, drop, slide, touch, press
Vibration	Buzz

device: lights blinking, beep, buzz; for input entry from user: press of a button, tap the device, slide gesture, a wrist movement (such as rotation, shake, and knock). The output responses from the system are often supported by a graphical user interface. To define these interfaces and the navigation flow between them, a second paradigm has been defined [50].

Multidimensional User Interfaces (MUIs)

The physical constraints inherent to wrist-worn graphical displays demand for user interfaces that contain only essential contents to end users, employing a simplified, manageable, and minimalist approach. To be able to convey information and meet these requirements, the set of graphical user interfaces must be organized to present an information piece at a time, preferably focusing either on content, or on navigation control items, in small chunks. This approach seeks to avoid overloading the cognitive capabilities and attention levels of end users. It also seeks to enhance the readability of the GUI and to enable the user microinteraction to be completed within a 3 s long time window.

To employ such paradigm, the user interfaces must be designed as part of a three-axes interaction continuum. In an example of a wrist-worn device with a squared (or rectangular) display, three representation axes are the most intuitive for navigation: two horizontal (x,y) and a vertical one (y). The information presented in the user interface at a given moment should explore the concept of an infinite axis (interaction continuum) in which the information is presented sequentially, following the linearity of the axis to connect subtasks in a sequence, enabling wearers to complete their main interaction goals, such as checking the time, date, heart rate, number of steps, battery levels, sharing information, and reading an alert.

Figure 4.1 illustrates a graphic scheme of the multidimensional interaction paradigm. Across graphical user interfaces, users can navigate in three directions, along the horizontal (x,y) or vertical (y) axes. The horizontal axis provides users with the main interaction features of the device (e.g., checking notification messages and the device status, home, settings, activity data) and the vertical axis provides subtasks or more details about each of the main features, as well as navigation controls, such as sharing options. In this paradigm, the output contents are mainly presented by means of a GUI; however, the input command to navigate through the UIs can be given in any modality (e.g., touch, gesture, button press, dial turn). In a touch-based interactive screen, the horizontal navigation is given by user gestures of swiping either left or right, whereas the vertical navigation requires scrolling the user interface either up or down.

The infinite continuum provides designers flexibility to create user interfaces according to the number of features available in the wrist-worn device and system requirements (e.g., amount of data, level of tasks). The number of UIs and navigation path between them is decided based on the requirements of the system as well as on the functionalities that the device provides. This choice gives flexibility for designers to build their interaction space according to their needs.

Still, to fully exploit such flexibility, the interfaces must be organized and structured in a logical way, consistent to the wearer mental models, and striving to avoid high complexity levels in the user interaction. Larger dimensions of the design space will naturally lead to higher complexity in the interaction which can consequently make users loose track of their interaction paths in a virtual hyperspace. This approach also enables designers to provide circular navigation paths, in an infinite continuum, along the x- and y-axes with main features or along the z-axis with more detailed features and navigation controls.

4.4.3 Head-Mounted Devices

Interaction paradigms like multidimensional user interfaces are also well suited for head-mounted devices, including the examples of devices presented in Fig. 4.2, and regardless of the interface modality used for output—be it graphic (for virtual reality headsets) or auditory (for earpieces and headphones). For augmented reality glasses, such as Google Glass, the input entry commands given by end users consisted of a horizontal swipe in a touchpad (to the left or right direction) or voice commands issued to a microphone, also positioned along the arms of the device frame [52].

For audio feedback, when multiple audio sources of different positions are combined in a circular space surrounding the user, he or she may use head gestures for input selection, controlling the interaction process [17]. 3D auditory radial pie menus (also named as egocentric sounds) instantiate the multidimensional user interface paradigm by placing the user's head in the middle of the "pie" (or Bullseye) and presenting sounds or speech for menu items structured in a plane around the wearer head. In this context, the users' nod gestures in the direction of the sounds correspond to a selection of items according to the sounds of user choice [17].

For design of interaction and evaluation purposes, it is worthy noting that wearers may need to wear glasses or contact lens during interaction. Some users may be able to use the head-mounted displays without any optical support [51]. If that is not an

Fig. 4.2 Head-mounted
devices vary from virtual
reality displays that immerse
users in a
computer-generated
environment, augmented
reality glasses that project
information on the user's
view to enhance it, and
headsets and earpieces used
mostly for audio feedback

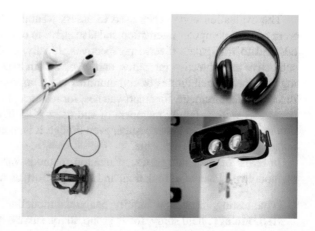

option, the device must be calibrated to accommodate the visualization according to
potential visual impairments users may have.

4.5   Evaluation Approaches

Once a version of technology, including an interface or interaction component, is
designed and implemented, the stakeholders focus on evaluating its wearability and
usability with end users. The evaluation process verifies, whether or not the implementation as well as the changes incorporated are useful and usable in theory and in
practice [5]. Usually, the evaluation with end users is preceded by tests and benchmark
assessments to ensure that the device, its applications, and functionality are suffi-
ciently operational to be assessed by end users. Tests can be manual, when executed
entirely by humans or automated, for instance, using simulations and scripts. A combination of both approaches leads to more comprehensive results, since automated
and manual methods are complementary. In an example of automated evaluation, to
assess the sustainability of a wearable bracelet, MATLAB simulations were used.
In those, the investigators explored various interaction scenarios, and used a set of
diverse measurements to analyze power consumption and energy harvested [53].

Investing time and resources to complement automated evaluation with user
research is critical, even when short periods of time can be dedicated to it. The
evaluation with end users helps to find a solution that properly matches users' needs.
In this process, the choice of methodology, data analysis, and approach to communicate findings is essential to report the ideas and find a consensus among end users
and stakeholders, including interaction designers and product designers, marketers,
senior officers, and venture capital shareholders in case of companies. User studies
inform decision-making regarding the form and features of a wearable technology
[38].

The evaluation approaches used to assess wearable technologies are inherited from human–computer interaction and also strive to combine complementary methods and to triangulate diverse perspectives. Ideally, evaluation methods combine subjective and objective measures, and involve both experts and end users, including also their social circles or communities when appropriate. In an assessment of functional requirements for smartwatches, for instance, Dibia et al. [54] interviewed parents as well as family members of end users [54]. The triangulation of evaluation methods leads to better results, even though it is more costly, concerning time, budget, and personnel available.

In terms of their categories, evaluation methods vary according to their type, methodology, level of automation, and human effort, as follows [32]:

Type: testing, inspection, inquiry, analytical modeling, and simulation;
Methodology: field study, focus group, diary, survey, and observation;
Level of automation and effort: automated, manual, or hybrid.

Focus groups, diaries, or surveys are considered to be inquiry methods [32]. When using diaries, study participants take regular notes about their events, expressing their thoughts, feelings, and behaviors using their own words [32]. Although diary studies are more time-consuming than surveys, they yield results that could not be gathered with surveys, observations, or even focus groups.

In terms of planning, evaluation often begins with IRB approval, followed by pilot studies, the recruitment of participants, debriefing session, task execution, assessment, data collection, analysis, and dissemination. Depending on the findings of the evaluation, the technology is iteratively redesigned to address issues encountered, improve its quality levels, and refine it until an acceptable version is achieved. Guidelines, design implications, and principles can also be derived from this iterative evaluation approach [47].

In terms of experimental design and the planning of evaluation methods and study protocols, evaluation sessions may be driven by predefined hypotheses. Coca et al. [55], when assessing wearable sensors for firefighters, hypothesized that (a) the data collected with a wearable plethysmographic sensor vest would not be significantly different from the data obtained from the standard physiological monitoring equipment, and (b) the data on respiratory rates (RRs) and tidal volume (VT) could be used to accurately derive ventilation (VE) during exercises while users are wearing the firefighter ensemble [55].

Evaluation should begin in early design phases, thus even if a device is not fully operational, certain aspects of the technology can be already subject to preliminary evaluation. Weller et al. [51] asked participants to simply wear a wrist-mounted keyboard during the tests to assess its comfort and acceptability, focusing on physical aspects. The keyboard was worn on the left wrist, although it was also possible to wear it on the right wrist. For the experiment, there were no requirements given for participants concerning data entry [51].

Control groups allow for performance assessments and comparisons. For instance, asking ten participants to perform three tasks with the wearable device and comparing the group performance with a control group of other ten participants who performed the same tasks with traditional approaches [56]. In another study, the effects of a calming armband were assessed by comparing two user groups. In the experimental group, wearers used the device activated and in the control group, the device was turned off. The study participants were randomly assigned to each group prior to the study [57].

To gather initial users' insights and feedback early in the design process, interviews are well suited. High fidelity prototypes, on the other hand, allow for field studies and to gather more consolidated feedback. Also, interviews after the user has experience interacting with the technology can help to elicit information about comfort. After a wearable art installation, for instance, Nunez and Loke [31] interviewed participants and identified that "four out of nine participants expressed that the weight of the equipment was somehow uncomfortable for them" [31]. Cultural probes and log analysis of the application enable to gain knowledge on the user experience during interaction, as well as how technology impacts users on everyday life activities [58]. Besides facilitating the assessment of wearable devices, usability studies also enable the comparison of the user experience across technologies [33].

Concerning the duration of an evaluation study, familiarization needs to be considered, as well as potential biases related to participants' attention levels, fatigue, and distraction. There is an effect on the user performance at the very beginning of the session, as the participant gets used to the system, in comparison with his or her performance half way through the tests, when his or her concentration levels can deteriorate. Also, in the second half of and toward the end of the session, study participants become more tired and begin to loose focus [51].

In terms of generalizability, ecological or external validity, the findings and results from evaluation studies ideally should extrapolate beyond the sample of individuals or subjects who participated in the assessment, to also match the needs, requirements, wishes, profiles, and preferences of the same population from which the sample was recruited, or to represent other similar populations in terms of contexts [32].

4.5.1 Categories of Evaluation

Evaluation methods vary largely depending on their goals, purposes, stage of development of the technology, target audience, available time, budget constraints, location of the experiment, contexts of use in which the technology will be employed, among others. In general, the procedure followed for evaluation experiments includes preparation, warm-up, baseline, main study, and debriefing [47].

Evaluation approaches can be summative or formative, depending on *when* and *how often* they occur, and qualitative or quantitative, depending on the nature of the data collected. In an evaluation experiment involving runners and three form factors, to assess the user interaction and preferences, investigators combined several measurements, including questionnaires with open questions, analyzed qualitatively for content and sentiment, as well as numeric scales, analyzed quantitatively for orders of ranking regarding device preference [47]. Khakurel (2018) also combined multiple approaches, employing usability evaluation, where data were collected through a survey, observations collected in a think-aloud session, and information gathered from diaries to assess the users' perceptions on self-tracking wearable technologies [32].

1. **Frequency of Evaluation**: Concerning the *frequency* of evaluation, the methods can be **formative** or **summative**. Methods such as usability testing, inspection, and inquiry are suitable for both types of evaluation, but some approaches are more suitable for specific implementation stages [32]. Formative and summative methods are defined as follows:

   a. **Formative**
   Formative evaluations are conducted throughout the implementation process, to collect feedback that will shape and inform the design decisions before the technology is ready for deployment. Such an approach helps to detect whether the device is comfortable or intrusive, without overloading users by seeing and imagining the full functionality of the device [38]. Although there are limitations in the technology, wearers should be made aware of those and focus on quality factors that are actually possible to evaluate without having the fully functional, consolidated version of the device ready for deployment. The quality criteria to be selected for evaluation depend on the stage of implementation, they can include aesthetics, weight, comfort, and ergonomics.

   b. **Summative**
   Summative evaluations are conducted in the end of the evaluation process, once the prototype is fully implemented. Such evaluations aim at gathering end users opinion about the effectiveness of the device and usefulness of the application. Because the technology is fully functional, the wearer can interact with the device, assess it, and provide his/her opinion.

2. **Data Type:** Concerning the *type*, or nature, of data collected as well as its structure, the methods can be **qualitative** or **quantitative**, or **subjective** or **objective** defined as follows:

   a. **Qualitative**
   Qualitative assessment consists in asking wearers' opinions about the technology, without any numeric measurements associated. Qualitative evaluation relies on data that cannot be easily expressed in numbers, including data based on subjective opinions or participants' insights, verbal expressions of feelings, moods, or general descriptions of problems during interaction [5]. In qualitative research studies, the investigator is the main instrument for data collection, an agent of new interpretations, and a creator and source of new knowledge [32]. A pre-test questionnaire can gather qualitative data on participants' backgrounds, their general feelings and knowledge about IT and wearable computers [51]. There are usability scales that can be used to guide the evaluation criteria, for instance, asking users about their satisfaction level, acceptance, and usefulness of the technology. Although the qualitative measures are hard

for comparison purposes, they are informative in the design process, allowing wearers to contribute to the implementation of the technology with suggestions and recommendations that reflect their individual opinions and preferences.

b. **Quantitative**

Quantitative assessment involves collecting numeric values to be associated with absolute or relative metrics. Numeric measures include but are not limited to the time the user takes to complete a task (or set of tasks), the number of errors during an operation, the number of tasks completed in a given time to accomplish a goal, the number of steps required to complete a task or operation, and the number of attempts necessary to succeed in the task completion. Quantitative measurements can include also open questions to assess the users' demographics, opinions, and feelings [47]. The advantages of quantitative measures include allowing mathematical calculations and statistical analysis [5], and enabling comparisons, be those across participants, versions of the technology, study settings, contexts of use, or others. Quantitative measurements also include data from questionnaires, for instance, ratings or scores in a Likert scale that can be mapped to numerical values [5].

c. **Subjective**

Subjective assessments concern the perceived values that a technology has to the end user, similarly to qualitative measures, subjective assessment cannot be directly measured and require asking users about their opinions and preferences, for instance, regarding their levels of satisfaction, comfort, ease of use, usefulness, and so on.

d. **Objective**

Objective measures can be directly measured, be it through sensors that collect user data, or logs that record user interaction. Other objective approaches also allow for comparisons across groups of participants, device models, software versions, and diverse settings. The numeric values collected through objective assessment enable investigators to conduct statistical tests and to generate mathematical models from data analysis. Objective measures can be identified from prior work in the scientific literature, for instance, to measure gait stability, changes in running movements (magnitude and duration) [47], and log history [59].

3. **Participant Profile**: Concerning the *participant profile* for the evaluation, the methods can be applied involving either **end users** or **experts**, be those domain experts or wearability experts. Their roles are defined as follows:

a. **End users**

Evaluation with end users requires recruiting a representative sample of the target user population. Representativeness is achieved concerning the profile of the participants involved in the evaluation, concerning their gender, age, background, and ethnicity, among others. End user evaluation requires establishing and considering inclusion criteria to screen participants and invite them to assess the technology. The closer the participants' profiles are to actual end users' profiles, the more reliable the evaluation results will be, effectively reflecting the end users' opinions about the technology. Evaluation with users can be retrospective, if study participants already have experience interacting with and using the device, or prospective, if the study involves potential users. The number of participants recruited for evaluation will depend on the variables studied, method used for data collection and analysis, and size of the target population, among others [60]. While small sample sizes facilitate the recruitment of study participants and data collection, they also result in a low significance in the statistical analysis and can lead to inconclusive results that may not generalize for larger populations [61].

b. **Experts**

Evaluation with experts include stakeholders whose professional experience contributes to assess the technology. Potential experts are interaction designers, UX researchers, accessibility consultants, or even testers with expertise in a given domain of interest, such as health care or privacy. By involving domain experts or usability experts in an evaluation [5], the results obtained will complement the findings from the user evaluation; however, one methodology does not replace the other.

4. **Study Duration**: Concerning the *duration* of the evaluation, the methods can be considered as either **longitudinal** or **short term**. They are defined as follows:

a. **Longitudinal**

Long-term (or longitudinal) evaluation aims at understanding how time affects the usage of a device, helping to clarify whether users' feedback is influenced by novelty effects, and if wearers tend to sustain their engagement along time. Long-term evaluation also enables investigators to verify whether users reduce, increase, or expedite the usage of technology along time, or even if they abandon it after a certain period of time. Such evaluations help to investigate the learnability and the utility of the technology beyond the analysis from controlled studies constrained to lab settings. Longitudinal studies aid investigators to classify the interaction issues identified as short term, occasional, or long term [32].

b. **Short term**

Short-term studies are often carried out in a lab setting for a short period of time (e.g., 1 h). Such studies are the most common ones, due to their low cost and reduced efforts required to set up the space and to recruit users to participate in an evaluation session. Short-term studies aim at assessing mostly the feasibility of a technology, or a few factors under investigation. Still, the short-term nature of these experiments may jeopardize the validity of the results besides also making it difficult to extrapolate the research findings to long-term user interaction [62].

5. **Location**: Concerning the *location* where the evaluation is carried out, the methods can be considered as either **field** studies or **controlled settings**. These categories are defined as follows:

a. **Field**

Evaluation in the wild takes place in actual settings and aims at clarifying the impacts that different contexts of use have in the user interaction. Evaluation in the field assesses whether and how the light, noise, and user motion influence the interaction of the wearer with the technology. The specific locations of field studies vary depending on the device purpose, but can include a living room for virtual reality headsets, swimming pools for fitness trackers, and school settings [59], among others. When experimenting interaction modalities for a wearable that monitors swimmers, the choice of a public swimming pool for the evaluation sessions, allowed the investigators to assess the technology in real-world conditions [63].

b. **Controlled Settings**

Evaluation in controlled settings, like a usability laboratory, has the advantage of isolating external factors that may influence the user interaction with the technology. Also, they are suitable to assess the feasibility of devices, for users interacting with the wearable in stationary interaction scenarios [44], and to generate ground truth by annotating data collected in user study carried out in a stationary environment with a controlled stimulus [64]. Controlled studies are suitable for methods that require users to complete a set of tasks, and then capture the interaction process in an automated way, analyzing users' mental models, intentions, attitudes, behaviors, and interaction approaches, for instance, using a game to examine the use of explicit eye gestures for input control [44]. In a controlled setting, it becomes easier to instrument the user environment in a consistent way, for instance, using cameras and microphones, or a treadmill with optical motion capture technology[1] to analyze kinematics for a longer series of steps [47]. In controlled settings, it is easier to control for consistency in the environment across evaluation sessions (e.g., light and noise level, device position, wearer placement). Using a lab-based setting, investigators can rule out any external factors, such as obstacles, weather, bystanders, or uneven ground [47]. The drawback with controlled studies is related to ecological validity since the results obtained in constrained environments may not extrapolate to real-world scenarios. Quality criterion, such as annoyance and embarrassment will not necessarily apply when users are wearing the device alone, at home; however, they may experience such emotions in a populated room; the same applies for security, as wearers may not feel it in a controlled environment, but they may face it when running with the technology outdoors [6]. Lastly, short-term user studies in controlled settings may not accurately reflect long-term spontaneous wearable interaction in the wild [5].

As this section describes, several alternative methods are available to conduct the evaluation of wearable technologies, gather and combine perspectives from end users and experts as well. While investigators and stakeholders have the freedom to decide on a given experimental protocol and select evaluation criteria that best suit

---

[1] Optical motion capture technologies serve to track a number of retro-reflective markers which are placed on the participants' skin in an experimental setup.

a wearable, selecting existing scales and questionnaires is preferred to expedite the evaluation process. Among the scales available to assess wearables, two stand out: the Comfort Rating Scale, proposed by Knight et al. [1] and the Wearability Scale, proposed by Weller et al. [51]. These scales are defined as follows.

4.5.2   Comfort Rating Scale

To assess the level of comfort of the wearer using a technology, the comfort rating scale (CRS) was originally introduced by Knight et al. [1]. In the CRS, comfort is assessed over multiple dimensions, including emotional, perceptive, and physical components. For evaluation questionnaires, six items are recommended to be assessed using a 10-point Likert scale with semantic differential ranging from "strongly agree" to "strongly disagree" [18].

The CRS scale, listed in Table 4.3, is easy and rapid to apply, besides also enabling numeric comparisons across participants' groups, devices, versions of applications, and user experience throughout time. Numeric values gathered from CRS enable statistical analysis of the data collected, facilitating the interpretation of the participants' responses [6]. For Knight and Barber [6], the differences in the scores for the multiple comfort dimensions highlight differences among types of products [6]. Unlike prior studies, not all statements in the assessment questionnaire are negatively phrased, since this may bias the responses or prime participants' opinions. Ideally, the sentiment of the statements should be alternated to increase validity. Also, 10-point scales may be too wide as a range to ensure accurate responses from human subjects. Lastly, with an even range, participants do not have the option to select neutral choices if they are undecided.

Table 4.3 Six items of the comfort rating scale proposed by Knight et al. [1], adapted from [1]

Item	Statement
Emotion	I am worried about how I look when I am wearing this device. I feel tense or on edge because I am wearing the device
Attachment	I can feel the device on my body. I can feel the device moving
Harm	The device is causing me some harm. The device is painful to wear
Perceived change	Wearing the device makes me feel physically different. I feel strange wearing the device
Movement	The device affects the way I move. The device inhibits or restricts my movements
Anxiety	I do not feel secure wearing the device

4.5.3 Wearability Scale

Similarly to comfort levels, wearability is defined by several constructs. Such constructs are quality factors that affect the experience users have when wearing and interacting with a wearable device. It is up to the stakeholder to select criteria and requirements that suit best the domain of the application and the technology envisaged. More specifically, devices used by runners should be unobtrusive, whereas assistive wearables should strive for accessibility. The context of use and target user population help to inform design decisions and evaluation protocols.

Regardless of the criteria selected and the evaluation results, the technology is assessed according to its wearability levels. For Weller et al. [51], the wearability of a technology can be defined using a 5-point scale with semantic differential ranging from low and moderate, to large, very large, and extreme, as defined in Table 4.4 [51].

4.5.4 Examples of Evaluation

Demonstrating the feasibility of a wearable system should precede the conception of the design. When assessing the feasibility of a wearable support system, researchers need to demonstrate that users are able to perform tasks as effectively with the wearable as with traditional methods of working, if not more effectively. Investigators should also demonstrate that the technology addresses challenges existing in the work environment, considering, for instance, extremely loud noise, low visibility, or constrained physical spaces [56].

In a feasibility test to assess a wearable monitoring system that measures vital signs from children, an experiment was conducted with a 5-year-old participant. Wearing the device, body temperature and heart rate data were collected and monitored with the system proposed. For reference and comparison, the body temperature and heart rate of the study participant were also measured with a commercial medical device. The experiment was repeated 20 times and the results indicated that the error rates in the data collected were considered "acceptable" [65].

Table 4.4 5-point wearability scale proposed by Weller et al. [51], adapted from [51]

Level	Definition
Low	The system is wearable
Moderate	The system is wearable, but changes may be necessary, and further investigation is needed
Large	The system is wearable, but changes are advised
Very large	The system is not wearable, fatiguing, and very uncomfortable
Extreme	The system is not wearable, and potentially harmful

A similar experiment was carried out to verify the accuracy of data collected with wearable sensors. Investigators compared physiological data collected using a wearable plethysmographic sensor vest with standard laboratory physiological monitoring equipment. The study participants wore firefighting ensembles to help verifying how accurate the wearable plethysmographic sensor was [55].

In another experiment conducted to evaluate four wearable applications and to demonstrate how user testing helps quantifying the effectiveness of wearable systems, laboratory prototypes were used. For this experiment, investigators selected two metrics for assessment, namely, time on task and time/accuracy. The tests involved participants performing typical operations related to the user work, including troubleshooting and repairing operations on computing equipment [7].

To carry out individual user testing sessions, a wearable art installation was organized. In such installation, the wearable system projected colorful visualizations of heartbeat data on the wearer body to explicitly communicate intimate physiological data. During individual user testing sessions, nine participants were dressed with an undergarment equipped with the electronics. After their experience with the wearable systems, interviews were conducted to gather participants' feedback [31].

Seeking to refine the technology according to the participants' feedback, SensVest followed an iterative design and evaluation process. The shirt was refined with adjustments and modifications made to improve and finalize the product [1, 6].

To gather quick feedback on the perceived usability as well as the user attitudes toward the technology under evaluation, questionnaires are well suited [32]. In the evaluation of HealthGear, for example, in an experiment, the study participant wore the physiological sensor for one night at his or her home. First, the investigators met with each participant during 15 min to explain them how to use the system. Then, the participant borrowed the wearable hardware and wore it during one night. The system was returned the day after usage. In the end of the evaluation, participants were invited to fill in a second questionnaire, focused on rating the experience and the usability of the system [25].

In the evaluation of a body-area wearable system for military soldiers, Tharion et al. [14] provided study participants with a questionnaire. The questions concerned assessing the comfort of the device, its physical impact on the body, and acceptability. Additional questions concerned the fit of the technology, its impact on users' performance, and the durability of the system [14].

In the context of a wearable health monitoring system for kids, to elicit requirements of the potential users, Jalaliniya and Pederson (2014) employed an online survey colleting responses from 21 parents. The investigators also interviewed a medical doctor and discussed the idea of the wearable system proposed. The survey responses informed the design of the wearable system by indicating that most respondents found alert systems useful, and preferred to be informed by receiving an SMS or an e-mail from the system rather than seeing real-time information on a web page [65].

In the evaluation of a wearable master device, two experiments were carried out with an upper garment. The goal of the first experiment was for the participant to move a cursor to five target points. The goal of the second experiment was to use the device to control a mobile robot. The mapping function of the sensor data to the shoulder motions was controlled by an artificial neural network. Both experiments began with calibration so that when participants moved their right shoulders up, down, forward, or backward, the cursor (in the experiment one) or the robot (in the experiment two) moved forward or backward, or turned left or right, using four directions [66].

In the evaluation of EOG for eye tracking, five electrodes were placed on the participant's face for 45 min. Two horizontal EOG electrodes were placed on both temples, two vertical ones were placed above and below the left eye, and a reference electrode was placed on the top-center of the participant's forehead. Prior to the experiment, each participant received an explanation about the stimulus. The lighting in the room was dimmed and participants were instructed to neither talk nor smile during the study to minimize artifacts in the EOG signals. The eye tracker was attached to the participant's head, followed by the cap with the inertial measurement unit attached on top. The study began with a 9-point calibration procedure for the EOG. Besides the data logged from the devices, a questionnaire was employed for feedback after each experiment session [64].

In the evaluation of three form factors to assess the user interaction during running, a set of interactive tasks were simulated. After an audio signal, participants performed a swipe gesture on the device to request a symbol that was then shown on the device's display. A swipe gesture was available on all three devices: a watch, a glass, and a phone. The task also required observing and remembering the symbols presented to ensure that the participants paid attention to the display [47].

When using questionnaires to assess the user experience, investigators can combine validated questionnaires with customized questionnaires. For instance, the NASA TLX (Task Load Index) can be complemented with customized questions about participants' general fitness levels and health conditions, their running habits, and previous experiences with devices already used. A questionnaire can also invite participants to rank multiple devices based on their personal preference for usage in an experiment or while running [47].

Questionnaires serve to gather qualitative as well as quantitative data from participants, besides also allowing investigators to collect prospective and retrospective opinions of end users. For instance, to assess the wearability of a system for urgent care and gather information on the participants' impressions about the given system, a post-test was employed. The post-test was delivered to participants as a questionnaire structured in three parts and applied after the participants had already used the system. The first part of the questionnaire examined the energy cost, comfort, and visual fatigue of participants. The second part was based on the rapid entire body assessment (REBA) test and an additional measure of the wearability of the system, which was calculated based on the method proposed by Knight et al. [15]. The third part of the questionnaire focused on qualitative data, representing the general information about the participants' feelings after they evaluated the system. The data gathered with the questionnaire concerned the usability and acceptability aspects of the technology in an intensive care unit (ICU) [51]. Seven questions were asked to participants to assess these aspects, as listed on Table 4.5.

Table 4.5 Seven examples of questions to gather data about the usability and acceptability aspects of a wearable system in an ICU (intensive care unit) context, adapted from [51]

Questions	
1.	What is your general impression of the wearable computer?
2.	Do you find it useful for clinical work?
3.	What do you like about the equipment?
4.	What do you dislike about the equipment?
5.	Do you have any suggestions for improving the efficiency, usability, and wearability of the equipment?
6.	Did you feel ill during the tests?
7.	Do you find the level of concentration during the tests adequate considering the level of attention required during work in the unit?

In addition to questionnaires, phone interviews also help to understand users to construct preliminary profiles about them, to prepare a data-gathering team, and to inspire the development team before data gathering occurs [38]. Interviews consist of detailed, one-on-one conversations that follow a predefined protocol. By focusing on specific themes, such as potential drivers and barriers for user adoption, qualitative interviews are useful for thematic, rather than specific, guidance. Overall, the direct feedback from a target user population gathered through an interview helps stakeholders to decide on the design of a wearable, to assess users' reactions to physical prototypes, and to identify the ideas of a target audience [38]. Interviews with prospective users aid to understand their preferences for wearable technologies [54].

Interviews can be conducted asynchronously as well, by the exchange of e-mails between the researcher and the interviewee. To ensure more flexibility than paper surveys offer, semi-structured interviews enable both the researcher and the interviewee to ask for additional clarifications [67].

Other methods that allow investigators to better understand the mental models of end users are the think-aloud [32] and participatory design sessions [38]. The latter allows study participants to co-design the technology, while the former clarifies the rationale of end users during their interaction. Both methods inform design decisions during the creation process. While think-aloud sessions usually last less than 1 h, participatory design sessions can run for a few hours, and are structured in parts. The parts include introduction, discussions of self-documentation and products (meant to understand participants' lifestyle), interactions with prototypes (meant to understand desired functionality), and wrap-up. By videotaping the session and documenting the user interacting with a prototype, an analysis can be performed on the transcripts of the data collected, for instance, using keywords coded [38].

To complement qualitative methods, questionnaires of numeric scale can be used. When applied after the system evaluation, questionnaires can help participants to evaluate subjective metrics associated with in-task and post-task perceptions. The perceived stress level, for instance, can be assessed using a 7-point Likert scale ranging from (1) calm to (7) stressed. Besides the assessment of stress, a satisfaction survey can also be employed, helping users to assess their overall experience during the interaction [61]. Using a questionnaire after the study, participants can provide feedback on the comfort of the general setup, for instance, concerning the placement of wearable sensors, including electrodes and eye trackers used for EOG analysis [64].

Another usage of questionnaires involves assessing the technology acceptance levels. The TAM is a validated, well-known model to assess user acceptance in a quantitative way. By applying an online survey, investigators can measure the relationship among attitude, affective quality, relative advantage, mobility, availability, subcultural appeal, cost, intention to use, perceived usefulness, and perceived ease of use [32]. The reliability of these factors is tested using a confirmatory factor analysis, while the strength and direction of causal paths among the constructs are analyzed through structural equation modeling (SEM) [32].

To complement questionnaire and survey data with data from the user interaction, a log file can be used. A log records the user data from task performance for each evaluation scenario. To assess Mood Wing, the data collected from logs included time to complete the scenario, the number of accidents, the number of violations, the percentage of the time spent over speed limit, the percentage of the distance spent over speed limit, and the number of center line crossings [61].

Ideally, the evaluation of the technology begins early in the design process, steering decisions according to the user feedback. Also, it should occur often, and iteratively, gathering users' feedback, analyzing it, to refine and redesign the technology as needed. To address potential errors of setup and anticipated problems, a pilot study is recommended prior to conducting the studies [47]. The pilot studies not always require a fully functional implementation, and requires fewer participants for evaluation.

Evaluation sessions should combine perspectives from wearers and experts, and complementary methods for data collection and analysis, for instance, with interviews, participatory design sessions, and logbooks allowing for thematic information to be validated or refuted across categories. Not only the feedback of current users is informative, but prior to the design phases, prospective users can also be consulted. Dibia et al. [8], for example, used a smart watch as a technology probe to identify potential applications of wearable technology for adults with mild cognitive impairments. The main features highlighted were health support, family support, and productivity support [54].

Concerning gathering multiple perspectives from different stakeholders, when designing a wearable for kids, Jalaliniya and Pederson [65] distributed a survey among parents to understand user requirements. Also, they interviewed a medical doctor as a domain expert to elicit system requirements [65]. Triangulating findings from multiple methods helps to either confirm and complement results or to refute those, increasing the validity of the evaluation analysis and reducing potential biases.

To ensure ecological validity, i.e., that the technology is operational in the contexts of use where the user interaction actually occurs, the evaluation sessions should take place in real-world scenarios, where realistic settings are available. Also, the tasks and interaction scenarios given to participants to assess the technologies should reflect realistic conditions, use cases, and settings. When an evaluation in the real world, or in a realistic setting, is not feasible, some considerations and approximations are needed. For instance, when evaluating technologies in safety-critical settings, the nature of the application may raise ethical issues, limiting the options for testing in a realistic environment with standard evaluation techniques [51].

To ensure realistic settings in the evaluation of wearable technologies, users are often invited to conduct other tasks simultaneously. To simulate a busy clinical environment, Weller et al. [51] ensured that during their study, the participants (clinical staff) were either watching a DVD or playing on a game console (simulating a multitasking environment), while the patients' information was displayed using a wearable system [51]. Additionally, the study participants were also taken for a walk around the hospital and to a coffee shop while wearing the device seeking a more complete assessment of comfort and self-consciousness while users wear the technology [51].

Lastly, both the application domain and the characteristics and complexity levels of the wearers' tasks must be carefully considered during evaluation phases. Prior research indicates that there are inherent differences in wearable computing when compared to Desktop interaction, due to its specific constraints, users' mobility, primary tasks, and activities [5]. To assess an EOG goggle, for instance, in a controlled experiment, investigators asked study participants to stand and walk down a corridor while evaluating the device to ensure some levels of ecological validity [44].

To assess a stress monitoring wearable, driving was selected as evaluation scenario. Driving is a common, yet stressful activity that most people engage with in daily life. By providing users with MoodWings in a simulated driving environment, investigators assessed the management of participants' stress levels. In the evaluation, users completed two sets of driving scenarios. Each set included one easy, one mild, and one hard scenario [61].

To assess a wearable system in clinical settings for urgent care, a set of interaction scenarios were defined. Each scenario ran for 5, 15, and 30 min to allow for participants' familiarization, and then each scenario ended in a 90 min execution. The duration of the scenarios was defined based on the battery life of the technology. Each scenario includes predefined events that range from a single patient becoming slightly unstable to two patients deteriorating at the same time. Each change in the system state was displayed for 1 min [51].

Concerning devices worn on the go and the location and setup for evaluation, when wearers execute main tasks in parallel, it is essential to asses the device usage and interaction in its specific contexts of use. Even when the evaluation sessions are carried out in a laboratory or any type of controlled setting, the context of use should be considered. It is worthy noting though that laboratory studies fail to mimic precisely the activities and environment of the actual end user scenario [55].

To define the comfort scale (explained in Sect. 4.5.2), the investigators asked participants to carry out a range of activities that involved whole-body movements, such as sitting down, walking, and moving the body segments to which the devices evaluated were attached. Exploring a range of positions helped investigators to direct participants to adjust their posture and move, ensuring that they were able to evaluate the wearable device comfort in situations of regular movement and activity [6].

In addition to considering actual contexts of use in the evaluation, care are must be taken to prevent bias when designing evaluation experiments. Such considerations help to prevent influence from fatigue in the data collection [44], and to avoid novelty effects when short-term evaluation is conducted. For Khakurel [32], short-term usability issues, considering the first few days when participants interact with the device, tend to have a minimal effect on user acceptance. Even with usability issues throughout the studies, no dropouts may indicate that users can get used to short-term or occasional usability issues [32]. Another aspect that needs to be balanced in the evaluation is the complexity of the interaction, because the more fine-grained the user control, the more difficult for users to interact with input entry [66]. Thus, breaking complex goals in simple tasks facilitates the evaluation of unique characteristics of the user interaction with wearables.

Additional considerations in experimental design [47] include the following:

(1) Avoid order effects by counterbalancing the study conditions (e.g., interaction scenarios);
(2) Reserve familiarization time during warm-up and before each condition so that participants get used to the activity (e.g., treadmill running) and the devices worn;
(3) Allow for breaks between the conditions to prevent fatigue in the participants during conditions (monitored externally also through heart rate measurements, to check the level of physical effort of the participants and ensure their safety during the experiment); and
(4) Fasten the device to fit the user, by using off-the-shelf devices with standard functionality and typical dimensions concerning size, weight, and shape.

The appearance of the device as well as make and model may influence the perceptions users have about the application, and overall experience during their interaction. To avoid potential effects of brand and familiarity, Cho et al. [62] masked devices' brands and logos during a research experiment using a smartwatch device with a 1.6-inch screen (a Sony SmartWatch 2) which was paired to a mobile phone via Bluetooth connection [62].

Bias in the data collection can also be related to the participants' acquiescence and reactivity, and many other factors that should be controlled to the extent as possible, including tiredness, boredom, hunger, or inattention [32]. When interpreting evaluation results, misinterpretation of values should be avoided when using numeric scales in which semantic information is lacking.

To reduce the Hawthorne effect, or change in user's behavior due to observation effects, Khakurel [32] prepared a friendly environment engaging with participants in discussions that were not directly related to the experiments for ice-breaking, maintaining professionalism. During the experiment, the participants were observed from behind instead of a face-to-face setup [32].

While recruiting participants, stakeholders need to account for data loss and consider oversampling. In their evaluation experiment, Seuter et al. [47] had to discard data from seven participants due to random input received on the smartglasses. These artifacts occurred because of movement of the glasses' optical touch sensor through the system's infrared spotlights. They also needed to discard motion data that presented low quality from participants, for whom the motion captures failed [47].

As this section describes, evaluation approaches vary largely depending on *when* and *how often* the studies are conducted, *what* type of data is collected and analyzed, *who* is involved in the evaluation session, for *how long* the evaluation takes place, and *where* it occurs. To ensure reliability in the evaluation, design challenges must be properly addressed, and several considerations taken into account.

4.6 Design Challenges and Considerations

Challenges in the design of wearable interaction involve the manufacture of the device, application development, and cultural differences between sub-fields that affect hardware and software aspects of the technology [68, 69]. More specifically, the cultural background of end users affects how they perceive effectiveness, efficiency, and satisfaction [32].

Major design considerations involve taking into account the resource-constrained environment with low processing power, limited storage and communication capabilities, the reduced interaction surfaces, in addition to social and normative implications related to garments "worn" by users. These unique characteristics of the wearable realm make the existing set of interaction guidelines for devices like smartphones and tablets to be inappropriate within the wearable context [8].

For Siewiorek [37], key research challenges to be addressed concern deciding *when* and *how* the wearable computer should interrupt wearers as interruptions from notifications must be useful but not disrupt wearers. Also, wearables must value the user attention, determine carefully what data should be collected, control who has access to the data collected, how wearers can specify their preferences regarding the availability of the data, and for how long the data should be retained [37].

Reducing the cognitive load in the interaction design allows users to divide their attention between tasks in an easy and efficient way. Such design decisions are crucial for user interfaces of wearable computers [5], and particularly important in nonstationary contexts where wearers must monitor and navigate their surroundings, and have lower attention levels devoted to the interaction with the technology. In such scenarios, an interface that reduces workload is more likely to be successful [17].

In previous work, analyzing the literature [9], we identified 20 factors that should be considered by designers and developers when creating new wearable technologies. These considerations, presented in Sect. 4.2.3, are useful when stakeholders want to evaluate their solutions, besides also serving as a framework of reference for comparisons and assessment.

Another important consideration when designing and evaluating wearable technologies is the large number of existing trade-offs. To address such trade-offs and guide design decisions, priorities in requirements must be set. For Dunne [69], the trade-off between wearers' comfort and accuracy in the data collection poses a significant obstacle to successful application design [70]. Hence, experimental investigation is needed to balance inherent trade-offs between physical variables (such as accessibility, dexterity, and haptics) and cognitive variables (such as learnability, and input entry approach) [71].

Considering all the quality criteria simultaneously is neither feasible nor practical. Also, some quality factors can lead to conflicting design decisions. Therefore, it is recommended to prioritize the factors that are more important in a given project or select just the ones that are well suited for assessment and comparison of wearable technologies in a given domain. In scientific research, for feasibility purposes, the evaluation of wearable prototypes often focuses on few criteria, such as fit and comfort [72]. Alternatively, they concern the user expectations for performance and effort, social influence, drivers (or facilitating conditions), intention to use, and user behavior [32].

In the military, key requirements include minimal weight, recharge, and battery replacement. By reducing size, weight, and power requirements of a wearable device, the designer increases the wearer acceptability and enhances the usability of the system facilitating the deployment of relevant applications in the field [73]. The wearer safety and comfort are important, and thus the choice of materials and design of the components should strive to ensure those factors.

Concerning the choice of materials and assembly decisions, in the design of a belt, Amft et al. [29] deliberately chose stainless steel sheet aiming at dissipating the heat produced by the technology, and also the tight fit of the materials aimed at preventing dust or liquid leakage [29]. In designing EOG goggles for eye tracking, care was taken to not physically constrain the users neither distract them with the device [44].

For wearables used in a work place, Khakurel et al. [74] highlight that key challenges concern technological and social aspects, as well as privacy and security concerns. They also mention the importance of ensuring applications are easy to use and compliant with policies and standards for regulations. Lastly, for end users, they consider that economic challenges as well as data challenges may hinder acceptance [74].

For older adults, key barriers that prevent the adoption of wrist-worn wearables include issues with: data inaccuracy, limited functionality of devices, implications of use, and poor wearability of the device. Usability issues such as screen size, tapping detection, device size, interaction techniques, navigation, and typography have been indicated as some of the reasons for the low adoption of wearables among older adults [48].

For Fletcher [75], the involvement of experts from interdisciplinary domains is essential to discuss the priorities of each requirement in the light of the solution space of wearable technologies. For wearable health, doctors and engineers need to communicate, dialog, and collaborate to reach a consensus on the appropriate level of performance and cost of the technology so that it can actually meet the needs of future wearable health interventions [75]. Regarding human perceptions, prior studies indicate that different wearable-device-specific variables induce unique psychological effects among users, and therefore those should be also considered when assessing the user acceptance of wearables striving to design successful solutions [32].

Summary

This chapter presents a number of support tools and techniques to help stakeholders, including designers, developers, and investigators, in the design, development, and evaluation of wearable technologies. The chapter begins with highlights of the most important quality factors that ensure design decisions are suitable to address users' needs. A set of quality criteria not only guide design phases but also help stakeholders to assess whether the technology provides wearers with acceptable levels of comfort, fit, and usefulness, among others.

To ensure that the wearers are comfortable, the devices should have reduced size, height, and weight, besides also meeting the users' expectations concerning overall wearability and functionality. The list of quality criteria for design considerations is extensive, with wearability and comfort standing out, especially for long-term use [44]. Because some quality criteria may conflict with others, prioritization of requirements is needed. To that end, user involvement combined with advice from domain experts becomes essential in the design process.

Wearable principles seek to guide stakeholders to take decisions, as they inform the design from a high-level, abstract perspective. Principles serve wearable projects regardless of form factor, interaction modalities, and across application domains. Design guidelines, on the other hand, tend to be more specific, guiding stakeholders for specific approaches of output responses, feedback types, and devices.

From a theoretical perspective, this chapter presents interaction paradigms for wrist-worn wearables and head-mounted devices, since those are the most popular technologies in use today. Then, the chapter concludes with descriptions about the types of evaluation methods that can be used to assess wearable technologies, providing also examples of applications from the scientific literature. Lastly, a discussion on main design challenges and considerations for the design of wearables is also included.

References

 1. Knight JF, Baber C, Schwirtz A, Bristow HW (2002) The comfort assessment of wearable computers. In: ISWC 2002 Oct 7 (Vol. 2, pp 65–74)
 2. Dunne L (2008) Wearability in wearable computers. In: 2008 12th IEEE international symposium on wearable computers 2008 Sep 28 (pp 125–125). IEEE

3. Dunne LE, Profita H, Zeagler C, Clawson J, Gilliland S, Do EY, Budd J (2014) The social comfort of wearable technology and gestural interaction. In: 2014 36th annual international conference of the IEEE engineering in medicine and biology society 2014 Aug 26 (pp. 4159–4162). IEEE

4. Dunne LE, Brady S, Tynan R, Lau K, Smyth B, Diamond D, O'Hare GM (2006) Garment-based body sensing using foam sensors. In: Proceedings of the 7th Australasian user interface conference-Vol 50 2006 Jan 1 (pp. 165–171). Australian Computer Society, Inc

5. Witt H (2007) Human-computer interfaces for wearable computers. PhD thesis

6. Knight JF, Baber C (2005) A tool to assess the comfort of wearable computers. Human Fact 47(1):77–91

7. Smailagic A, Siewiorek D (2002) Application design for wearable and context-aware computers. IEEE Pervasive Comput 1(4):20–9

8. Dibia V (2015) An affective, normative and functional approach to designing user experiences for wearables. Normative and Functional Approach to Designing User Experiences for Wearables (July 14, 2015)

9. Motti VG, Caine K (2014) Human factors considerations in the design of wearable devices. In: Proceedings of the human factors and ergonomics society annual meeting 2014 Sep (Vol. 58, No. 1, pp. 1820–1824). Sage CA: Los Angeles, CA: SAGE Publications

10. Gemperle F, Kasabach C, Stivoric J, Bauer M, Martin R (1998) Design for wearability. In digest of papers. Second international symposium on wearable computers (cat. No. 98EX215) 1998 Oct 19 (pp. 116–122). IEEE

11. Angelini L, Caon M, Carrino S, Bergeron L, Nyffeler N, Jean-Mairet M, Mugellini E (2013) Designing a desirable smart bracelet for older adults. In: Proceedings of the 2013 ACM conference on Pervasive and ubiquitous computing adjunct publication 2013 Sep 8 (pp. 425–434). ACM

12. Svanaes D (2013) Interaction design for and with the lived body: some implications of merleau-ponty's phenomenology. ACM Trans Comput Human Interact (TOCHI) 20(1):8

13. Cho G (2009 Dec 23) Smart clothing: technology and applications. CRC Press

14. Tharion WJ, Buller MJ, Karis AJ, Mullen SP. Acceptability of a wearable vital sign detection system. In: Proceedings of the human factors and ergonomics society annual meeting 2007 Oct (Vol. 51, No. 17, pp. 1006–1010). Sage CA: Los Angeles, CA: SAGE Publications

15. Knight F, Schwirtz A, Psomadelis F, Baber C, Bristow W, Arvanitis N (2005) The design of the SensVest. Personal Ubiquitous Comput 9(1):6–19

16. Hoof C van, Penders J (2013) Addressing the healthcare cost dilemma by managing health instead of managing illness –An opportunity for wearable wireless sensors. In: 2013 design, automation and test in europe conference and exhibition (DATE) 2013 Mar 18 (pp. 1537–1539). IEEE

17. Brewster S, Lumsden J, Bell M, Hall M, Tasker S (2003) Multimodal eyes-free interaction techniques for wearable devices. In: Proceedings of the SIGCHI conference on Human factors in computing systems 2003 Apr 5 (pp. 473–480). ACM

18. Strohrmann C, Harms H, Troster G, Hensler S, Muller R (2011) Out of the lab and into the woods: kinematic analysis in running using wearable sensors. In: Proceedings of the 13th international conference on Ubiquitous computing 2011 Sep 17 (pp. 119–122). ACM

19. Siewiorek D, Smailagic A, Starner T (2008) Application design for wearable computing. Synth Lect Mobile Pervasive Comput 3(1):1–66

20. Karahanoglu A, Erbug C (2011) Perceived qualities of smart wearables: determinants of user acceptance. In: Proceedings of the 2011 conference on designing pleasurable products and interfaces 2011 Jun 22 (p. 26). ACM

21. Nazneen F, Boujarwah FA, Sadler S, Mogus A, Abowd GD, Arriaga RI (2010) Understanding the challenges and opportunities for richer descriptions of stereotypical behaviors of children with ASD: a concept exploration and validation. In: Proceedings of the 12th international ACM SIGACCESS conference on Computers and accessibility 2010 Oct 25 (pp. 67–74). ACM

22. Hansson R, Ljungstrand P (2000) The reminder bracelet: subtle notification cues for mobile devices. In: CHI'00 Extended abstracts on human factors in computing systems 2000 Apr 1 (pp. 323–324). ACM

23. Lin R, Kreifeldt JG (2001) Ergonomics in wearable computer design. Int J Ind Ergon 27(4):259–69
24. Baber C, Knight J, Haniff D, Cooper L (1999) Ergonomics of wearable computers. Mobile Netw Appl 4(1):15–21
25. Oliver N, Flores-Mangas F (2006) HealthGear: a real-time wearable system for monitoring and analyzing physiological signals. In: International workshop on wearable and implantable body sensor networks (BSN'06) 2006 Apr 3 (p 4-p). IEEE
26. Motti VG, Caine K (2015) Users' privacy concerns about wearables. In: International conference on financial cryptography and data security. Springer, Berlin, Heidelberg, pp 231–244
27. Lee W, Lim YK (2012) Explorative research on the heat as an expression medium: focused on interpersonal communication. Personal Ubiquitous Comput 16(8):1039–49
28. Buenaflor C, Kim H (2013) Six human factors to acceptability of wearable computers. Int J Multimed Ubiquitous Eng 8(3):103–114
29. Amft O, Lauffer M, Ossevoort S, Macaluso F, Lukowicz P, Troster G (2004) Design of the QBIC wearable computing platform. In Proceedings. In: 15th IEEE international conference on application-specific systems, architectures and processors, 2004. 2004 Sep 27 (pp. 398–410). IEEE
30. Tao X (ed) (2001 Oct) Smart fibres, fabrics and clothing: fundamentals and applications. Elsevier 4
31. Nunez-Pacheco C, Loke L (2014) Crafting the body-tool: a body-centred perspective on wearable technology. In: Proceedings of the 2014 conference on Designing interactive systems 2014 Jun 21 (pp. 553–566). ACM
32. Khakurel J. Enhancing the Adoption of Quantified Self-Tracking Devices. (Doctoral dissertation, University of Technology, Lappeenranta, Finland) ISBN 978-952-335-318-3
33. Zucco JE, Thomas BH (2016) Design guidelines for wearable pointing devices. Front ICT 27(3):13
34. Apple Watch—Human Interface Guidelines (2015). https://developer.apple.com/library/prerelease/ios/documentation/UserExperience/Conceptual/WatchHumanInterfaceGuidelines/
35. Samsung Gear 2—UI Design Guideline (2014). http://img-develop-er.samsung.com/contents/cmm/SamsungGearApplication_UIDesignGuideline_1.0.pdf
36. Android Guidelines—Building Apps for Wearables (2015). https://developer.android.com/training/building-wearables.html
37. Siewiorek D (2017) Wearable Computing: Retrospectives on the first decade. GetMobile: Mobile Comput Commun 21(1):5–10
38. Forlizzi J, McCormack M. Case study: User research to inform the design and development of integrated wearable computers and web-based services. In: Proceedings of the 3rd conference on Designing interactive systems: processes, practices, methods, and techniques 2000 Aug 1 (pp. 275–279). ACM
39. Rekimoto J (2001) Gesturewrist and gesturepad: Unobtrusive wearable interaction devices. In: Proceedings Fifth international symposium on wearable computers (pp. 21–27). IEEE
40. Oakley I, Lee D (2014) Interaction on the edge: offset sensing for small devices. In: Proceedings of the SIGCHI conference on human factors in computing systems 2014 Apr 26 (pp. 169–178). ACM
41. Xu C, Lyons K (2015) Shimmering smartwatches: exploring the smartwatch design space. In: Proceedings of the Ninth international conference on tangible, embedded, and embodied interaction 2015 Jan 15 (pp. 69–76). ACM
42. Ashbrook DL. Enabling mobile microinteractions (Doctoral dissertation, Georgia Institute of Technology)
43. Houben S, Marquardt N (2015) Watchconnect: a toolkit for prototyping smartwatch-centric cross-device applications. In: Proceedings of the 33rd annual ACM conference on human factors in computing systems 2015 Apr 18 (pp. 1247–1256). ACM
44. Bulling A, Roggen D, Troster G (2008) It's in your eyes: towards context-awareness and mobile HCI using wearable EOG goggles. In: Proceedings of the 10th international conference on Ubiquitous computing 2008 Sep 21 (pp. 84–93). ACM

45. Martin T, Healey J (2007) 2006's wearable computing advances and fashions. IEEE Pervasive Comput 6(1):14–6
46. Toney A, Dunne L, Thomas BH, Ashdown SP (2003) A shoulder pad insert vibrotactile display. IEEE
47. Seuter M, Pfeiffer M, Bauer G, Zentgraf K, Kray C (2017) Running with technology: evaluating the impact of interacting with wearable devices on running movement. Proc ACM Interact Mobile Wearable Ubiquitous Technol 1(3):101
48. Khakurel J, Knutas A, Melkas H, Penzenstadler B, Porras J (2018) Crafting usable quantified self-wearable technologies for older adult. In: International conference on applied human factors and ergonomics. Springer, Cham, pp 75–87
49. Rawassizadeh R, Price BA, Petre M (2015) Wearables: has the age of smartwatches finally arrived? Commun ACM 58(1):45–7
50. Motti VG, Caine K (2015) Micro interactions and multi dimensional graphical user interfaces in the design of wrist worn wearables. In: Proceedings of the human factors and ergonomics society annual meeting 2015 Sep (Vol. 59, No. 1, pp. 1712–1716). Sage CA: Los Angeles, CA: SAGE Publications
51. Weller P, Rakhmetova L, Ma Q, Mandersloot G (2010) Evaluation of a wearable computer system for telemonitoring in a critical environment. Personal Ubiquitous Comput 14(1):73–81
52. Powell C, Munetomo M, Schlueter M, Mizukoshi M (2013) Towards thought control of next-generation wearable computing devices. In: International conference on brain and health informatics. Springer, Cham, pp 427–438
53. Magno M, Brunelli D, Sigrist L, Andri R, Cavigelli L, Gomez A, Benini L (2016) InfiniTime: multi-sensor wearable bracelet with human body harvesting. Sustain Comput: Inf Syst 1(11):38–49
54. Dibia V, Trewin S, Ashoori M, Erickson T (2015) Exploring the potential of wearables to support employment for people with mild cognitive impairment. In: Proceedings of the 17th international ACM SIGACCESS conference on computers & accessibility 2015 Oct 26 (pp. 401–402). ACM
55. Coca A, Roberge RJ, Williams WJ, Landsittel DP, Powell JB, Palmiero A (2009) Physiological monitoring in firefighter ensembles: wearable plethysmographic sensor vest versus standard equipment. J Occup Environ Hygiene 7(2):109–114
56. Gobert D (2002) Designing wearable performance support: Insights from the early literature. Techn Commun 49(4):444–8
57. Azevedo RT, Bennett N, Bilicki A, Hooper J, Markopoulou F, Tsakiris M (2017) The calming effect of a new wearable device during the anticipation of public speech. Sci Report 7(1):2285
58. Matassa A, Rapp A, Simeoni R (2013) Wearable accessories for cycling: tracking memories in urban spaces. In: atelier of smart garments and accessories, held in conjunction with 2013 ACM international joint conference on pervasive and ubiquitous computing (UbiComp 2013) 2013 (pp 415–424). ACM
59. Zheng H, Motti VG, Giwa-Lawal K, Evmenova A, Evaluating Graff H, WELI: A Wrist-Worn Application to Assist Young Adults with Neurodevelopmental Disorders in Inclusive Classes. In, (2019) IFIP Conference on Human-Computer Interaction. Springer, Cham, pp 114–134
60. Caine K. Local standards for sample size at CHI. In: Proceedings of the 2016 CHI conference on human factors in computing systems (pp 981–992). ACM
61. MacLean D, Roseway A, Czerwinski M (2013) MoodWings: a wearable biofeedback device for real-time stress intervention. In: Proceedings of the 6th international conference on PErvasive technologies related to assistive environments 2013 May 29 (p 66). ACM
62. Cho H, Yoon H, Kim KJ, Shin DH (2015) Wearable health information: effects of comparative feedback and presentation mode. In: Proceedings of the 33rd annual ACM conference extended abstracts on human factors in computing systems 2015 Apr 18 (pp. 2073–2078). ACM
63. Bachlin M, Forster K, Troster G (2009) SwimMaster: a wearable assistant for swimmer. In: Proceedings of the 11th international conference on Ubiquitous computing 2009 Sep 30 (pp 215–224). ACM

64. Vidal M, Bulling A, Gellersen H (2011) Analysing EOG signal features for the discrimination of eye movements with wearable devices. In: Proceedings of the 1st international workshop on pervasive eye tracking & mobile eye-based interaction 2011 Sep 18 (pp 15–20). ACM
65. Jalaliniya S, Pederson T (2012) A wearable kids' health monitoring system on smartphone. In: Proceedings of the 7th Nordic conference on human-computer interaction: making sense through design 2012 Oct 14 (pp 791–792). ACM
66. Lee K, Kwon DS (2000) Wearable master device for spinal injured persons as a control device for motorized wheelchairs. Artif Life Robot 4(4):182–7
67. Virkki J, Aggarwal R (2014) Privacy of wearable electronics in the healthcare and childcare sectors: a survey of personal perspectives from Finland and the United Kingdom. J Inf Secur 5(02):46
68. Berglund ME, Duvall J, Dunne LE (2016) A survey of the historical scope and current trends of wearable technology applications. In: Proceedings of the 2016 ACM international symposium on wearable computers 2016 Sep 12 (pp 40–43). ACM
69. Dunne L (2010) Smart clothing in practice: key design barriers to commercialization. Fashion Pract 2(1):41–65
70. Dunne L (2010) Beyond the second skin: an experimental approach to addressing garment style and fit variables in the design of sensing garments. Int J Fashion Des Technol Educ 3(3):109–17
71. Peshock A, Duvall J, Dunne LE (2014) Argot: a wearable one-handed keyboard glove. In: Proceedings of the 2014 ACM international symposium on wearable computers: adjunct program 2014 Sep 13 (pp. 87–92). ACM
72. Erickson K, McMahon M, Dunne LE, Larsen C, Olmstead B, Hipp J (2016) Design and analysis of a sensor-enabled in-ear device for physiological monitoring. J Med Devices 10(2):020966
73. Friedl KE (2018) Military applications of soldier physiological monitoring. J Sci Med Sport 21(11):1147–53
74. Khakurel J, Melkas H, Porras J (2018) Tapping into the wearable device revolution in the work environment: a systematic review. Inf Technol People 31(3):791–818
75. Fletcher RR, Ming-Zher Poh RR, Eydgahi H (2010) Wearable sensors: opportunities and challenges for low-cost health care. In: Proceedings of the 2010 Annual international conference of the IEEE engineering in medicine and biology society. pp 1763–1766

Chapter 5
Future Trends in Wearable Computing

Abstract This chapter concludes the book by presenting a critical view about novel interfaces for wearable technologies, focusing on the miniaturization of devices as well as on-body interfaces that employ multiple modalities. The examples of technology presented include electronic tattoos and implanted devices that are seamlessly connected to the users' body to facilitate data collection and user interaction.

While substantial advances have contributed to mature wearable computing as a discipline, there are several considerations in the design of wearable interaction that should be taken into account. To shed light into these considerations, the contents presented here provide materials, definitions, examples, and recommendations to help designers, developers, and investigators in the design of wearable devices by carefully considering human factors. The multidimensional aspects discussed include individual aspects, device characteristics (software, hardware and application level), cutting across technological, social, and ethical aspects.

5.1 Acceptance, Adoption, and Sustained Engagement

The considerations of multiple factors in the design of wearable computers, along with a closer and iterative user involvement, aim at lowering the barriers related to the device characteristics, reliability, and validity regarding the accuracy of the data collected, as well as improving the drivers that lead users to higher acceptance, adoption, and sustained engagement rates [1].

5.2 Methodological Approaches

Wearable technology heightens and brings attention to the mutual shaping of the user body, the environment, and technologies [2]. Despite ongoing efforts to facilitate the implementation and assessment of wearable technologies, a systematic approach for

© Springer Nature Switzerland AG 2020   149
V. G. Motti, *Wearable Interaction*, Human–Computer Interaction Series,
https://doi.org/10.1007/978-3-030-27111-4_5

the design, implementation, and evaluation of wearable user interfaces is still needed [3]. Although design methods have been created to facilitate the design and evaluation of wearable interfaces, novel approaches are still needed to allow efficient interaction designs, evaluation, and comparisons to assess the suitability and appropriateness of interfaces for wearable computers of diverse forms.

Additionally, mechanisms to build reusable repositories, interface libraries, and widgets could enable application developers to effectively and efficiently implement appropriate user interfaces for wearable applications by exchanging information on best practices, lessons learned, and design guidelines and patterns.

Concerning methodological approaches for design and evaluation, because human users are an integral part of the system, techniques such as user-centered design, rapid prototyping, and in-field evaluation should be iteratively employed to identify and refine user interface models that are useful across sectors [4]. Novel methods that carefully consider dynamic contexts of use and transient requirements are also needed in the design and evaluation phases.

5.3 Smart Garments

For Schneegass and Amft [5], smart garments shape the way in which users interact with computing systems [5]. For them, the wearer interaction has to shift from touch and press with finger tips to a more intimate and seamless body contact. Implicit interaction, including physiological signals, posture, and user intentions, should dominate the approach for implicit, passive input entries. Further advances in technology, for instance, concerning noncontact electrodes that can detect biosignals, like EMG, ensure that technology becomes even more wearable, or even seamlessly integrated with clothing, requiring minimal or no efforts for user input [6].

Recent trends have also steered away from garment-based forms focusing more toward accessory and jewelry forms, which have a miniaturized format [7]. For Berglund et al. [7], the maturity of wearable technologies still puts more emphasis on more applications of wristband-form sports and fitness functions as well as style and fashion statements. Instead, more efforts of research and development should be placed on a broader range of garments and functionality-specific equipment [7].

5.3.1 On-Body Interfaces

Wearable devices are expected to provide users' continuous access to computing and communication resources, preferably in an intelligent way in which user intention is accurately predicted, so that resources, services, and information are delivered seamlessly to wearers in the right time, approach, and amount [8].

For MacLean et al. [9], future system designs should carefully consider how to deliver constant, real-time feedback responses to end users discreetly, in a localized ubiquitous and personalized approach [9].

To address this vision, biocompatible electronics that can be seamlessly embedded in the users' skin are needed. The key advantages of such devices include not requiring additional maintenance, for instance, for energy recharges, besides also enabling an intimate integration with end users to collect data or to provide them with feedback.

5.3.2 Post-WIMP Interfaces

Although significant progress has been made in wearable interaction, innovation is needed to generate interaction paradigms, such as brain–computer interfaces that are even more unobtrusive and closer to mental models of end users, reducing the requirements for training as well as the efforts and costs associated to input entry and output responses for both end users and technological solutions (in terms of energy consumption, hardware and software requirements).

The speech-based interaction has also evolved substantially in the past, and became more popular (for instance, for personal assistants), still it presents some limitations, especially to interpret accents, complex sentences, to handle ambiguity, irony, or sarcasm. Therefore, alternative "post-WIMP" interfaces should be further explored in the landscape of wearables, including natural user interfaces using eye tracking or lip-reading. These interaction paradigms are still under development, and thus their performance is limited and require further efforts to be proven as acceptable among end users, especially considering the limited hardware resources of wearable computers [10].

5.3.3 Advantages of Wearable Computing

The literature discusses extensively the benefits of wearable computers for social good, high quality of life, increased self-awareness, behavior change, improvements in learning, and health care [1].

More specifically, for behavior changes, the users' feedback indicates that they are motivated due to increased awareness about their daily steps and sleep patterns. Wearers also consider it is "fun to meet challenges" and to become more "aware to move and not to be sedentary for long periods of time" [1].

For work environments, wearable technologies have potential to increase work efficiency among employees, to improve workers' physical well-being and to reduce work-related injuries [11]. More concrete benefits highlighted by Khakurel et al. [11] include monitoring psychological and physiological factors of employees, enhancing operational efficiency, collaborating through wearable HMD, promoting work environment safety and security for employees, task support when performing industrial and product design, and improving workers' health [11].

In educational settings, wearables have potential to improve the diversity of the student pool by introducing practical application topics. Wearable computing motivates diverse students to learn technology and computing, since students can not only design and craft the clothes but also enhance those with electronic components, including sensors and LEDs. By providing a space for students to exercise their creativity, wearable computing also teaches them about technology and programming [12].

For behavior change, the application of vibration as output response for a calming armband has shown a significant calming effect in both physiological measures of arousal and subjective reports of anxiety for wearers executing tasks that are known to induce social stress. Thus, wearables have potential to enable users to remain calmer and feel less anxious [13].

For work support, wearables are capable of facilitating hands-free or hands-limited interaction when users are executing other tasks [14].

5.3.4 Design Directions

Although a substantial progress can be noted in the domain of wearable computing regarding interaction design, research, and development, the existing guidelines are still preliminary. For Nunez and Loke [2], by following a body-centered approach to design wearable technologies, new directions open up allowing stakeholders to engage in an emergent area of design research that emphasizes the iterative body-tool observance as well as personal growth. This exploration will lead to wearable technologies that establish connections to the wearer, besides also promoting opportunities for self-awareness and transformation [2]. In exploring this venue, several questions must be addressed by future research and development on wearables. Specific aspects of the wearer interaction that deserve further attention in future research [15] include the following:

- **User goals**: Targeting either navigation or checking the screen for information access in different contexts of use.
- **Placement of the device, or sensors, and user** posture: To investigate the relation between the user interaction and the different positions of the user body, or different ways in which wearers carry a device, be it by holding the device in hand or attaching it using bands, straps, and clips.
- **Input entry approach**: Alternative input methods, including taps, swipes, drawing a circle, or voice recognition, are important components to be considered, particularly studying the interaction performance of users when they are moving.

The new generation of wearables is expected to help augmenting human intelligence in multiple dimensions—spatial, musical, logic-mathematical, linguistic, and so on [8]. Driven by the idea that the body is not like other equipment, and thus requires permanent monitoring to attend to the endless task of self-improvement, Nunez and Loke [2] state that when designing for somatic awareness and self-cultivation, body-centered wearable technologies have a promising potential to improve the wearer quality of life [2].

In the wearable realm, future design directions steer toward more natural user interfaces, benefiting from electronic textiles and electronic ink. Devices that are implanted, embedded, or injected on the user skin, as well as digestible pills are also promising as next-generation technology. Those concepts are defined as follows:

1. **Natural user interfaces**: Natural user interfaces, including those with gestural interaction, are an emerging area for design and development of wearables that can allow for cursor control and input entry interaction in a more passive and implicit way, demanding for less obtrusive approaches [14].
2. **e-Textiles**: Electronic textiles are smart technologies that combine fabric with electronics to create "smart" clothes. E-textiles have potential to ensure that wearable computers become truly wearable so that end users start perceiving them as actual garments and accessories, instead of computers. Examples of e-textile applications include shirts that communicate via infrared, temperature-sensing hats, and wearable LED displays, such as bracelets and shirts. Shifting from wearable devices to electronic clothes facilitates compliance with medical and industrial applications besides also ensuring higher acceptability among consumer applications [16].
3. **e-Tattoos**: Electronic ink is placed (or printed) on the users' skin to create an integrated circuit that is seamlessly embedded with the user body. Such an approach requires no, to low, maintenance levels, as users do not have to remember to carry or recharge a device.

   a. **Injectables** are devices that are inserted on the user's body, remaining under his or her skin. They also require no, to low, maintenance, and are currently used for identification or as medication dispenser.
   b. **Digestibles** include pills that have electronic components placed inside them, enabling medical examinations, diagnostics, and treatments with sensors in specific medical conditions. Such electronics benefit from miniaturized components and biocompatible materials that are safe for end users to ingest.
4. **Implantables**: are technologies that are inserted on the user skin, and remain in the user body for an extensive period of time. The next logical step for electronics is the reduction from wearable devices to implants, seeking to further improve the wearers' comfort [17].

The potential of wearables to improve user's quality of life is associated with their ability to automatically track users' data and as such inspire goal setting in order to facilitate behavior changes [18].

5.3.5 *Vision*

In the wearable computing vision, the technology creates an intimate wearer–computer symbiosis in which its respective strengths are combined [8]. However, to ensure users' adoption, both convenience and compatibility are important factors [19]. Acceptance, adoption, and sustained engagement are greatly influenced by external forces as well, including influences from peer pressure, trends, and perceived social prestige [19]. For wearers, considerations about their "internal contexts" taking into account user emotions, learning new behavior, and transformation in motivation are important to ensure high wearability [1].

For devices that are integrated to the user's body, further advances are needed to ensure safety and biocompatibility, preventing harming users. Advances are also needed to address requirements related to energy consumption and recharges as well as connectivity and data transmission issues.

For wrist-worn wearables, specifically, Khakurel (2018) demonstrated that there is a strong link between internal context (wearer profiles) and external context (device characteristics). Thus, device characteristics impact the internal context of end users regardless of age group. Usability issues affect not only the internal context (or how users perceive a device) but they can also hinder the acceptance of devices, including commercial smartwatches and pedometers [1].

Despite wearables being still niche in terms of usage, as they become more mature, and specific guidelines for wearable interaction of target user populations emerge, wearable computers are expected to continue migrating to a wider consumer base and becoming mainstream, similarly to what occurred with mobile users [8].

As extensively discussed in this book, to address this vision of wearables for all, there is a number of open challenges that remain to be explored in future research and development. Six of those challenges include the following:

- **Power**: Even with considerable advances in wearable technologies [20], battery life remains among the biggest user's concerns [21], and is yet a challenge to be addressed so that stakeholders are able to fully exploit a vision of unobtrusive devices that support user's life and well-being without requiring regular maintenance [20]. Optimization of energy consumption involves design decisions of software, hardware, and functionality level so that users can interact with the technology for as long as possible, and have a continuous and seamless experience without major frustrations [22, 23].
- **Utility**: Understanding the most important motivations and benefits for users to adopt the technology helps to ensure high acceptance and adoption rates. The utility of a wearable defines how users perceive its usefulness. Along with user behavior and intention to use, the utility of a device also informs the decisions about device type (form factor) and its purpose [1]. However, given the large variety of form factors and device purposes, it is still unclear "which devices are suitable for which purposes" [1]. While there are certain limitations in existing technologies, just by identifying when the technology benefits outweigh its costs, stakeholders are able to propose new devices and applications that have high success rates

among different users and across application domains. Along those lines, if end users need the devices for healthcare purposes or as assistive technologies, the wearable interface naturally becomes part of their everyday lives.

- **Attitude**: Attitude strongly influences the user acceptance, affecting also the users' intention to use a device. If the user perceives that the device is usable, this further motivates him or her to do more physical activities, for instance, in case of behavior change. The technology also has potential to foster a positive mindset about the physical activities engaging users with features such as data visualization, gamification, and self-awareness [1].
- **Form factors**: The expectation in terms of hardware is that new form factors will emerge, or at least become feasible to implement. The projected form factors include but are not limited to hearing aids, contact lenses, and general devices with reduced sizes and dimensions [22]. Next-generation devices will benefit from flexible electronics, more efficient power sources that enable stand-alone devices whose batteries last longer, and miniaturized components that are biocompatible and thus safe to use in a symbiotic mode with the wearer.
- **Sustainability**: An issue of great concern is ensuring that devices are used continuously, for a long term, besides being also able to be reused afterward, and not disposed, or ultimately disposed in an ecologically friendly way. Short-term adoption and obsolescence both have a negative impact on the environment because of e-waste [1]. The choice of materials and assembly process may help to ensure that the electronic components can be discarded in safety or even reused later on for an extended life.
- **Standards**: Even though some sensors available in commercial devices have been already validated through the American National Standard (e.g., ANSI/AAMI EC13:2002) [24], FDA approvals remain as an open question for several wearables that have been used in the healthcare domain [22]. The lack of standards on wearable computing is considered to be a barrier for the implementation and widespread adoption of novel devices [1]. Devices used as fitness trackers or for "wellness" purposes typically do not receive FDA approval. There are important errors in the data collected with such devices, as well as in the estimated values in readings that make them unsuitable being used as medical devices. Stakeholders and end users must be aware of that when creating and using devices, accounting for potential deviations in actual values measured by sensors.

5.3.6 Gaps

There are extensive opportunities to further advance research and development in wearable computing. As the next sections describe, those opportunities include standards, demographic profiles, and personalization to the end users, besides also involving applications for behavior change.

Standards, lessons learned with past experiences, and knowledge gained from prior work and experiments unfortunately are not readily available in a unified way to serve as guidelines and principles for stakeholders implementing new applications. However, these recommendations are valuable to inform a design process. Because experimental evaluation results focus on very specific design aspects, user populations and profiles, or application domains, they are not disseminated as universal guidelines for developers. By being often tightly coupled to a specific application, they do not have broad applicability. Still, such findings are informative for similar interface developments, and more effort should be placed to establish and validate guidelines, principles, and interaction standards for wearable computing [3].

Given the vast potential of wearables to help with chronic illnesses and behavior change, identifying the drivers for user adoption is crucial. An important question to be addressed concerns how to continuously motivate patients to use the devices and sustain their engagement for long periods of time [25]. At an individual level, more users can become involved in healthier life styles, engaging with physical activities, striving for immediate as well as long-term health benefits.

At the organizational level, employers can fulfill corporate social responsibilities, by reducing healthcare costs, retaining healthy employees, and increasing productivity. Wearers can improve their well-being. At the government level, wearable devices can also help decreasing healthcare expenditures by ensuring healthier communities. In conclusion, wearable technologies have a promising potential to become valuable assets at the individual, organizational, and government levels [1].

Another area that has been overlooked in prior work is the impact and influence of the demographic profile of end users (including age group, gender, and culture) on user acceptance, adoption, and engagement with technology [1]. To address this issue, investigators need to acquire an in-depth understanding of the target user population as well as the drivers and barriers for technology usage.

An important set of questions that must be asked before designing wearable interfaces, and that guides future research and development in the field [4], striving to make wearable computing effective include the following:

- How do stakeholders develop social and cognitive models of applications?
- How do stakeholders integrate input from multiple sensors and map them into user social and cognitive states?
- How do stakeholders anticipate user needs?
- How do stakeholders interact with the user?

The optimization of design decisions is also a relevant topic for research and development. Not only the number of sensors should be optimized, but also how data is collected, processed, transmitted, and stored. Developing processing algorithms and data abstraction techniques that are optimal facilitate practical deployment of wearable technologies, while avoiding hindering daily activities of users with devices that are bulky to use [26].

5.3.7 Privacy

The variety of sensors that are incorporated in wearables, summed with a continuous opportunity for data collection, increases the potential for privacy breaches. Because the landscape of wearable computers is still under development, most consequences and risks to the users' and data privacy are still unclear and unknown. But, in practice, privacy breaches refer to the access that unauthorized agents have to users' data that are sensitive and confidential. The technologies users rely on and trust for the most sensitive information about themselves carry a heavy weight regarding security and privacy expectations [27].

Hence, stakeholders must be careful to ensure users' privacy, appropriately managing related concerns when creating wearable devices [25]. Such concern is especially important when sensitive data and vulnerable populations are involved and there is a risk of privacy invasion, data misuse, and exploitation [1]. Although privacy is a complex question to address, users value such considerations when purchasing a device. Along with technology and purposes, privacy stands out as one of the most important factors influencing the user acquisition and adoption of wearable devices commercially available [21], especially in healthcare contexts [1].

Wearers must be made aware of the policies of vendors, regulatory frameworks, and the practices regarding data collection, sharing, and usage. While there is a lot of potential to mine information from large repositories and gain knowledge about user behavior, data analysis must ensure that private data is protected and that no individually identifiable information is disclosed without users' awareness, consent, and approval. Also, governmental regulations may be applicable. In the European Union, the data protection for individuals (GDPR) states the requirements regarding how any organization can collect and process personal data at the consumer level [1]. Recently, more research has been completed in this domain as well [28, 29], but still several questions remain open regarding what users want to share, with whom, when, and why, as well as what are the motivations, rationale, and benefits of disclosing user information in specific contexts of use.

In addition to that, there is a blurred line as to what is deemed acceptable for end users to disclose and what is not on end users' perspectives. This uncertainties make privacy-preserving solutions actually challenging to define [19]. The questions that help to inform design decisions in this context concern understanding the level of sensitivity and confidentiality of the data, the benefits and utility of sharing information from the end user's perspective, as well as the users' groups and contacts with whom users would be comfortable sharing information.

Privacy in wearables can be improved by providing users with a sense of disassociability, predictability, accessibility, and manageability. Such concepts are defined as follows [1]:

(1) **Disassociability** aims at actively protecting or preventing the disclosure of an individual's self-tracking data.
(2) **Predictability** informs individuals about how their information is being handled.

(3) **Accessibility and Manageability** allow users to control what is collected, when and how, as well as how data is shared.

For Cranny and Hawkin [30], the materiality of wearable technology and the body has no clear distinction, even though they can produce mutual effects. For them, "it is an intense and specific engagement with the materiality of the interface (wearable technology) by the located, embodied subject that provides the greatest opportunity for creative development of this technology" [30].

5.3.8 Final Remarks

Wearable technology has faced a significant growth in the last few years [7] thanks to a rapid evolution of technology. The versatility of the applications, form factors, and sensors increases the possibility of wearable computers to be employed across different domains and to support multiple tasks of daily life [8].

Despite a wider adoption, both the usability and durability of wearable systems still need to be improved, concerning hardware as well as software interfaces. Also, the design process for the computing systems has to be facilitated, with appropriate tools and methods that allow domain experts in addition to software engineers to create wearable systems [10].

This book provides readers with a theoretical basis and concrete examples of applications that aim at guiding stakeholders, be those designers, developers, or investigators, throughout the implementation of wearable systems. Given the complexity of the design spaces for wearable computers, it is crucial to understand in-depth the users' needs, tasks, and contexts of use where the interaction takes place.

It is equally important to involve end users early and often in the design phases. By being actively and closely involved throughout the implementation process of the devices, stakeholders are able to bridge potential gaps between what the wearable technology offers to end users and what users effectively need from technology. Such an approach can improve users' commitment, trust, and control, while reducing their resistance to change and anxiety to adopt the device. A lack of knowledge about what users want and need jeopardizes the future innovation and long-term adoption of wearable devices [1].

Lastly, the future trends of embedded interfaces will enable the wearer to not carry a bulky, rigid input device [8], pointing to a next generation of wearable computers that ultimately become indistinguishable from everyday clothing [8].

Summary
This chapter concludes wearable interaction by presenting a number of future trends in the domain of wearable technologies, among those we can highlight the following:

   a The miniaturized devices that are embedded, implanted, or injected in the user body, ensuring a synergistic experience that requires no effort from the users' part in order to maintain the device.

   b The electronic tattoos, which are placed directly on the skin of the user, also ensuring prompt access to the electronics from anywhere and at anytime.

   c Digestible pills which benefit from electronic components, such as micro-cameras and antennas, and serve to facilitate medical diagnoses.

As presented throughout the book, wearable computing provides an extensive number of solutions that support daily activities of end users across sectors. Besides the large potential of wearable technologies with a range of applications and numerous benefits, designing wearable devices is not always a simple endeavor. The design process involves cross-cutting concerns, and stakeholders creating the technology need to carefully take design decisions that affect the device regarding its shape, size, dimensions, weight, functionality, user interaction, and interfaces. While the industry continues to propose novel wearable devices [1], their design phase has to carefully consider the users' perspectives and contexts of use ensuring that the technology is built in compliance with their requirements, suiting their specific needs to sustain long-term adoption and user engagement [1].

To bring light into the wearable interaction, this book provides a comprehensive view on application domains, interaction modalities, guidelines, and principles across form factors, sensor, and network usage, as well as users' populations. This book discusses key design concerns, including interaction, motivations, and features. Overall there is a lot of enthusiasm about the potential opportunities and purposes for novel wearable technologies; however, the design of their interaction requires considerations of multidimensional concerns. While understanding users' requirements, wishes and interests may be a challenging task, bringing their insights and opinions front and center in design phases, iteratively, is the key to improve the acceptance, adoption, and sustained engagement of end users.

References

1. Khakurel J. Enhancing the adoption of quantified self-tracking devices. (Doctoral dissertation, University of Technology, Lappeenranta, Finland) ISBN 978-952-335-318-3
2. Nunez-Pacheco C, Loke L (2014) Crafting the body-tool: a body-centred perspective on wearable technology. In: Proceedings of the 2014 conference on Designing interactive systems 2014 Jun 21 (pp. 553–566). ACM
3. Witt H (2007) Human-computer interfaces for wearable computers. PhD thesis
4. Smailagic A, Siewiorek D (2002) Application design for wearable and context-aware computers. IEEE Pervasive Comput 1(4):20–9
5. Schneegass S, Amft O (2017) Smart textiles. Springer, Cham, Switzerland

6. Cannan J, Hu H (2012) A wearable sensor fusion armband for simple motion control and selection for disabled and non-disabled users. In: 2012 4th computer science and electronic engineering conference (CEEC) 2012 Sep 12 (pp. 216–219). IEEE
7. Berglund ME, Duvall J, Dunne LE (2016) A survey of the historical scope and current trends of wearable technology applications. In: Proceedings of the 2016 ACM international symposium on wearable computers 2016 Sep 12 (pp. 40–43). ACM
8. Billinghurst M, Starner T (1999) Wearable devices: new ways to manage information. Computer 32(1):57–64
9. MacLean D, Roseway A, Czerwinski M (2013) MoodWings: a wearable biofeedback device for real-time stress intervention. In: Proceedings of the 6th international conference on PErvasive technologies related to assistive environments 2013 May 29 (p. 66). ACM
10. Burgy C, Garrett JH (2002) Wearable computers: an interface between humans and smart infrastructure systems. Vdi Berichte 1668:385–98
11. Khakurel J, Melkas H, Porras J (2018) Tapping into the wearable device revolution in the work environment: a systematic review. Inf Technol People 31(3):791–818
12. Lau WW, Ngai G, Chan SC, Cheung JC (2009) Learning programming through fashion and design: a pilot summer course in wearable computing for middle school students. ACM SIGCSE Bull 41(1):504–508. ACM
13. Azevedo RT, Bennett N, Bilicki A, Hooper J, Markopoulou F, Tsakiris M (2017) The calming effect of a new wearable device during the anticipation of public speech. Sci Report 7(1):2285
14. Zucco JE, Thomas BH (2016) Design guidelines for wearable pointing devices. Front ICT 27(3):13
15. Seuter M, Pfeiffer M, Bauer G, Zentgraf K, Kray C (2017) Running with technology: evaluating the impact of interacting with wearable devices on running movement. Proc ACM Interact Mobile Wearable Ubiquitous Technol 1(3):101
16. Martin T, Healey J (2007) 2006's wearable computing advances and fashions. IEEE Pervasive Comput 6(1):14–6
17. Scheffler M, Hirt E (2004) Wearable devices for emerging healthcare applications. In: The 26th annual international conference of the IEEE engineering in medicine and biology society 2004 Sep 1 (Vol. 2, pp. 3301–3304). IEEE
18. Chuah SH (2019) You inspire me and make my life better: investigating a multiple sequential mediation model of smartwatch continuance intention. Telemat Inf 10:101245
19. Virkki J, Aggarwal R (2014) Privacy of wearable electronics in the healthcare and childcare sectors: a survey of personal perspectives from Finland and the United Kingdom. J Inf Secur 5(02):46
20. Hester J (2019) Why wear a battery? the future of wearables may be batteryless. In: The 5th ACM workshop on wearable systems and applications 2019 Jun 12 (p. 3). ACM
21. Motti V. G., Caine K (2014) Understanding the wearability of head-mounted devices from a human-centered perspective. In: Proceedings of the 2014 ACM international symposium on wearable computers 2014 Sep 13 (pp. 83–86). ACM
22. Burnham JP, Lu C, Yaeger LH, Bailey TC, Kollef MH (2018) Using wearable technology to predict health outcomes: a literature review. J Am Med Inf Assoc 25(9):1221–7
23. Magno M, Brunelli D, Sigrist L, Andri R, Cavigelli L, Gomez A, Benini L (2016) InfiniTime: multi-sensor wearable bracelet with human body harvesting. Sustain Comput: Inf Syst 1(11):38–49
24. Banos O, Villalonga C, Damas M, Gloesekoetter P, Pomares H, Rojas I (2014) Physiodroid: combining wearable health sensors and mobile devices for a ubiquitous, continuous, and personal monitoring. Sci World J
25. Torous BJ, Gualtieri L (2016) Knowns and Unknowns. Psychiatric Times, Wearable Devices for Mental Health, pp 4–7
26. Atallah L, Lo B, King R, Yang GZ (2010) Sensor placement for activity detection using wearable accelerometers. In: 2010 international conference on body sensor networks 2010 Jun 7 (pp. 24–29). IEEE

27. Goyal R, Dragoni N, Spognardi A (2016) Mind the tracker you wear: a security analysis of wearable health trackers. In: Proceedings of the 31st annual ACM symposium on applied computing—SAC'16, 131–136. https://doi.org/10.1145/2851613.2851685

28. Motti VG, Caine K (2015) Users' privacy concerns about wearables. In: International conference on financial cryptography and data security. Springer, Berlin, Heidelberg, pp 231–244

29. Lowens B, Motti VG, Caine K. Wearable privacy: skeletons in the data closet. In: 2017 IEEE international conference on healthcare informatics (ICHI) 2017 Aug 23 (pp. 295–304). IEEE

30. Cranny-Francis A, Hawkins C (2008) Wearable technology. Vi Commun 7(3):267–270

Bibliography

1. Bernaerts Y, Druwe M, Steensels S, Vermeulen J, Schoning J (2014) The office smartwatch: development and design of a smartwatch app to digitally augment interactions in an office environment. In: Proceedings of the 2014 companion publication on Designing interactive systems 2014 Jun 21 (pp 41–44). ACM
2. Li Y, Chen X, Tian J, Zhang X, Wang K, Yang J (2010) Automatic recognition of sign language subwords based on portable accelerometer and EMG sensors. In: International conference on multimodal interfaces and the workshop on machine learning for multimodal interaction 2010 Nov 8 (p 17). ACM
3. Lowens B, Motti V, Caine K (2015) Design recommendations to improve the user interaction with wrist worn devices. In: 2015 IEEE international conference on pervasive computing and communication workshops (PerCom Workshops) 2015 Mar 23 (pp 562–567). IEEE
4. Lyons K, Profita H (2014) The multiple dispositions of on-body and wearable devices. IEEE Pervasive Comput 13(4):24–31
5. Mann S, Nolan J, Wellman B (2003) Sousveillance: inventing and using wearable computing devices for data collection in surveillance environments. Surveill Soc 1(3):331–55
6. Mann S (1997) Wearable computing: a first step toward personal imaging. Computer 30(2):25–32
7. Mencarini E, Leonardi C, De Angeli A, Zancanaro M (2016) Design opportunities for wearable devices in learning to climb. In: Proceedings of the 9th Nordic conference on human-computer interaction 2016 Oct 23 (p 48). ACM
8. Mistry P, Maes P (2009) SixthSense: a wearable gestural interface. In: ACM SIGGRAPH ASIA 2009 sketches 2009 Dec 16 (p 11). ACM
9. Motti VG, Caine K (2015) An overview of wearable applications for healthcare: requirements and challenges. In: Adjunct Proceedings of the 2015 ACM international joint conference on pervasive and ubiquitous computing and proceedings of the 2015 ACM international symposium on wearable computers 2015 Sep 7 (pp 635–641). ACM
10. Ugulino W, Cardador D, Vega K, Velloso E, Milidiu R, Fuks H (2012) Wearable computing: accelerometers' data classification of body postures and movements. Brazilian symposium on artificial intelligence, 20. Springer, Berlin, Heidelberg, pp 52–61
11. Zheng H, Motti VG (2017) Wearable life: a wrist-worn application to assist students in special education. International conference on universal access in human-computer interaction. Springer, Cham, pp 259–276

© Springer Nature Switzerland AG 2020
V. G. Motti, *Wearable Interaction*, Human–Computer Interaction Series,
https://doi.org/10.1007/978-3-030-27111-4

Index

Fall, 11, 22, 25, 30, 50
Familiarization, 119, 129, 140, 141
Family, 6, 26, 112, 128, 139
Farming, 19, 50, 54
Fashion, 20, 26, 27, 42, 100, 112, 114, 150
Fatigue, 13, 18, 28, 66, 67, 87, 93, 98, 129, 137, 141
Feasibility, 83, 109, 110, 132, 133, 135, 143
Feasible, 14, 70, 102, 123, 140, 143, 155
Features, 1, 2, 8, 10, 13, 18, 20, 21, 24, 25, 29, 31, 41, 43, 44, 46, 51, 52, 54–56, 60, 68, 92, 94, 95, 97, 114, 115, 125–127, 139, 155, 159
Feedback, 25, 28–30, 46, 49, 51, 52, 56, 65, 71, 75, 84–88, 90–93, 103, 112, 114, 115, 123, 124, 126, 127, 129, 130, 132, 136–139, 144, 151
Feelings, 65, 66, 113, 128, 130, 131, 137
Fiber, 14, 16, 48, 53
Field, 1, 4, 5, 7, 31, 41–43, 46, 58, 59, 75, 85, 95, 97, 120–123, 128, 129, 132, 133, 142, 143, 150, 156
Filter, 52
Finger, 6, 10, 12, 13, 44, 48, 67, 85, 90–92, 122, 150
Finger-mounted, 6, 30, 90
Firefighters, 10, 28, 30, 128
Firmware, 49, 52
Fit, 8, 14, 67, 82, 91, 96, 101, 102, 113, 116, 117, 120, 122, 136, 141, 143, 144
Fitness, 1, 2, 9, 18, 19, 24, 25, 28, 30, 31, 46, 54, 55, 61–64, 67, 70, 71, 86, 123, 133, 137, 150, 155
Fixed, 23, 49, 50, 58, 73, 100, 122
Fletcher, 3, 11, 13, 15–19, 21, 22, 43, 59, 64, 73, 100, 143, 144
Flexibility, 12, 14, 44, 67, 126, 138
Flexible, 3, 4, 9, 44, 57, 58, 95, 113, 155
Font, 68, 84, 89, 95, 121
Foot, 12, 13, 17, 24, 26, 49
Forearm, 18, 29, 30, 95, 101, 118
Form, 1, 2, 5, 8, 9, 15, 17, 19, 24, 26, 31, 41, 44, 45, 49, 50, 52, 58, 62, 65, 68–70, 72, 81–83, 88, 92, 95, 98, 100, 102, 103, 113, 115, 117, 118, 127, 129, 137, 144, 150, 154, 155, 158, 159
Frameworks, 4, 8, 74, 97, 157
Freedom, 13, 14, 113, 133
Frequency, 11, 14, 26, 51, 52, 67, 68, 73, 92, 93, 121–123, 130
Function, 1, 8–10, 19, 21, 44, 50, 60, 64, 88, 90, 92, 97, 99, 112, 113, 137, 150

Functionality, 2, 5, 9, 10, 12, 14, 21, 41, 42, 44, 51, 52, 57, 58, 73, 91, 99, 101, 112, 113, 118, 122, 123, 126, 127, 130, 138, 141, 143, 144, 150, 154, 159
Fundamental, 1, 4, 11, 22, 31, 44, 65, 66, 115
Fusion, 29, 48, 50, 52, 53, 59

G
Game, 5, 29, 92, 97, 133, 140
Gaming, 2, 9, 19, 62, 88, 98
Garment, 1, 8–12, 16, 17, 20, 27, 45, 56, 58, 64, 65, 67, 71, 99–101, 120, 136, 142, 150, 153
Gaze, 14, 49, 92, 97
Gender, 64, 66, 68, 131, 156
General-purpose, 23, 84, 98
Generation, 44, 60, 69, 82, 94, 152
Generic, 64, 68, 112, 115, 117
Gestural, 86, 92, 153
Gesture, 7, 11, 15, 23, 29, 31, 45, 53, 54, 56, 62, 67, 68, 71, 81, 83, 85–87, 91–93, 96, 97, 100, 103, 111, 116–119, 122, 125, 126, 133, 137
Gioberto, 22, 44, 45
Glass, 5, 7, 8, 13, 26, 27, 29, 30, 95, 97, 98, 126, 127, 137, 141
Glove, 9, 26, 28–30
Goggle, 9, 10, 14, 29–31, 49, 52, 53, 119, 140, 143
Google, 7, 8, 99, 126
GPS, 10, 12, 15, 47
Graphic, 2, 18, 50, 67, 69–71, 81, 82, 85, 86, 88, 89, 91, 93, 95, 96, 98, 103, 111, 120, 124–126
Graphical, 4, 47, 123, 125
Gravity, 14, 90, 100
Ground, 52, 55, 133
Groups, 22, 43, 54, 63, 114, 117, 128, 129, 131, 134, 154, 156, 157
Growth, 2, 3, 6–8, 152, 158
GSR, 10, 12
GUI, 125, 126
Guideline, 109, 110, 115–120, 128, 142, 144
Gyroscope, 10, 12, 16, 25, 46, 48
Gyroscopic, 119

H
Habits, 18, 20, 21, 24, 30, 68, 122, 137
Hand, 10, 12, 16, 17, 29, 43, 45, 48, 58, 62, 64, 67, 70, 72, 82, 83, 87, 89, 91, 93–

Printed in the United States
by Baker & Taylor Publisher Services